iDentities

BRITISH ENGLISH EDITION

STUDENT'S BOOK **2**

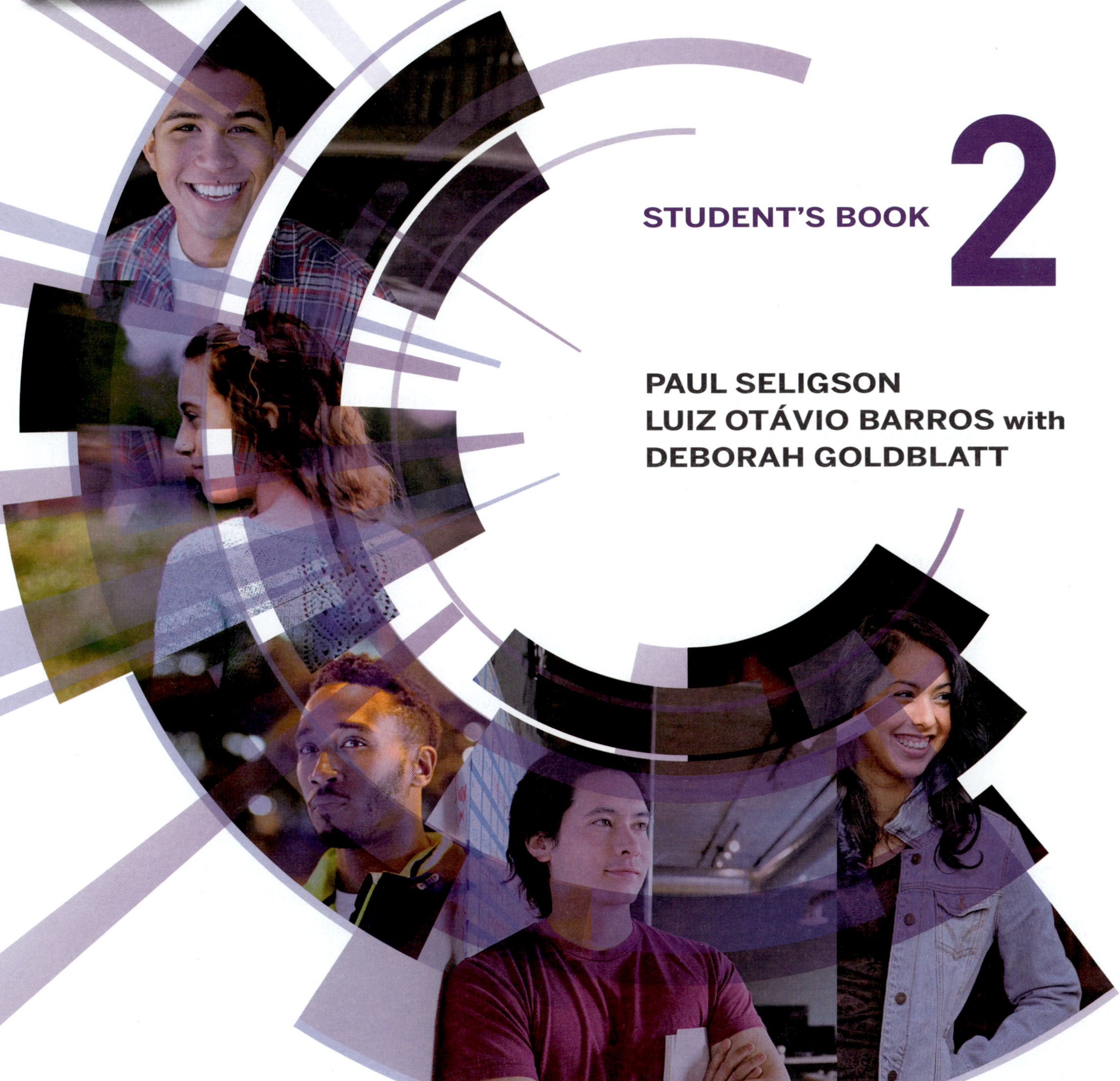

PAUL SELIGSON
LUIZ OTÁVIO BARROS with
DEBORAH GOLDBLATT

Richmond

To the student

High-intermediate and advanced students often face a challenge when they study English: continuing to make steady progress in their skills and fluency. In iDentities, we've tried to address that challenge in ways we hope you'll enjoy.

iDentities offers you rich content in each of the four skills – reading, writing, listening, and speaking – as well as grammar, pronunciation, and vocabulary. Here are just some of the ways we try to make all of these areas useful for you.

Natural, authentic, and entertaining audio and visual material continues to develop your listening comprehension. To help you, iDentities is unique in offering 'Listen to check' activities throughout the unit. Good pronunciation improves your understanding, too, and you'll find new pronunciation points, fully integrated with speaking activities. Pink syllables in the longer reading texts show you how to stress new poly-syllabic words.

Of course, you want to keep improving your speaking skills, too, so you will find relevant and realistic ...

- *Make it personal* activities, where you can express your ideas and talk about yourself.
- *How to say it* activities to introduce you to more advanced conversational strategies and expressions.
- A *Keep talking* section in the last lesson to consolidate and use the language you've learned.

What's more, every lesson offers a song lyric linked to the content to help you remember the lesson.

iDentities fully develops your reading skills through high-interest authentic articles, blog posts, and interviews on many new topics, which help you to understand main ideas quickly, focus on reference words, make inferences, and more.

Every unit also offers contextualised writing practice that follows directly from the topics you will discuss in *Keep talking*. The activities give you a chance to practise the kinds of tasks you may need to do in real life.

Finally, iDentities recognises your need to keep improving your grammar and expanding your vocabulary.

- Grammar points in every unit focus on usage and form, as well as introducing you to aspects of more formal written English.
- Grammar boxes give you a chance to discover rules by yourself so they stay with you.
- New structures are *always* presented in context so you can see exactly how they are used in natural conversation.
- *Grammar Expansion* section allows you to work on even more challenging structures.

Vocabulary-development activities introduce you to high-frequency words, expressions, and phrasal verbs, which are always in context. The *Phrasal Verb list* on page 164 will also help you build your vocabulary, and the *cyber teacher* audio sections help reinforce the meaning of new words and phrases in a unique, fun way. You will also find frequent *Common mistake* boxes, covering grammar points and vocabulary, as well as purple language boxes with helpful information on more aspects of English.

As you work through iDentities, you will notice that it's both serious and fun. We hope you will notice increased fluency and accuracy after every unit. And, above all, we hope attending English class will be your favourite weekly activity!

Language Map

		Speaking / Topic	Grammar	Vocabulary / Strategies	Writing
1	1.1	What are your earliest memories of school?		Expressions for reminiscing; Phrasal verbs with *off*	
	1.2	What innovative businesses do you know?	Subject-verb agreement: portions and indefinite pronouns; units of measurement, collective nouns, asides, and verbs as subjects		
	1.3	How many ways can you use a brick?		Figurative expressions for ideas (*pop into your head, hit you*, etc)	
	1.4	What do the 2000s make you think of?	Using perfect tenses: past simple vs present perfect; present perfect vs present perfect continuous; past perfect vs past perfect continuous	Uses of *set* (*put, design, establish, schedule*)	
	1.5	Have you ever had a dream come true?		Informal responses (*That's for sure; I'll say*, etc.)	An autobiographical narrative: functions of the word *as*, both neutral and slightly more formal
2	2.1	What would you change about your lifestyle?		Expressions for decision making; Expressions for expressing goals	
	2.2	What's the biggest house you've ever been to?	Avoiding repetition: affirmative and negative statements (*but I really should have; but my friends aren't*, etc)	Plural-only nouns	
	2.3	Do you like to spend time on your own? (Authentic reading: article on dining and travelling alone)		Understanding metaphor; Common verb / adjective + noun collocations (*convey an idea, ubiquitous presence*, etc)	
	2.4	Are you more of a morning or an evening person?	Using *so* and *such*: *so, so much, so little, so many, so few, such* and *such a(n)*		
	2.5	Can an apartment be too small?		Expressions from video for discussing city problems	A compare-and-contrast email: considering two things together, adding supporting points, and offering contrast
Review 1 *p.26*					
3	3.1	What language would you least like to learn?		Expressions to discuss learning (*out of your depth, pick something up*, etc)	
	3.2	Are you into tweeting?	Information focus: subject and object clauses (*What I did was to … ; Why … is unclear I'm not really sure.*)	Making your attitude clear (*to put it mildly, to say the least*, etc)	
	3.3	Can someone learn to be a good speaker? (Authentic reading: article on public speaking)		Expressions with *word* (*by word of mouth, get a word in edgewise*, etc)	
	3.4	What's the ideal age to learn a language?	Using participle clauses to express result, time, and reason (*When driving to work, I used to … ; Supported by his parents, Ben is in no hurry …*); Perfect participles (*Having played the trombone …*)		
	3.5	What can't you learn through practice?		Expressions related to giving advice (*Practice makes perfect; You need to hit a middle ground*, etc)	An expository essay: participle clauses for linking ideas; making suggestions with modal verbs
4	4.1	How often do you remember your dreams?		Productive suffixes (*-conscious, -friendly, -related*, etc)	
	4.2	Do you believe everything you're told?	Emphatic inversion: inverted subject and verb (*Rarely do we find such realistic sound effects, Not since … has there been so much excitement.*)		
	4.3	When did you last hear something illogical? (Authentic reading: article on why people believe in conspiracy theories)		Nouns and adjectives from phrasal verbs (*break-in, throwaway*, etc)	
	4.4	How would you describe your personality?	Formal relative clauses with *which* and *whom* (*most of whom, about which*, etc)		
	4.5	Would you ever hire a former criminal?		Expressions for honesty (*be up front, on the table*, etc)	A letter to the editor: fixed expressions to support arguments in formal writing
Review 2 *p.48*					

Language Map

		Speaking / Topic	Grammar	Vocabulary / Strategies	Writing
5	5.1	Why do good plans sometimes fail?		Expressions for failed plans (*on the verge of, call something off*, etc); Talking about disappointments	
	5.2	Do you ever make resolutions?	Formal conjunctions and prepositions for reason and purpose (*in view of; with the aim of; so as to*, etc)		
	5.3	How well do you deal with failure? (Authentic reading: article on making peace with failure)		Expressions for evaluating success (*keep in perspective, take stock*, etc)	
	5.4	Have you ever had a wrong first impression?	Levels of formality in nouns, object pronouns, and possessive adjectives + *ing* form (*I appreciated him / his considering our project*, etc)		
	5.5	How bad are drivers where you live?		Expressions for making proposals (*airtight, rationale*, etc)	A proposal: adverbs and adverbial expressions to link ideas and signal the next point; Formulaic expressions for formal proposals and emails
6	6.1	Do you still read paper books?		Phrasal verbs with *out*	
	6.2	Do you ever watch dubbed films?	Adverb clauses of condition (*in case, even if, as long as*, etc)	Using the expression *out of*	
	6.3	Who are your favourite authors? (Authentic literature: short story by Roald Dahl, *The Way Up to Heaven*)		Evocative language: vivid verbs	
	6.4	What do you think of graffiti art?	Emphasis with auxiliaries (*I really did like it*, etc)		
	6.5	Are musicals popular where you live?		Expressions for making recommendations	A book review: techniques and expressions to capture the reader's attention and maintain suspense
Review 3 *p.70*					
7	7.1	What are our most important years?		Expressions for describing milestones (*come of age, make it through*, etc)	
	7.2	Would you like to live to be 100?	Future perfect vs future continuous	Expressions for clarifying opinions (*What I mean is that … , What I was trying to say is that … ,* etc)	
	7.3	Do babies ever surprise you? (Authentic reading: article on surprising things babies can do)		Adjective-noun collocations in writing and speech	
	7.4	Do you seem younger or older than you are?	Cleft sentences: subject and object (e.g. *It's my grandmother who can walk three miles.*)		
	7.5	What would your ideal job be?		Expressions for making formal requests	An application letter: more formal alternatives to cleft sentences (*Working in a hotel is rewarding*, etc)
8	8.1	What makes a restaurant special?		Expressions with *take* for discussing events; Describing negative experiences	
	8.2	Are you a demanding customer?	Subjunctive: verbs and expressions (*I insist that … , it's important that …* etc)		
	8.3	What are the worst aspects of air travel? (Authentic reading: article about amazing customer service)		Expressions of help (*took it upon himself to, went to great lengths to*, etc)	
	8.4	Have you ever borrowed money?	Information focus: adverb clauses to emphasise conditions or contrasts (*As useful as the manual may be, it didn't help; However reasonable the price may seem, its too high*, etc)	Money terms (*borrow, loan, profit, inherit, tax*, etc.)	
	8.5	What was the last complaint you made?			A formal complaint letter (formulas: *to no avail, to resolve the matter*, etc; passive expressions: *It was my understanding that … , I was led to believe that …* , etc)
Review 4 *p.92*					

Language Map

	Speaking / Topic	Grammar	Vocabulary / Strategies	Writing
9 9.1	Would you like to be a teacher?		'Out-verbs' (*outsmart*, *outnumber*, etc); Drawing tentative conclusions	
9.2	What is alternative medicine?	Passive expressions with active and passive infinitives (*The treatment is thought to work well*, *Patients are known to have been helped*, etc)	Three-word phrasal verbs (*come down with*, *give up on*, etc)	
9.3	What unconventional families do you know? (Authentic reading: article about single parenting)		Common collocations and compounds (*fictitious belief, fairytale ending*, etc)	
9.4	How often do you work out?	Overview of verb patterns: with base forms, infinitives, and *-ing* forms	Fitness words (*treadmill*, *stretching*, etc); Verbs ending in *-en* (*whiten*, *lengthen*, etc)	
9.5	What are the pros and cons of dieting?		Reacting to new information (*I should reserve judgment*, *Did I hear you correctly?*, etc)	A report on pros and cons: using consistent style in lists
10 10.1	Why do friends drift apart?		Expressions with *say* and *tell* (*it goes without saying*, *truth be told*, etc); Friendship idioms (*the life of the party*, *a breath of fresh air*, etc)	
10.2	Who's the oldest person you know?	Degrees of comparison with *the ... the*, *more / ... er*, and *as ... as* (*the more friends you have, the happier you'll feel*, *friends are nowhere near as important as family*, etc)		
10.3	How easy is it to make friends where you live? (Authentic reading: the nature of American friendship)		Words with both prefixes and suffixes (double affixation) (*dis-*, *il-*, *im-*, *iln-*, *ir-*, *un-* + root + *-able*, *-al*, *-ful*, *-ible*, *-ive -ity*)	
10.4	Have you ever met someone new by chance?	Inverted conditional sentences for present, past, or future time (*Had she not gone to the party, we wouldn't be married today*, etc)	Expressions with odds (*What are the odds that ...?*, etc)	
10.5	How persuasive are you?			A persuasive opinion essay: logically building an argument (review of topic sentences; words appealing to common sense, conjunctions, and time markers)
Review 5 *p.114*				
11 11.1	What was the last risk you took?		Risk-taking expressions (*play it safe*, *err on the side of caution*, etc); Expressing hesitation and encouragement (*There's just too much at stake*, *What do you have to lose?*, etc)	
11.2	Do you enjoy cycling?	Special uses of modals (expectation, suggestion, refusal, annoyance)	Expressing danger and fear (*He froze in his tracks*, *He screeched to a halt*, etc)	
11.3	Are you in favour of online dating? (Authentic reading: article on online dating safety)		Strategies for whether to look up words (guessing words in context, deciding whether they're for active use, etc)	
11.4	What does the sea make you think of?	Definite and indefinite articles: general and specific use (count and non-count nouns, first mention, adjective + number, shared knowledge, adjective for a group)		
11.5	Have you ever had an allergic reaction?		Talking about symptoms (*itching*, *swelling*, etc)	A statistical report: subject-verb agreement (fractions, percentages, *half*, *one*, *a number*, *the number*, etc)
12 12.1	What brands are the wave of the future?		Verbs describing trends (*skyrocket*, *plummet*, etc.); Expressing cause and reason (*stem from*, *is closely related to*, etc)	
12.2	What songs have changed the world?	Passive forms with gerunds and infinitives (*I remember being told about it*; *New facts seem to be discovered all the time*, etc)	Transitive and intransitive phrasal verbs	
12.3	What futuristic programmes have you seen? (Authentic reading: predicting the future 100 years ago)		Looking up words	
12.4	How unpredictable has your life been?	The passive with *get* and *be*; the causative with *get* and *have* (*get* passive to express informality, emphasis, negative intent, and unintended consequences)	Expressions with *worth* (*worth the effort*, *worth my time*, etc)	
12.5	What will make a better society?		*Whatsoever* to emphasise negative ideas	An opinion essay: using verb phrases and noun phrases to avoid repetition
Review 6 *p.136*				

Grammar expansion *p.138* **Selected audio scripts** *p.162* **Phrasal verb list** *p.164*

1 » What are your earliest memories of school?

1 Listening

A 1.1 Ben is telling his friend Lucy about a memorable experience. Look at the photos. Then listen to the first part of their conversation and guess what happened.

B 1.2 Listen to the second part. T (true) or F (false)? What would you have done in Ben's shoes?

1 Both the students and headteacher thought the lesson was fascinating.
2 Ben's lesson was interrupted by someone screaming.
3 Only some of the children had left by the end of class.
4 Ben was hired without doing a sample lesson.
5 We know for sure that Ben was hired because of a shortage of teachers.

> I think I might have called for help. But if it had been a snake, I think I would have fainted.

C Make it personal Share a story about a first time.

1 1.3 **How to say it** Complete the table. Listen to check.

Reminiscing	
What they said	**What they meant**
1 As ________ as I can recall, ...	From what I remember ...
2 I can still see it as ________ it were yesterday.	It's still fresh in my mind.
3 It's completely ________ my mind.	I've completely forgotten.
4 I've got a vague recollection ________ ...	I've got a distant memory of ...
5 But come to ________ of it, ...	In retrospect ...

2 Choose a topic from the list and note down ...

a *who, what, when, where,* and *why.*
b which images, sounds, and smells are the most vivid.
c any additional details.

Your first ...

day at school · driving lesson · day in your current home · English lesson
job interview · time speaking in public · sports event · wedding

3 In groups, share your experiences. Use *How to say it* expressions. Whose story was the most interesting?

> I'll never forget my first driving lesson. I can still see it as if it were yesterday.

> What was so unusual about it?

> I remember showing up early because I was so excited. And then just when ...

2 Vocabulary: Phrasal verbs with *off*

A 1.4 Complete 1–6 with the correct form of these verbs. Use your intuition. Listen to check.

doze	go	pull	rush	take	wear

1 I even tried it for a year after I got my degree, but the initial enthusiasm ________ off (= disappeared) after a while.
2 Yeah, I suppose I don't regret that my teaching career never really ________ off (= succeeded).
3 Even the headteacher was yawning and looking as if he was about to ________ off (= fall asleep).
4 Anyway, it doesn't really matter because I never even had the chance to ________ it off (= make it happen).
5 Tables overturned, papers everywhere ... It was like a bomb had ________ off (= been activated).
6 Well, by then they'd all ________ off (= left in a hurry) and left me and the headteacher in an empty classroom.

B In pairs, take turns retelling the story in 1A as if you were a) the headteacher, b) a student. Use at least four of the phrasal verbs.

Common mistake

Class is over. The bell just ~~went off~~ rang.

C 1.5 Listen and complete the mind maps. Which collocations were you familiar with?

1
____
enthusiasm → **wear off** ← ________

3
____
lesson ← **pull off** → ________

2
____
career → **take off** ← ________

4
____
bomb → **go off** ← ________

D Make it personal In groups, share a funny story about the last time you did something. Use phrasal verbs and collocations from C. Anything in common?

sat through a boring film — were delayed travelling by bus / train / plane — managed to do something difficult — were really into a fashion or fad for a while — overslept / were late / delayed for something critical

I had a big day coming up: a hiking date with someone I hoped would be my boyfriend. But my alarm clock never went off!

Oh, no! Then what?

Well, I had to think of something creative fast! So I ...

3 Language in use

A 1.6 Listen to the start of a podcast. What's it about?

☐ People who want to innovate and turn their ideas into a small business.
☐ Big companies that try to meet people's changing needs.

B 1.7 In pairs, look at the photos and the slogans. What exactly do you think each start-up does? Listen to the rest to check. How close were you?

C In pairs, which start-up would be more successful where you live? What kinds of problems might each one face?

> *Lists and Twists* would be a hard sell. Maybe it's just me, but I'd hate to wear something that's been worn before.

4 Pronunciation: Final consonant clusters

A 1.8 Read and listen to sentences 1 and 2. Cross out the letters you hardly hear at all, or don't hear, in the highlighted words. Then circle the correct word in the rule.

1 IT manager Elena Fernández left her job and created *Lists and Twists*, a company that has shipped more than 100,000 dollars in products since 2015.
2 The app asks where you're going and tracks you as you make your way to your destination – just like your parents used to do at the weekend.

A consonant cluster is a group of consonants with no vowels between them. In final clusters ending in /sts/, /kts/, /sks/, /nts/ and /ndz/, the [**first / second / third**] consonant is very weak or not pronounced.

B 1.9 Listen and complete 1–4 with words that end in consonant clusters. Then listen again and repeat.

1 One of our ________ ________ seven articles of clothing. ☐
2 Our team ________ new clothes based on your ________ and purchase history. ☐
3 If 60 dollars ________ like a lot of money, that's nothing compared to what most designer clothing usually ________. ☐
4 The feedback we've been getting from our ________, as well as the number of positive press reviews, ________ our commitment to excellence. ☐

C **Make it personal** Complete 1–6 to create your own innovations. Which is the class favourite?

I'd like to see a start-up / an NGO / an app / a robot that ...

inspects [1]______ free of charge. scans our hard disks for [2]______.
looks for the best discounts in [3]______. lists [4]______ in our area.
reinvents the way we [5]______. defends the rights of [6]______.

> I'd like to see a robot that inspects my car free of charge. I'm tired of getting ripped off by mechanics!

5 Grammar: Subject-verb agreement

A Read the grammar box and complete the rules (a–c) with *singular* or *plural*.

Subject-verb agreement: Portions and indefinite pronouns		
1 Portions and count vs non-count	Some of the company's advertising	is very innovative.
	A lot of their strategies	are brilliant.
	A few of their apps	are unique also.
2 Indefinite pronouns	No one in our group	likes my new logo.
	Only one of us	thinks it works.

a *Both, many, several,* and *a few* always take a ________ verb.

b *All, any, more, most, a lot, some, a half, a third,* etc take a singular verb when the noun is ________ and a plural verb when the noun is ________.

c *One, each, everyone, no one, someone,* and *anyone* always take a ________ verb.

B Read the rest. Then write the correct numbers from A and B (1–6) next to the sentences in 4B.

Units of measurement, collective nouns, asides, and verbs as subjects		
3 Units of measurement	Sixty pounds	seems like a lot.
	Two months	is an eternity.
4 Collective nouns	The agency	wants a deposit.
	In general, people	don't like having to park.
5 Asides	The start-up, as well as its competitors,	is making a lot of money.
6 Verbs as subjects	Having good ideas	takes a lot of courage.

Grammar expansion p.138

C Circle the correct alternative in these quotes.

1 'Everyone [**have** / **has**] talent. What is rare is the courage to follow the talent to the dark place where it leads.' Erica Jong

2 'An invasion of armies can be resisted, but not an idea whose time [**have** / **has**] come.' Victor Hugo

3 'One of the advantages of being disorderly [**are** / **is**] that one is constantly making exciting discoveries.' Abraham Maslow

4 'Man's mind, once stretched by a new idea, never [**regain** / **regains**] its original dimensions.' Oliver Wendell Holmes

5 'The achievement of excellence can only occur if the organisation [**promote** / **promotes**] a culture of creative dissatisfaction.' Lawrence Miller

6 'If you're having difficulty coming up with new ideas, then slow down. For me, slowing down [**have** / **has**] been a tremendous source of creativity.' Natalie Goldberg

D **Make it personal** In groups, choose your two favourite quotes from C and ...

1 explain what they mean and why you like them.

2 think of concrete examples to illustrate them.

The second really struck a chord with me.

I'm not sure I understood it well.

Well, basically he's saying that ...

6 Reading

A Read the first paragraph. In pairs, what creative ideas or solutions have occurred to you in the shower? List as many as you can in two minutes.

I've figured out the solution to some crossword clues.

You're in the shower, shampooing your hair, when – bam! – an idea pops into your head. Maybe you finally figure out a way around a problem at work. Or perhaps it becomes clear why a family member or friend has been acting out of character. Or maybe the perfect end-of-year project suddenly comes to mind. It seems that those aha! moments hit us when we least expect them and elude us when we need them the most.

Most brain research has traditionally focused on the downside of letting your mind wander, highlighting the negative effects of daydreaming on our work and academic performance. [1]But if tuning out is as bad as has been suggested, why do we spend up to 50% of our time–according to some estimates–thinking about tasks other than those in front of us? Surely this wouldn't make sense in evolutionary terms.

A few recent studies have tried to shed new light on the nature of creativity. In 2012, a team of American researchers asked 145 students to list as many uses as possible for everyday objects, for example, toothpicks and bricks. One group of participants took a break during the task and engaged in recreational, undemanding activities. When these students returned, their creative ability to think of uses for the everyday objects had improved by 41%. Creativity, it seems, requires an incubation period. [2]But are there any biological mechanisms at play here?

As it turns out, our brains are not necessarily most active when we focus and try to zero in on a task. Things that make you switch to autopilot, like showering, working out, or even scrolling through your newsfeed, tend to relax the prefrontal cortex (the 'feel good' centre of the brain) and release hormones that can boost creativity. In other words, when our minds wander, ideas we might never have consciously connected seem to come together. This, of course, begs the question: [3]If our brains are not wired to be constantly attentive, why is tuning out usually considered such a bad thing?

We're immersed in a culture of attention and mindfulness, which puts a premium on the ability to 'stay on top of things' as we juggle busy schedules, multiple technologies, and children demanding attention. [4]How can you allow yourself to simply space out when your project is unfinished and there's a deadline looming? If recent research is anything to go by, it looks as if maybe you should. You may have the idea of a lifetime!

B 1.10 Read and listen. In pairs, match the questions (1–4) in the article to the most likely answers (a–e). There's one extra.

a ☐ We are expected to be focused.
b ☐ Creative ideas need time to develop.
c ☐ Students who daydream get better marks.
d ☐ It's the best way to have a creative idea.
e ☐ When you're distracted, the pleasure centres of your brain react positively.

C Find 1–5 in the article and circle the most likely meaning in the context.

1 elude (paragraph 1): We [**escape from / fail to achieve**] them.
2 shed new light on (paragraph 3): They [**explain / define**] it in a new way.
3 boost (paragraph 4): They [**amplify or increase it / push it up from below**].
4 looming (paragraph 5): It [**appears as a large form / is about to happen**].
5 is anything to go by (paragraph 5): It [**can be followed / should be obeyed**].

D Make it personal In groups, debate which statements are good advice. Find evidence in the article for or against. Has anyone ever said them to you?

1 'Stop daydreaming! You won't get your homework done in time again.'
2 'Take a short break. Come back to it when you're fresh, and something will occur to you.'
3 'You have to learn to concentrate or you won't get ahead!'
4 'Stop worrying so much about the deadline. Let's go out and have some fun. You might have a brilliant idea!'

My parents used to say number 1 all the time.

But look, in paragraph 3, it says ...

7 Vocabulary: Figurative expressions for ideas

A Look at the highlighted expressions in the article in 6A. Then match them to pictures 1–6.

B In pairs, explain what the expressions mean. Use an online dictionary, if necessary. Then add them to the table. Which images in A best help you remember them?

Having an idea	Getting distracted	Staying focused

One meaning of *pop* is to 'explode' or 'burst open', so if an idea pops into your head, it 'explodes' or 'appears suddenly'.

Yes, like a burst of energy. So if I say, 'An idea popped into my head', it means it was very sudden and wasn't there before.

C Share true sentences about yourself using at least three of the expressions in B.

Yesterday when I was walking home from school, a great idea hit me ...

D Make it personal In pairs, share your creative process.

1 Think of a time when you couldn't think of an idea.
2 Where / When / How did the solution finally come to you?
3 Have you applied your strategy to any new situations since then? Did it work?
4 Have you ever used any of the suggestions in the article?

I took a very demanding art course, and it was hard to stay on top of all the projects. One day, an idea just wouldn't come to me.

So what did you do?

8 Language in use

A 1.11 In pairs, decide the historical significance of 1–3. Then listen to a radio interview to check. Were your reasons the same?

Wikipedia has changed the way I learn about new things.

FAMOUS FIRSTS This week: The 2000s BY ROY MARTÍNEZ

1 

A non-Hollywood film wins eight Oscars for the first time.

2 

New technological words are invented.

3 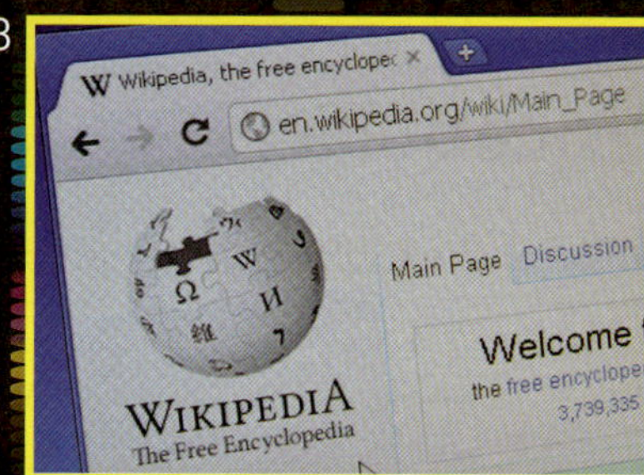

The first user-created encyclopedia is introduced.

B 1.11 Read *Uses of* set. Complete 1–5 with the most logical words from the box. Listen again to check.

Uses of *set*

Set is one of the most flexible verbs in English, with meanings as varied as *put*, *design*, *establish*, and *schedule*:

a In the 90s, the Japanese **set** (= established) the standard for small cars.

b The 2020 Olympics are **set** (= scheduled) to take place in Tokyo.

Set is also the verb in fixed expressions and idioms:

Nelson Mandela was **set free** (= released) in 1990.

fire	motion	record	release	rules	stage

1 *Slumdog Millionaire* set a new world ________: It was the first time an international production had won so many Oscars, and this set in ________ a number of important changes.

2 You may feel some of these new words didn't exactly set the world on ________ initially, but by 2010, everyone had been using words like 'texting' and 'to Google' for years.

3 Maybe some of these early words set the ________ for more new ones. 'To Google ' and 'cloud computing' were invented in 2007 and 'Twitter' in 2008.

4 Since it was introduced in 2001, Wikipedia has set new ________ for how we build and share knowledge.

5 I've been working on a new book, and it's different from anything I've ever written. It's set for a December ________.

C **Make it personal** In groups, do you agree with Roy's 'famous firsts'? Consider these questions.

1 What percentage of films included in the Oscars should be foreign? Considering that the Academy Awards are a US ceremony, how important is it for them to be international?

2 How important are language changes and the addition of new words? Was the addition of technological words a groundbreaking 'first'?

3 What do you think of Wikipedia? How accurate do you think it is?

Wikipedia definitely set the stage for a new way of accessing information.

Yes, entries in two different languages on the same topic are sometimes completely different.

Really? Let's try it!

9 Grammar: Using perfect tenses

A Read the grammar box and tick (✔) the correct rules 1–3. Find an example of each rule in 8B.

Past simple vs present perfect; present perfect vs present perfect continuous; past perfect vs past perfect continuous

I	**watched**	the Oscars last year.
	've seen	some great foreign films lately.
	've been going	to the cinema a lot.
Our view of language	**has changed.**	We now expect new words.
	has been changing	slowly.
I	**'d sent**	a text message before I got home.
	had been using	the word 'texting' for years when I saw it in a dictionary.

1 When the action is complete, use the ☐ **past simple** ☐ **present perfect** if you say when the action happened.

2 The ☐ **present perfect** ☐ **present perfect continuous** sometimes means the action is complete, but the ☐ **present perfect** ☐ **present perfect continuous** always means it's in progress.

3 The ☐ **past perfect** ☐ **past perfect continuous** is used to talk about actions in progress when the action occurs before another point in the past.

» **Grammar expansion p.138**

Common mistake

I ~~saw~~ *'ve seen* some great films lately. I saw a really good one at the festival.

You can only use the past simple if you say 'when' or 'where'.

B Complete the discussion forum. Circle the best choice (1–7).

WHAT ABOUT MUSIC IN THE 2010S? Any defining moments?

Alanis7

To me, it was the release of Adele's *25* in 2015. Her *21* album [1][**had been setting** / **had set**] the charts on fire a few years earlier, and no one thought she'd be able to match that kind of success. Turns out she did. *25* [2][**sold** / **has sold**] something like 3.5 million copies in the opening week alone! This is a big deal because it's shown the industry that even though album sales [3][**fell** / **have been falling**] year after year, not everybody is into singles. There's still a place for complete albums.

TaylorFan

Agreed. The last few years [4][**had been** / **have been**] really good for Taylor Swift, too. She [5][**'d won** / **won**] like a million awards in 2014–15, but, truth be told, she [6][**'s been breaking** / **'d been breaking**] record after record long before that.

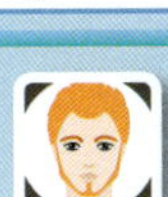
RiccoW

Well, album sales are down because most people [7][**stopped** / **have stopped**] downloading albums completely. Why buy an album when you can stream it on Spotify?

C **Make it personal** What's your most important defining moment of the 2010s?

1 Choose a topic. Search on 'Top defining moments of the 2010s' for more ideas.

the arts   history   technology   sport   a personal moment

2 In groups, explain what was special about the defining moment. Use expressions with *set* as well as perfect tenses to talk about actions in the past and to bring the listener up to the present.

For me, it was the last *Harry Potter* film.

What was so special about that?

It was the end of an era. JK Rowling set a record for unknown writers: 40 million books translated into 67 languages and eight films!

10 Listening

A 1.12 Listen to Leon and Amy discussing cross-cultural relationships. Tick (✔) a or b.

It can be inferred that the couple in the article ...

a ☐ may not have talked about cultural differences early on.

b ☐ were aware from the beginning that culture can be very important.

B 1.13 Listen to the next part. Does Leon express these opinions? Y (yes), N (no), or NI (no information)?

1 Almost nothing is universal, and all aspects of life have to be talked about.
2 The things people say are unimportant might hide cultural assumptions.
3 People usually give up their old cultural assumptions when they move to a new country.
4 The need for security is personal, not cultural.
5 If you really try, you can change someone.

C 1.14 Guess whether the couple stayed together. Listen to the end to check. Note down two reasons for the outcome.

11 Keep talking

A 1.15 Read *Informal responses*. Then complete the table. Listen to check.

Informal responses

In conversation, it's important to know how to respond appropriately. Some responses are neutral in register, while others can be very informal, for use with friends and family.

I'm not sure I agree. (neutral) *You're joking! (informal)*

	What they said	What they meant
Very informal	1 That's what I'm ________ you.	I just said that.
	2 That's for ________. OR I'll ________.	Definitely! I know.
	3 You're ________ me? How ________ I know?	I don't know.
Neutral	4 Let's ________ it.	You have to consider this.
	5 Just give it a ________.	Don't decide in advance.

B In groups, discuss these questions. Use expressions from A.

1 Did anything that Amy and Leon said surprise you? Why (not)?
2 What other sorts of conflicts can you imagine between cross-cultural couples?
3 Is a cross-cultural relationship a 'first' experience you've tried or would like to try?

C **Make it personal** What unusual 'firsts' have you tried? Make notes and share your story. Whose was most surprising?

Common mistake

It ~~went~~ was bad / awful.

I love danger and last summer I decided to try rock climbing. I was a bit nervous, though.

I'll bet! How did it go?

Well, it didn't go very well.

12 Writing: An autobiographical narrative

A Read the narrative and answer 1–3. Underline examples.

Which tense(s) does the writer primarily use to ...

1 give background information?
2 introduce and describe the events?
3 bring the reader up to the present?

B Read *Write it right!* Match the highlighted *as* in the narrative to the meanings 1–4 below.

Write it right!

As is a versatile word that has many functions:

Slightly more formal

1 **As** we're from different cultures, Mayumi and I have some cultural differences. (= because)
2 **As** a student, I used to like French. (= when I was a student)

Neutral

3 I ran into Laura. She's working **as** a shop assistant. (= in the role of)
4 I used my jacket **as** an umbrella. (= for the purpose of)

1 because
2 when
3 for the purpose of
4 in the role of

C Complete these expressions with *but* from the narrative.

1 It was ________ but sheer luck.
2 I couldn't ________ but overhear.
3 I was ________ but certain.
4 I did ________ but study.

D **Your turn!** Write a four-paragraph autobiographical narrative (250 words) on a first experience.

Before
Plan background information, introduce and describe the events, and bring the reader up to the present.

While
Write four paragraphs following the model in A, adding a summary as the fourth paragraph. Be careful with narrative tenses. Include at least two examples with *as* and an expression with *but*.

After
Post your narrative online and read your classmates' work. Whose narrative was most surprising?

If I can do it, so can you!

By Mitch Pebble

I'd always dreamed of having a sailing boat. I love the water, and as a child, I'd learned to swim by the time I was four. But I never, ever thought I'd have the chance to live on one until I moved from my home in Miami to the Caribbean island of Grenada. The most astonishing part of all is that I went there to take a temporary job as a waiter over the winter break. After that, it was nothing but sheer luck!

One night, as I was serving customers in the capital city, St George's, I couldn't help but overhear the word 'sailboat' in a conversation. Of course, my ears pricked up immediately, and I got up the courage to introduce myself. Lo and behold, it turned out that a young couple from Grenville, the island's second largest city, were looking for someone to take care of their boat as they were going to be abroad for a year. They explained that they needed an experienced 'captain', who could also handle repairs. I wasn't a certified captain, and I was all but certain I had no chance at the job. Still, I couldn't let this marvellous opportunity pass, so instead of meeting friends when my shift ended, I did some research and enrolled in a sailing exam-preparation course.

I had a lot of work ahead of me, and for two months, I did nothing but study. In the end, though, I passed the test with flying colours. I had to refresh my knowledge of astronomy and meteorology. But now it's over, and I can do nautical calculations using the sun and stars as a reference. At the beginning of May, I moved ... into their sailboat! My new home is a bit small, and my parents are a bit disappointed that I haven't gone back to school, but I've never been happier.

My friends always told me to follow my dreams, and at first, I was a bit sceptical. Now I couldn't agree with them more!

Common mistake

I had the experience of a lifetime. ~~I've~~ I'd never felt that way before.

Remember to maintain tense consistency in your writing.

2 What would you change about your lifestyle?

1 Listening

A 2.1 Look at the 'vision board'. Guess what it is and what it's used for. Listen to the start of Luke and Julia's conversation to check. How close were you? Do you like the idea?

It might have something to do with lifestyles.

I wonder if it's an app.

B 2.2 Listen to the second part. Infer Luke's two main objections. Do you agree?

Luke thinks 'vision boards' are ...

☐ boring. ☐ illogical. ☐ time-consuming. ☐ unscientific.

C 2.3 Listen to the end. Circle the photos in **A** Julia talks about. Which goal(s) is she definitely going to pursue?

D **Make it personal** Talk about your own 'vision board.'

1 2.4 **How to say it** Complete the table. Listen to check.

Decision-making	
What they said	What they meant
1 I'm ________ (to get it published).	I'm definitely going to ...
2 My ________'s made up.	I'm convinced.
3 I'm ________ between (an MA in literature) and (an MBA).	I can't decide between ...
4 There's a lot at ________.	There's a lot that could be lost.
5 I need to give it some more ________.	I need to think about it some more.
6 I've been ________ with the idea of (selling this house).	I've slowly been considering ...

2 Think of at least four personal goals and note them down for these categories:

a short-term (definitely) b short-term (maybe) c long-term (definitely) d long-term (maybe)

3 Compare your ideas in pairs. Use *How to say it* expressions. Anything in common?

I'm determined to take a trip abroad next year. My mind's made up! I want a freer lifestyle.

Where will you get the money?

2 Vocabulary: Expressing goals

A Complete the extract from the dialogue with a–g. Check in AS 2.2 on p.162. Are you more like Luke or Julia?

LUKE: In other words, you're saying that a vision board really can help you [1] __________?

JULIA: Exactly.

LUKE: The whole idea seems so [2] __________! You can stare at a picture of a new car till you're blue in the face, but it won't just [3] __________. It's not enough just to [4] __________. You've got to do your part and [5] __________ – you know, save money for a long time, if necessary.

JULIA: Yes, of course, you've got to [6] __________ your goals, even if they seem [7] __________. But our minds help us do that.

- a **go the extra mile**: make a special effort
- b **work towards**: move gradually towards your objectives
- c **meet your goals**: achieve your objectives
- d **put your mind to something**: be determined to achieve something
- e **far-fetched**: (adj) unlikely (e.g. an idea)
- f **fall into your lap**: happen without any effort
- g **unattainable**: (adj) cannot be reached or achieved (e.g. a goal)

B In groups, describe the memes in 1A using the vocabulary from A. What's your (least) favourite one? Why?

Let's see. 'Goals: keep your eye on the prize.' It's saying if you really work towards something, you can achieve it.

I think that's quite obvious.

C 2.5 Complete collocations 1–4 with words in red from A. Then listen to check. How many collocations were you familiar with?

1
story | explanation
a(n) __________
example

3
a (tight) deadline | the requirements
____
someone's expectations

2
objective | wish
a(n) __________
(sales) target

4
a (law) degree | a solution (to a problem)
____
a career in (journalism)

D Make it personal Choose a collocation from C and a topic below. Then tell your partner something about yourself. Stop before the collocation. Can he/she guess what you had in mind?

a degree   a job problem   a personal goal   a news item   a teacher   your boss

My boss is incredibly demanding. It's nearly impossible to meet …

Meet her expectations?

Exactly. Can you believe she …

3 Language in use

A 2.6 Barry and Crystal have just moved into a new place. Listen and choose the right photo. Which one do you like better?

> I grew up in a small flat, so I don't actually know what a big house would be like.

B 2.6 Listen again. What can you infer about Barry and Crystal? Do they remind you of anyone you know?

1 ☐ They've always lived in relatively small spaces.
2 ☐ He's probably more open to change than she is.
3 ☐ They don't work anymore.
4 ☐ Most of Crystal's friends are about her age.

C 2.7 Listen to the rest. Order Crystal's arguments about small homes 1–3. There's one extra. Do you think she convinced him?

1 ☐ more affordable
2 ☐ emotionally freeing
3 ☐ cosier
4 ☐ easier to maintain

D 2.8 Read *Plural-only nouns*. Then complete excerpts 1–4. Listen to check.

Plural-only nouns

Some nouns are only used in the plural. They include articles of clothing and tools / instruments that have two sides or pieces:
jeans, trousers, pyjamas, shorts, glasses, earphones, scissors

Other plural nouns include:
congratulations, likes and dislikes, possessions, savings, stairs, surroundings

1 CRYSTAL: The one we kept near the ________? I threw it out.
BARRY: You what?! I loved that painting. You did, too.

2 BARRY: I have to admit I like the ________, especially these tree-lined streets.
CRYSTAL: I knew you would!

3 BARRY: Well, I suppose we can downsize. Especially now that we're living off our pension and ________!
CRYSTAL: It's a new phase of life.

4 BARRY: Some of our ________ won't fit in this apartment.
CRYSTAL: I'm sure most of them will.

E Make it personal In groups, answer 1–4. Any big surprises?

1 What would be your top priority when choosing a new home?

price size surroundings space for your possessions noise parking

2 How easy would it be for you to get used to living in a smaller space?
3 If you had one extra cupboard, what would you put in it?
4 Is the saying, 'Less is more' always, sometimes, or never true? Why?

> Size is definitely number 1 for me. I've got tons of possessions!

> I'm not so sure. I'd put ... first.

4 Grammar: Avoiding repetition

A Read the grammar box and tick (✔) the correct rules (1–4). Then underline the parts of the sentences in 3D that avoid repetition. What words are missing?

Avoiding repetition: affirmative and negative statements	
I'm worried about finding a place to live,	but my friends **aren't**.
I've never lived in a house,	but my boyfriend **has**.
I haven't started looking for a flat,	but I think I **might** soon.
I didn't rent a flat of my own,	and I really **should have**.
I'd love to have more space,	but I may never be able **to**.
I love this neighbourhood,	and my sister **does, too**.
I've never lived on my own,	and my girlfriend **hasn't, either**.

1 To avoid repetition, use ☐ **a main verb** ☐ **an auxiliary or modal verb**.
2 The missing words are in the ☐ **first** ☐ **second** part of the sentence.
3 The verbs in both parts ☐ **always** ☐ **sometimes** refer to the same time period.
4 You ☐ **can** ☐ **can't** use a contracted form when the final verb is affirmative.

» Grammar expansion p.140

B ▶2.9 Cross out the unnecessary words in 1–4 and complete 5–8 with an auxiliary or modal verb. Listen to check.

Common mistake

I have an MBA, and my sister ~~has~~ *does*, too.

HOLLY: I didn't know you had so many CDs!
TOM: Yeah. Some are mine, and some I inherited from my brother when he went off to college.
HOLLY: Do you still listen to them?
TOM: [1]**No, I haven't ~~listened to them~~ in years**, [2]**but I might listen to them one day**. Who knows?
HOLLY: Why would you? I mean, you're on Spotify, right?
TOM: [3]**I am on Spotify**.
HOLLY: So, why don't you give them away?
TOM: [4]**I can't bring myself to give them away**.
HOLLY: Why not? Do they bring back memories or something?
TOM: Some of them [5]__________, yeah. This one was a gift from my grandmother.
HOLLY: *One Direction*? Do you actually like them?
TOM: I [6]__________ when I was younger. But, you see, it's not about the music.
HOLLY: It [7]__________?
TOM: No. It's the memory that counts! I mean, look at Grandma's note on this one.
HOLLY: Well, you could always pick the ones that mean something special and get rid of the rest.
TOM: Yeah, I guess I [8]__________ if my brother was OK with that, too.

C Make it personal Your prized possessions! Role-play a conversation with a future flatmate.

1 You're about to rent a very small flat. Make a list of things you can't do without.

books   music   art / photos   clothes / shoes   appliances / devices of my own   sentimental objects

2 Decide on at least two things you will each throw out to save space. Which one was most difficult?

3 Role-play the conversation again with a new partner. Be sure to avoid repetition where possible.

I have no idea where to start.

Of course you do! What big appliances do you have?

5 Reading

A 2.10 Read and listen to the article. Circle the correct answer.

Its main aim is to [**describe** / **question** / **argue against**] a trend.

Going it alone: more popular than ever

Travellers to the United States are sometimes struck by a phenomenon they don't see frequently at home – or, at least, one they don't think they see – the sheer number of people dining alone in restaurants. They are wrong to think this trend is limited to the US. In fact, it's spreading and becoming harder to miss – wherever one goes. A 'single' in Amsterdam can even enjoy dining at Eenmaal, a restaurant featuring tables for one. What's more, solo dining has become common in upmarket locations, as well. Long gone are the days when a diner stating 'one, please' might have been ushered out of the way and into an empty room. These days, solo dining is good for business. In fact, Open Table reports that between 2013 and 2015 alone, the number of single reservations rose by 62 per cent. It looks as if the solo diner is becoming more and more ubiquitous.

Another increasingly familiar presence is the solo traveller. Tour companies have gone out of their way to convey a clear message that single customers are welcome, and the success rate for their efforts is high. Among those 45 and older, according to the American Association for Retired People (AARP), more than 80 per cent of those who have taken a solo trip plan to do it again.

What could possibly account for these trends? For one thing, it turns out that the number of people living alone has grown exponentially. To cite just a few examples, more than half of all homes in New York City are occupied by just one person; in London, a third; in Paris, more than half; and in Stockholm, 60 per cent. As of 2012, one in five US adults over the age of 25 had never been married, as opposed to one in ten in 1960. No longer a last resort, living alone has become a coveted choice for many who savour their solitude. While some singles may be avid chefs, many would rather 'people gaze' than cook for just one person. As solo living has become more prevalent, solo dining has spread. And for those with a bit more disposable income, it's a short hop, skip, and jump to solo travel.

Companies planning solo tours don't only cater to those who are single, however. Increasingly, solo travellers may be half of a couple whose holiday schedules clash, or anyone who wants a taste of independence and craves new experiences. A solo holiday is, in many cases, a ticket to a week of freedom.

Where has this desire for freedom come from? Some say it may have arisen in childhood. As more children have their own rooms and spend time alone after school, they have become increasingly comfortable with a solo existence. Today, colleges are inundated with requests for single rooms. At Montclair State College in New Jersey, for example, a full 1,500 dorm rooms out of 5,000 are single rooms. Of course, it can be argued that with social media always available, students are never very far away from those they are closest to. Dining, travelling, or living on our own, it is easy enough to 'reach out and touch someone', just as the phone company adverts once suggested.

B Sentences 1–4 are true, according to the writer. Find the evidence in the article. Do any surprise you?

1 Solo diners have become not only commonplace, but an identifiable market.
2 Children who grow up alone have less of a need for company.
3 Living alone can be a positive lifestyle choice.
4 Solo travellers are not necessarily single.

C Read *Understanding metaphor*. Then identify the metaphors in the underlined phrases in the article. In pairs, explain their meaning in that context.

Understanding metaphor

Authentic texts often include metaphors, where non-literal meanings are used to add power and imagery. For example: A diner might have been **ushered** into an empty room.

Doesn't *usher*, as a verb, usually mean 'to show someone to a seat', like in a theatre? So here the meaning is extended to a restaurant.

D **Make it personal** In groups, what are the pros and cons of these experiences? Any disagreements?

having your own room as a child   having a flatmate at university
living alone as an adult   living separately from your partner / spouse

I can't see any advantages to couples living separately. He or she might meet someone else!

6 Vocabulary: Common verb / adjective + noun collocations

A 2.11 Complete the table with the highlighted words in the article. Listen to check.

	Word	Meaning	Examples of common collocations
1	________	make known, communicate	an idea, a sense of (freedom), an impression
2	________	long for, want greatly	excitement, attention, peace and quiet
3	________	widespread	influence, presence, fashion
4	________	supply what a specific audience desires or requires	a (young) audience, (students') needs, (different) interests / tastes
5	________	appealing to those with money	neighbourhood, restaurant

B Complete 1–4 with collocations from **A**, changing the forms of the words as needed. Which sentences might be true for you?

City vs country life: Four reasons why I went back to São Paulo!

1 I'm not cut out for country life. When I lived in Itu, I missed São Paulo and ________ the ________ of a big city.
2 *Avenida Paulista*. It ________ a unique ________ of energy and freedom that's hard to put into words. Not to mention the ________ ________ of street musicians on every other corner!
3 How I missed the food! Not the ________ ________, but the small, affordable ones, which are just as good – and sometimes even better.
4 Oh, and the nightlife! It ________ everyone's tastes and ________, tourists and locals alike.

C **Make it personal** In groups, create a poster with four reasons for making one of the lifestyle changes below. Use collocations from **A**. Whose is the most convincing?

ditch social media   do yoga   never get married   save money instead of taking holidays   work from home

I crave peace and quiet, so it would be great to work from home.

OK, so number 1: If you crave peace and quiet, you'll never have unwanted interruptions.

7 Language in use

A 2.12 Listen to the start of a conversation with a sleep expert. What's it about?

☐ insomnia ☐ sleep patterns ☐ morning routines

B 2.13 In pairs, are 1–3 good ways to start your morning? Listen to the rest to check. Were you right?

1 drinking coffee as soon as you get up
2 making your bed first thing, before taking a shower
3 checking email on your phone right after you wake up

I see nothing wrong with drinking coffee. Do you?

C 2.13 Listen again. True (T) or false (F)? Correct the false statements.

1 It's not very important how you start your morning.
2 Postpone coffee because cortisol provides natural energy.
3 Your first task should be something achievable.
4 It's sometimes OK to skip breakfast.
5 A good time to answer email is when you first get up because you're alert.

D Complete what the participants said with the correct form of a word or expression from the box. Which person is most like you?

boost (n)	drag (v)	drowsy	hectic	not sleep a wink

I was such a night owl that I wrote most of my assignments between 1.00 and 4.00am. Sometimes, I [1]__________ before exams! I looked like a zombie, but it was so much easier to study at night!

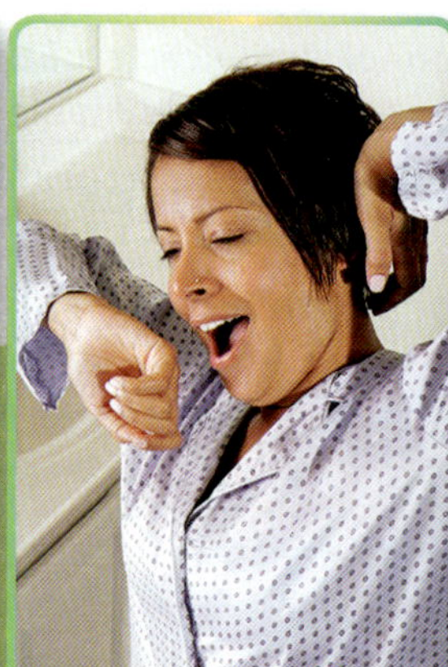

I looked for studies on sleep habits, but there were so few that it was hard to figure out how morning habits could ruin your day – you know, when time [2]__________ and you can't think straight.

If you drink coffee as soon as you wake up, you end up with so much energy that you run out of stamina faster. But if you drink it later in the day, you get an extra energy [3]__________. It's such useful advice.

You see, my mornings are so [4]__________ I have to skip breakfast sometimes. There's just no time. In fact, there's so little I have to run for the bus.

All too often I have so little time and so many urgent messages, it's hard to put them on hold, even though I know it's not a good idea to handle email when I'm still [5]__________.

E **Make it personal** In pairs, what's your typical morning routine? Does it affect the rest of your day?

In my case, I usually sleep the morning away because I'm a night owl.

But aren't you drowsy if you have to be somewhere early?

8 Grammar: Using *so* and *such*

A Read the grammar box and tick (✔) the correct rules (1–4). Then find examples of the rules in 7D.

so, so much, so little, so many, so few, such and *such a(n)*		
It's	**so** comfortable	sleeping in this bed.
It's	**such** useful information	(that) I always remember it.
It makes	**such a** big difference	to wake up early.
It's	**so much** better	than staying up late.
I have	**so many** things to do	I don't know where to start.
There are	**so few** ways	to get a good energy boost.
They're charging	**so much** (money)	I can't even consider it.
As for free time, I have	**so little** (time)	I can barely have lunch.

1 Use ☐ **such** ☐ **such a** before non-count nouns.
2 Use **so many / so few** with ☐ **count** ☐ **non-count** nouns, and **so much / so little** with ☐ **count** ☐ **non-count** nouns.
3 Use ☐ **so** ☐ **so much** before a comparative.
4 You can delete the noun after *so much, many,* etc.
☐ **When it is in the sentence or understood.**
☐ **Only when it is in the sentence.**

Grammar expansion p.140

Common mistakes

This article has such ~~a~~ useful **information / advice**.

I have such ~~a~~ strange **dreams** that I'm always scared.

B Complete 1–3 using the blue words in the grammar box. Then join the underlined sentences in 4–5 using the bold words and *that*.

FIVE WAYS TO BECOME MORE PRODUCTIVE!

1 Drink more water. If you're dehydrated, you'll have ________ energy you'll barely make it through the day.

2 Use your commuting time to do something productive. There are ________ good audio books on Amazon and iTunes! You can even learn a new language while you're stuck in traffic.

3 Make yourself unavailable for a few hours, and turn off your devices, so you can work in ________ way that there are as few interruptions as possible.

4 Stop multi-tasking. Research shows there are a lot of distractions invading our lives. They're changing the way our brains work.

5 Have fewer and shorter meetings. Long meetings waste a lot of time. Some companies have switched to stand-up meetings.

C Make it personal In groups, share opinions on productivity.

1 What's your immediate reaction to the tips in B? Why? Use some of these expressions with words from A.

Number ___ is [1]________ true!	Number ___ is [2]________ nonsense!
Number ___ is [3]________ a misconception!	There's [4]________ truth to number ___ .
Number ___ is [5]________ a no-brainer!	

Number 4 is such nonsense! Multi-tasking is a great way to get more done.

Yes, but if you tried doing one task at a time, you might find ...

2 When are you most / least productive during the week / day?

3 Are you as productive as you could be? If not, what would you need to change in your lifestyle?

9 Listening

A 2.14 In pairs, brainstorm some ways your city (or one you know) has changed in recent years. Then listen to / watch (to 1.12) Shawn Groff talking about his micro apartment. Answer the questions.

1 Where does Shawn live?

2 Why has he chosen to live in a micro apartment?

> Here in ... there are a lot more people than there used to be!

B 2.14 Listen to / watch the second part (1:12 to 3:22). Number the reasons for micro apartment in the order mentioned. There's one extra.

a ☐ Life expectancy has increased.

b ☐ Cities are growing in size.

c ☐ More people are living alone.

d ☐ People spend less time at home than they used to.

e ☐ There is an inadequate amount of housing.

f ☐ People are marrying later and divorcing more often.

C 2.14 Complete 1–6 with words from the box. Listen to / watch the third part (3:22 to the end) to check.

addressing	backlash	geared	higher	priced out	target	voiced

1 Recent college graduates ... might otherwise be ____________ of the city.

2 There has been ____________. In Seattle, community groups have ____________ concerns.

3 [The apartments] are really ____________ toward young, high-income people.

4 [The apartments] aren't ____________ the needs of lower-middle income workers.

5 A lot of these pilots that are happening in cities are definitely on the ____________ end.

6 And you can ____________ different populations [with micro apartments].

D 2.14 Listen to / watch again (3:22 to end). In pairs, summarise two key criticisms of micro apartments. What answers to the criticisms are given? Use expressions from C.

> I think a reason there's been backlash is that ...

10 Keep talking

A Watch to 1.12 again with the sound off. Note down the features of the apartments that appeal to you most.

B In groups, discuss which statements in 9B are true where you live. Would micro apartments be a good solution? Which features from A might be most appealing?

> There's definitely overcrowding here, but on the other hand, I think there would be backlash if we ...

C Search on 'innovative solutions to city problems'. Share one in groups. Be sure to present the pros and cons of each solution.

> I read that in Japan, they're addressing overcrowding in Tokyo by moving jobs elsewhere.

> Yes, but what about leaving your friends and family? I think it's better to ...

11 Writing: A compare-and-contrast email

A Read Marta's email to her friend Ann. Write the numbers of the paragraphs.

In paragraph ...

a [ ], she compares the two flats to others available.

b [ ], Marta first establishes that she's asking for something.

c [ ], she mainly compares good and bad points of one flat, but mentions a similarity for both.

d [ ], she only compares good and bad points of one flat.

Ann Johnson (ann.johnson@allmail.com)

Help me decide!

Hey there Ann,

1 Hope everything has been going well. It's been a while, hasn't it? Some big news from my end: I'm just about to rent my first flat, and I wondered if you wouldn't mind giving me your opinion. I mean, there's so much at stake! And you always have such good practical advice!

2 I've seen two flats. Each has its pros and cons, so my mind isn't totally made up. The first one is right in the centre of town, only a ten-minute walk from my job, and the price is reasonable, too. In addition, the neighbours I've met were all very friendly. <u>However</u>, while the neighbourhood has many amenities, including lots of shops and even a cinema, this flat also has some key drawbacks. For one thing, it's small and dark. Even in the morning, I'd have to keep the lights on, which would inevitably raise my electricity bill. <u>Moreover</u>, it's a studio flat with tiny wardrobes. Although there's a separate kitchen, the stove has only two burners, and there's no oven. <u>Finally</u> – wait till you hear this – one of the neighbours said he had mice last year, even though he assured me the problem has been solved!

3 The second flat, on the other hand, is modern, light, and spacious, with a stunning view of the park. It's in an upmarket neighbourhood. It's also a one bedroom with fairly large closets and, of course, a full kitchen. You're probably thinking it's a no-brainer, aren't you? If only it were that simple. <u>The two flats are more or less identical in price</u>, <u>but</u> the commute from the second one is horrendous. I'd have to switch trains every morning, not to mention take a bus just to get to the train. I estimate my commute would take a good hour and a half. Even so, in spite of these disadvantages, I'm thinking about it seriously. Yet it worries me that I may find I don't have much of a social life as there's very little to do in the neighbourhood.

4 So what do you think? <u>Both flats</u> are good deals compared to others that are available, so I'm really torn. <u>The main difference between</u> them would be one of lifestyle. You know me really well. You may not want the responsibility of answering this question, but where do you think I'd be happiest?

Looking forward to hearing from you. I have to pay a deposit tomorrow!

Love,
Marta

B Read *Write it right!* Then match the underlined words or expressions in the email to 1, 2, or 3.

Write it right!

Words and expressions used to compare and contrast fall into three categories:

1 Considering two things together: *Each has its pros and cons.*
2 Adding additional supporting points: *In addition*, the neighbours I've met were all very friendly.
3 Offering a contrast: The second flat, *on the other hand*, is modern, light, and spacious.

C The modal verbs *may* and *might* can be used to speculate about the reader's reaction. Find two examples in the email.

D Your turn! Write a four-paragraph compare-and-contrast email (250 words) on one of the topics discussed in 10C.

Before
Note down the pros and cons of both options, and decide which you will cover together in the same paragraph.

While
Write four paragraphs following the model in A, making sure to include a summary paragraph. Use expressions to compare and contrast, and at least one example of *may* or *might* to speculate.

After
Post your email online and read your classmates' work. Whose presents a contrast more clearly?

Review 1

Units 1-2

1 Speaking

A Look at the vision board on p.16.

1 In pairs, share everything you can remember about it, using these expressions.

fall into your lap far-fetched go the extra mile meet your goals put your mind to something meet someone else's expectations work toward unattainable

2 In groups, share highlights of what you learned from your own vision boards.

3 Summarise your discussion for the class, using some of these expressions.

I learned I really didn't want to have to meet someone else's expectations.

a lot of us some of us a few of us only one of us no one in our group some of us

No one in our group has unattainable goals. ...

B Make it personal Choose three question titles from Units 1 and 2 to ask a partner. Ask at least three follow-up questions for each. What did you learn about each other?

What are your earliest memories of school?

I have a vague recollection of not wanting to play with anyone.

C Search on 'first day of school' and, in groups, make a list of the best advice.

If you want to pull off having a totally new image, don't wear last year's clothes.

2 Listening

A R1.1 Listen to the beginning of a lecture on fashion and lifestyle. Choose the correct answer.

The main purpose of the teacher's lecture is to ...

a describe new fashion trends in China.

b illustrate the meaning of 'lifestyle'.

c compare East and West.

B R1.2 Listen to the whole lecture and take notes on 1–2.

1 Why is fashion important?

2 In what other areas of life might fashion trends in China lead to a more open lifestyle?

C Make it personal With a partner, share your answers to B. What does the way you dress say about your own personal lifestyle?

Fashion is important because it ...

I've never thought about that before, but it's true. For example, the fact that I wear ... shows that ...

3 Grammar

A Tick (✔) the correct sentences, and correct the mistake in the incorrect ones.

1 Some of this book's grammar exercises is a bit difficult.
2 Two hundred pounds really are a lot for a hotel room.
3 Everyone in our class has unusual 'first' experiences.
4 Only one person in my family live alone.
5 Being organised require lots of planning.
6 A few of the apps on my phone are really innovative and unusual.
7 Having new experiences, as well as learning from them, are a sign of maturity.
8 In general, most people is very impatient in shops.

B Make it personal In pairs, share your answers and explain the incorrect ones. Then make the sentences true for you.

The first sentence should be 'are': 'Some of this book's grammar exercises are a bit difficult.'

Actually, I think some of this book's grammar exercises are a bit easy. But then I really love grammar!

4 Writing

Write a paragraph about a 'first' experience a classmate told you. How much do you remember about him / her?

1 Use a range of tenses to give background information, describe the events, and bring the reader up to the present.
2 Use at least two different meanings of the word *as*.

5 Self-test

Correct the two mistakes in each sentence. Check your answers in Units 1 and 2. What's your score, 1–20?

1 I can picture that party yet like it were yesterday.
2 My fatigue hasn't gone off, and, in fact, I slept off in class this morning.
3 I saw some great films lately and I've gone to a really good one last weekend.
4 Today most people stopped using their landline phones and had been using a mobile phone exclusively.
5 Like we both didn't study enough, we thought the test went awful.
6 Your dream of being a chef won't seem inattainable if you really put your head to it.
7 I wasn't familiar with my new surrounding, and I fell going down the stair.
8 I didn't take the flat, but I think I should have taken because now I'm having trouble finding a place, and my flatmate has too.
9 This TV programme has such a useful information and so much suggestions.
10 There are so little ways to tell the twins apart, but the main difference from them is their eyebrows.

6 Point of view

Choose a topic. Then support your opinion in 100–150 words, and record your answer. Ask a partner for feedback. How can you be more convincing?

a You thought the 2000s were a really innovative decade until the 2010s came along. OR
You think the 2000s definitely had more 'firsts'.
b You think deep down people are the same regardless of where they live. OR
You think cross-cultural relationships can be really challenging.
c You think never getting married is a valid lifestyle choice. OR
You can't imagine living and travelling alone and think marriage is a wonderful way of commiting to someone.
d You think choice of neighbourhood is far more important than the size of your flat. OR
You think a very small flat is never worth it, even if the neighbourhood is exciting.

3 What language would you least like to learn?

1 Listening

A Which way of learning a foreign language (photos a–d) have you found most effective / enjoyable? Why?

Well, I'm really into American sitcoms, but I'm not sure I've learned a lot of English from TV.

a ☐

b ☐

c ☐

d ☐

B 3.1 Listen to part of an English class. Which photo (a–d) best illustrates the way Bartek learned French?

Common mistake

I ~~think~~ *don't think* learning grammar rules ~~isn't~~ *is* effective.

C 3.2 Listen to the second part. What can you infer about Bartek, Sylwia, and the teacher? Complete 1–5 with the correct names. Check in **AS** 3.2 on p.162. What sentences made you decide?

1 ________ doesn't read a lot in a foreign language.
2 ________ finds language learning a challenge.
3 ________ and ________ feel hard work is essential for language learning.
4 ________ connects emotionally to English online.
5 ________ thinks living abroad makes you almost feel like a native.

D **Make it personal** In pairs, discuss 1–4. How much do you have in common?

1 Which phrase best describes your experience learning English? Why?

a bumpy ride a necessary evil a whole new world Fun, fun, fun!

2 Are you more like Bartek or Sylwia? How much English have you learned through interaction? How about reading / listening for pleasure?
3 How much progress have you made in the past year in listening and speaking? Do you have any useful tips?
4 When did you first realise you could really speak English?

Well, at first I thought English was just a necessary evil. But now it's a whole new world.

I agree. As soon as I started understanding song lyrics, I was hooked!

2 Pronunciation: Stress in noun / verb homographs

A 3.3 Read and listen to the rules and examples. Can you think of any other homographs?

> Homographs are words that have the same spelling, but may be different in meaning or pronunciation. When the pronunciation isn't the same, nouns are stressed on the first syllable and verbs on the second:
> I like to **record** (v) myself speaking English. My **record** (n) is a two-hour video!
> But many nouns and verbs are pronounced the same:
> My teacher **comments** (v) on my written work every week. Her **comments** (n) are very helpful.

B 3.4 Do you remember the stressed syllable in the bold words (1–5)? Listen to check. Which do you agree with?

1 I think you need to spend some time in an English-speaking country to have a really good **command** of the language.
2 I **suspect** you learn a language more easily when you're an extrovert.
3 If you're willing to go the extra mile, you can make a lot of **progress**, whether or not you're naturally good at languages.
4 Why do you need to live abroad when you can **access** the Internet and immerse yourself in a foreign language without leaving your home?
5 Reading for pleasure is the only way to **increase** your vocabulary.

I disagree with the first one. Remember how our teacher told us she'd never lived abroad.

3 Vocabulary: Learning expressions

A 3.5 Listen to six conversation excerpts from 1B and 1C. After you hear a 'beep', match each one to the teacher's response (a–g). There's one extra. Continue listening to check your answers.

a ☐ Yes, it's improved by leaps and bounds!
b ☐ You mean you picked it up naturally by talking to native speakers?
c ☐ Yes, I know you have! You've put a lot of effort into your work!
d ☐ So your French is a bit rusty ...
e ☐ Well, it's natural to feel out of your depth sometimes.
f ☐ You mean you could get by?
g ☐ That's debatable.

B **Make it personal** Learning can be a bumpy ride!

1 In pairs, role-play conversations about these other learning experiences. Use learning expressions from A.

1

My serve is getting much better.

2

I really struggled when I first joined the orchestra.

3

I used to depend on my spell checker till I joined the spelling club.

4

I've worked very hard on this painting.

2 Choose at least two topics. Share true information. End by answering question 1 in 1D.

art maths music spelling sport

I've started playing the violin again. I was really rusty, but I've been putting a lot of effort into my technique.

That's fantastic! Are you enjoying it?

In a way I am. It's a whole new world.

4 Language in use

A 3.6 What are the blue words in the tweets called? How can they help you search for information? Listen to the start of a talk on digital literacy and check your answers.

> I think you can search by typing ..., both in Twitter and other applications like ...

1 Having lunch at Au Bon Pain. Love this place! #lunch

2 Very interesting article on global warming: www.globalwarming_whatweknow #climatechangeisrealandweshouldactnow

3 Wonder if Rihanna thinks of Pinocchio when she sings 'I love the way you lie'. #funny

B 3.7 Listen to the second part. Complete a student's notes.

Reasons to use hashtags:
- Stronger messages, which reflect your [1]_________ and [2]_________ identity.
- Gives your message a humorous [3]_________
- Easier to express non-verbal [4]_________.
- Political and [5]_________ significance.
- A clearer sense of belonging to a larger [6]_________.

C 3.8 Guess the problems (a–c) for the hashtags (1–3) in A. Listen to check.

a ☐ It's hard to read. b ☐ It doesn't offer new information. c ☐ It assumes you agree.

D **Make it personal** What do you think of hashtags?

1 3.9 **How to say it** Complete 1–6 with the words in the box. Listen to check.

extent	mildly	respects	say	speak	will

Making your attitude clear

What they said	What they meant
1 Hashtags let you search by topic, which, to a certain _________, filters out some of the less relevant results.	This is only partially true.
2 Hashtags are an integral part of online communication – and, in some _________, of our culture at large.	
3 What a hashtag can do is give your text more colour and depth – like a clever punchline, if you _________.	I'm speaking figuratively.
4 They're just noise so to _________, and, honestly, why people use them is beyond me.	
5 This hashtag is confusing to _________ the least, and how it can help the reader isn't clear.	It's worse than I'm suggesting.
6 Personally, I find that tweet a bit lame – to put it _________ – but that's beside the point.	

2 In groups, discuss a–d.

a Do you find hashtags helpful? How often do you use them?
b How would you improve the hashtags (1–3) in A?
c How important is it for you to get lots of likes and retweets?
d What point is the cartoon trying to make? Do you agree?

> I think the people in the building are all trying to pass the responsibility to someone else!

> I don't really agree. In the digital age ...

5 Grammar: Information-focus clauses

A Read the grammar box and tick (✓) the correct rules. Then underline three more examples in 4D.

Information focus: subject and object clauses

To prepare the listener for new information, we sometimes use a subject clause:		
Subject	**How often** people post	increases their influence.
	What she did to simplify her life	was (to) unfollow lots of people.
To explain something further, we can use an object clause:		
Object	**Why** my writing is unclear	I'm not really sure.
	Whether slang should be used	we think is a question of personal style.

1 The verb in the information-focus clause can be ☐ **active** ☐ **passive** ☐ **active or passive**.
2 The verb starting the main clause is ☐ **singular** ☐ **plural** ☐ **singular or plural**.

» Grammar expansion p.142

B Correct two errors in each sentence. Can you think of any other ambiguous emoticons?

TWO POPULAR EMOTICONS YOU MIGHT BE USING WRONG!

Many people assume this is a tear drop, but what is it meant to be are a sweat drop that shows you're stressed out. I spent years misusing this one!

This one's used to convey triumph rather than anger. Why did they decide to make it look like an angry bull remain a mystery!

Common mistakes

How ~~does~~ my sister ~~manage~~ *manages* to be so funny I'll never understand!

Why Bob has so many followers ~~remain~~ *remains* a mystery.

C Write sentences with information-focus clauses using the prompts 1–6. Use the correct tense and verb form, and add words, as needed.

4 old-fashioned slang terms I wish would make a comeback!

The thing about slang is that it's unpredictable. A new word or expression may catch on quickly, but [1][how long / last / no one / know]. It may disappear in a year or two or stick around for decades. Here are four old-fashioned slang terms you might still hear:

1 DOLL UP: I love this one! You might think it has to do with dolls, but [2]**[what / mean / be / 'get dressed up']**, as in 'I got all dolled up for the party.' Now, [3]**[how / friends / react / if / say this / mystery!]**

2 DOUGH: Slang words for 'money' come and go, but 'dough' is my favourite. [4]**[When / originate / surprise you]**: The first printed records date back to the mid 1800s!

3 SWANKY: If you describe something as swanky, you're saying it's expensive and fashionable. [5]**[Whether / really / be / people / decide / for themselves]**.

4 WHAT'S EATING YOU? This one means 'What's bothering you?' [6]**[Where exactly / hear / first time / not / remember]**. It might have been in a film. Or maybe my grandfather used it.

D Make it personal In groups, discuss 1–3.

1 What are the most popular slang terms at the moment where you live?
2 How much slang do you use? When? Where? Why?
3 Do your parents / grandparents / children ever use slang you don't recognise?

Have you heard the expression ...?

6 Reading

A In pairs, how do you feel when you have to speak in front of a group of people?

> I feel kind of self-conscious, but I never panic.

> Lucky you! I usually start to sweat and forget what I was about to say.

B Read the first paragraph. Predict at least three strategies the article might give for overcoming nervousness when speaking to a group. Continue reading to check. Were your ideas mentioned?

Better Public Speaking:

Becoming a Confident, Compelling Speaker

BY MINDTOOLS.COM

1 **Whether we're talking in a team meeting or presenting in front of an audience, we all have to speak in public from time to time. We can do this well or we can do this badly, and the outcome strongly affects the way that people think about us. The good news is that, with thorough preparation and practice, you can overcome your nervousness and perform exceptionally well. This article explains how!**

2 **Plan appropriately:** Think about how important a book's first paragraph is; if it doesn't grab you, you're likely going to put it down. The same principle goes for your speech: from the beginning, you need to intrigue your audience. For example, you could start with an interesting statistic, headline, or fact that pertains to what you're talking about and resonates with your audience. You can also use story telling as a powerful opener.

3 **Practice:** There's a good reason that we say, 'Practice makes perfect!' You simply cannot be a confident, compelling speaker without practice. If you're going to be delivering a presentation or prepared speech, create it as early as possible. The earlier you put it together, the more time you'll have to practise. Practise it plenty of times alone, using the resources you'll rely on at the event, and, as you practise, tweak your words until they flow smoothly and easily.

4 **Engage with your audience:** When you speak, try to engage your audience. This makes you feel less isolated as a speaker and keeps everyone involved with your message. If appropriate, ask leading questions targeted to individuals or groups, and encourage people to participate and ask questions. Also, pay attention to how you're speaking. If you're nervous, you might talk quickly. This increases the chances that you'll trip over your words, or say something you don't mean. Force yourself to slow down by breathing deeply. Don't be afraid to gather your thoughts; pauses are an important part of conversation, and they make you sound confident, natural, and authentic.

5 **Cope with nerves:** How often have you listened to or watched a speaker who really messed up? Chances are, the answer is 'not very often'. Crowds are more intimidating than individuals, so think of your speech as a conversation that you're having with one person. Although your audience may be 100 people, focus on one friendly face at a time, and talk to that person as if he or she is the only one in the room.

6 **Watch recordings of your speeches:** Whenever possible, record your presentations and speeches. You can improve your speaking skills dramatically by watching yourself later, and then working on improving in areas that didn't go well. Are you looking at the audience? Did you smile? Did you speak clearly at all times? Pay attention to your gestures. Do they appear natural or forced? Make sure that people can see them, especially if you're standing behind a podium.

7 If you speak well in public, it can help you get a job or promotion, raise awareness for your team or organisation, and educate others. The more you push yourself to speak in front of others, the better you'll become, and the more confidence you'll have.

C ▶3.10 Re-read and listen to the article. T (true) or F (false)? Underline the evidence.

1 First impressions are critical.
2 There's no such thing as too much rehearsal.
3 Audience participation can be distracting.
4 Eye contact should be random, and it's best not to look at people.
5 You can recognise and correct your own mistakes.

D Scan paragraphs 1–4. Find words that mean ...

1 result (n): ________ (paragraph 1)
2 complete (adj): ________ (paragraph 1)
3 appeal to: ________ (paragraph 2)
4 persuasive: ________ (paragraph 3)
5 collect: ________ (paragraph 4)

E Make it personal In groups, discuss 1–3.

1 Who's the best / worst public speaker you see on TV? Why?
2 Which advice in the article seems most useful? Have you ever tried any of it?
3 What additional problems do people face when speaking in public in a foreign language? What can they do to cope?

In a foreign language, you could forget words or make grammar mistakes.

Yes, and if you have a strong accent, your audience might not understand you!

7 Vocabulary: Expressions with *word*

A Read paragraph 4 again. Underline an expression that means 'to stumble' or 'have trouble saying' your words.

B Read the quotes. Can you figure out what the **highlighted** expressions mean?

1 'They say 90% of the promotion of a book comes **by word of mouth**. But you've somehow got to get your book into the hands of those mouths first!.' (Abraham Cahan)
2 '**Keep your word**. It creates a life of never having to explain who you are.' (Cleo Wade)
3 'Happiness is a choice, not a destination. **Spread the word**.' (Unknown quote)
4 'No, you can't **take back your words**. Because once you've said them, there's no refund.' (Francine Chiar)
5 'I got well by talking. Death could not **get a word in edgewise**, grew discouraged, and travelled on.' (Louise Erdrich)
6 'I believe that unarmed truth and unconditional love will **have the final word** in reality.' (Martin Luther King, Jr.)

I think *by word of mouth* just means 'by talking'. So, number 1 means you have to read the book first to be able to talk about it.

C Make it personal Which quotes do you agree with? How many similar opinions?

I agree with the first. Most of the books I've read recently have been recommendations from friends.

Common mistakes

I couldn't get ~~the~~ *a* word in edgewise.

It spread by ~~the~~ word of mouth.

He was at a loss for ~~the~~ words.

8 Listening

A In pairs, what advantages can you imagine to growing up bilingual?

> Well, a big plus is that you can communicate with more people.

Caroline Erdos

B 3.11 Guess the true statements. Then listen to / watch speech pathologist Caroline Erdos to check.

1 Bilingual children solve problems more easily.
2 Later in life, bilinguals are less likely to develop Alzheimer's disease.
3 There must be only one language at home and one at school.
4 It's natural for children to mix languages, even when the parent doesn't understand both.
5 Bilingual children learn to speak a bit later than monolingual children.
6 Special-needs children with language difficulties should remain monolingual.
7 To become bilingual, children need to be exposed to proficient speakers at least 30% of the time.

C 3.11 Listen / Watch again. In pairs, correct the false statements in **B**. Any surprises? Which facts seem the most logical?

> I was really surprised by number ... because I thought ...

9 Language in use

A 3.12 Read the discussion forum for people raised bilingual, and put 1–4 back into the posts. Listen to check. There's one extra sentence.

1 Having studied Italian informally, I've now learned the grammar
2 Taught in both languages, I felt I was always in close contact with my roots
3 Living in a city like Rio, though, I still use my German every now and then, too
4 Maybe that's why, when talking to my mom, I find it hard to discuss very abstract ideas

Anita

Having been raised in Brazil by an Australian mother and German father, I learned how to navigate between languages comfortably from a very early age. Today, I use both Portuguese and English at work. _________, even if it's only to help tourists with directions and things like that.

Fred

I grew up in Chicago, speaking English with my dad and Italian with my mom, almost exclusively. When I went to school, my English surpassed my Italian, of course. _________ My conversations with Dad, on the other hand, tend to be more profound – unless, of course, I switch to English with Mom.

Marco

Growing up in a multicultural home in Buenos Aires, I've always cherished my heritage. My mother is Argentinean, and my dad is American. We spoke both English and Spanish at home, and when I was six, my parents enrolled me in a bilingual school. Looking back, it was the best thing they could have done. _________

B **Make it personal** In pairs, answer 1–4. Any interesting stories?

1 Do you know anyone who grew up bilingual?
2 If you know bilingual people, do they mix languages? Do they switch easily from one to the other?
3 Do you think bilinguals have a favourite language? Do they think mainly in one?
4 Do you agree with the video that bilingualism has only advantages?

> I'm not sure I agree with number 4. I knew this guy who couldn't speak either language well.

> But did he have enough input? Remember the video said that ...

10 Grammar: Using participle clauses

A Read the grammar box and tick (✔) the correct rules (a–c).

Participle clauses to express result, time, and reason

1 **Knowing** some English,	I never have trouble getting by.
2 **Growing up** in a family of artists,	Gwen eventually became an actress.
3 **When driving** to work,	I used to listen to audio books.
4 **Supported** by his parents,	Ben is in no hurry to find a job.

Participle clauses, which are very common in written English ...

a describe the ☐ **past** ☐ **present or past**.

b refer to the ☐ **subject** ☐ **object** of the main sentence.

c are ☐ **always active** ☐ **either active or passive**.

» Grammar expansion p.142

B Choose the correct meaning (a–d) for the example sentences (1–4) in the grammar box. Then rephrase the participle clauses 1–3 in 9A beginning with a conjunction, too.

a As I [**know** / **knew**] some English, I ...

b She [**grew up** / **is growing up**] in a family of artists, so ...

c When I [**drive** / **drove**] to work, I ...

d Because he [**is** / **was**] supported by his parents, he ...

Common mistake

Growing up as an only child, ~~my time was spent writing~~ *I spent a lot of time writing*.

Participle clauses must have a clear subject: Your time didn't grow up – you did.

C Complete 1–5 with participle clauses, using the verbs in the box.

begin	educate	inspire	watch	win

The apple doesn't fall far from the tree

1 ____________ her mother perform across the globe for decades, singer and actress **Liza Minnelli** went on to become one of the world's most successful entertainers.

2 ____________ by his grandfather's collection of jazz records, crooner **Michael Bublé** decided he wanted to become a singer at a very early age.

3 ____________ his musical career at the age of five with a story on Yoko Ono's 1981 album, *Season of Glass*, **Sean Lennon** went on to become a musician and singer in his own right.

4 **Laila Ali**, daughter of world champion Muhammad Ali, became a professional boxer at age 18. ____________ all the fights she ever took part in, **Laila Ali** retired from the ring in 2007.

5 ____________ in Miami from the age of seven, **Enrique Iglesias**, son of Spanish singer Julio Iglesias, sings in both Spanish and English.

D Read *Perfect participles*. Then rephrase 1–5 in C.

Perfect participles

You may use a perfect participle to emphasise that an action happened before another one:
Having played the trombone when I was younger, I already knew how to read music.
After having left university, I started looking for a job in my field.

E **Make it personal** In groups, answer 1–3. Any interesting stories?

1 List a few of your special skills, talents, and accomplishments.

2 Which did you pick up mostly from your (a) family, (b) friends, (c) teachers?

3 Do you know anyone with a special talent that became clear early in life?

Yes, my nephew started writing music when he was just 12. Growing up in a musical family, he was exposed to music all the time.

11 Listening

A 3.13 Listen to part one of a conversation between two friends, David and Paula. In pairs, answer 1–2.

1 What did the musician do during the concert?
2 Why did he do it?

B 3.14 Listen to part two. Then tick (✔) Paula's advice, a or b. Do you agree with her reasons?

1 a ☐ Think about your audience during a performance. You need to be concerned with people's reactions.
  b ☐ Don't worry too much about your audience. People tend to be more accepting than we give them credit for.
2 a ☐ Don't try too hard. It will just make you nervous.
  b ☐ Try to do the best you can. It's important to be good, but within reasonable limits.
3 a ☐ Don't focus on talent. Learning is mainly motivation and practice.
  b ☐ Consider if you have talent. If not, choose something else to learn.

C 3.15 Fill in the missing words in these expressions. Listen to check.

1 Practice makes ________, remember?
2 I really have my ________ about my playing! I can't even ________ to imagine giving a concert.
3 You're setting yourself impossibly high ________.
4 Don't go to the other ________. You need to hit a middle ________.
5 Do your very ________, but don't worry about being perfect.
6 Do you think I could learn to ski if I put my ________ to it?
7 Yeah, I do. Why not give it a ________?

12 Keep talking

A Choose or invent something you've been unable to learn. Think about these questions:

1 Why did you have trouble learning it?
2 How often / hard did you try?
3 Might you give it another shot in the future?
4 What would you do differently?

B In groups, take turns presenting your problem for the others to offer advice. Use the expressions in 11C and those below.

In addition to ..., you might want to ...	Have you thought about ...?
You might not ..., but you can still ...	

I've been unable to learn how to swim! I can't even begin to imagine being in the deep end of the pool. Maybe you can give me some advice.

Have you thought about relaxation techniques? Maybe you're scared.

"I CAN'T READ BUT I HAVE EXCELLENT TV VIEWING SKILLS."

13 Writing: An expository essay

A Read the essay on an online site for language learners. Find ...

1 a sentence that creates initial interest.
2 the topic sentence.
3 three concrete techniques the essay offers.

B A good expository essay maintains the theme in a paragraph. In paragraphs 3–5 underline seven time words and expressions that help link ideas.

C Read *Write it right!* Then find three more participle clauses that the writer uses to link ideas. What is the subject of each one?

Write it right!

Expository essays use a variety of structures to create interest. Participle clauses with *-ing* are one way to link ideas or create suspense.

Before downloading a full album, I would look at the lyrics to see if the language seemed 'useful'.

D Combine 1–5 with participle clauses. Check all sentences to be sure the subject is clear!

1 You need to be motivated. In addition, you need to go the extra mile.
In addition to being motivated, you need to go the extra mile.
2 I love listening to music. My friends tell me I can improve my English that way.
3 I bought some new albums. I started to listen to them every day.
4 I imagined visual scenes as I listened. I felt as if I was in the UK.
5 I've learned a lot more colloquial language. My listening skills have improved.

E Your turn! Choose a topic you role-played in 12 and write an essay giving three pieces of advice in about 280 words.

Before
Choose three pieces of advice. Note down details to support your arguments.

While
Write six paragraphs following the model in A. Use at least two participle clauses and two other linking words or expressions.

After
Post your essay online and read your classmates' work. Who had the best advice?

What worked for me when I was studying Russian

1 We've all seen announcements from language programmes that promise we can learn English (or another language) in '20 easy lessons'. Naturally, that's false. But you might well be wondering what exactly the best way to learn a language really is.

2 Just as there are multiple kinds of intelligences, there are multiple ways of learning a foreign language. Your personal techniques have a lot to do with your personality and your learning style. What you need is lots of patience – and, of course, motivation. These three techniques helped me tremendously with Russian, when I was studying it at university.

3 I'm the kind of person who likes to listen. In fact, my friends tell me I'm a good listener, and they often choose me when confiding their problems. So, I decided to apply my listening skills to learning Russian. First, I had some Russian friends recommend popular music to me. Before downloading a full album, I would look at the lyrics to see if the language seemed 'useful'. Then listening to the songs over and over, I would compare the lyrics with the English translation I had also downloaded. Over time, I started to pick up new words and expressions, and what's more, I even heard them used when I had a chance to practise my Russian with native speakers.

4 As well as focusing on music, I thought TV could be useful for language learning. So even though I don't really like TV, I decided to pay extra to have access to the local Russian channel, too. Then I began to watch films with the English subtitles on. In the beginning, I understood very little. The actors talked so fast! But in no time at all, I started to follow the dialogue because my favourite soap opera had a predictable plot.

5 There was no way I was going to do grammar exercises in my free time, but I love to read. So, after a while, in addition to listening to music and watching TV, I decided to read novels to improve my grammar. I would look closely to see if I could recognise the structures taught in class, and sometimes made a mental note to use parts of sentences myself in conversation. In a matter of weeks, I was trying out new expressions! You could try this technique, too. But be careful! It only works with modern novels. If you read Tolstoy or Dostoyevsky, you may start sounding as if you were born in the 1820s!

6 These are just a few fun and useful ways you can improve your language skills in any language. You might want to try them, too!

4 How often do you remember your dreams?

1 Listening

A 4.1 Listen to the start of a radio show with a psychologist. Circle the correct answer.

Scientists [**are fairly sure** / **only suspect**] that some dreams may reveal certain things about our personalities.

B 4.2 Guess what dreams 1–3 represent. Listen to the second part and write the numbers. There's one extra choice. Any surprises?

☐ anger ☐ perfectionism in your work
☐ anxiety or guilt ☐ unassertiveness

1

2

3

C 4.2 Listen again and complete the table.

In which conversation(s) does Dr Wallace ...	1	2	3
1 reassure the caller things will be OK?			
2 offer two different interpretations of the same dream?			
3 ask for further details about the dream?			
4 avoid committing to a point of view?			
5 seem to have trouble convincing the caller?			

D 4.3 Listen to the end of the show. Summarise Dr Wallace's last point in one sentence.

E **Make it personal** In pairs, discuss these questions.

1 Have you ever had a dream that came true? What happened?

2 Have you recently dreamed about ...?

fire water flying falling being trapped
being unable to move missing a plane / train failing in school

Common mistake

I dreamed ~~with~~ *about* falling last night.

3 Search online for an interpretation. Does it make sense?

I've had dreams about falling, but I don't feel insecure and anxious like the website says.

It can mean other things, too. Maybe you were afraid of failing at love.

2 Vocabulary: Productive suffixes

A 4.4 Read about productive suffixes. Then complete 1–6 with the correct suffixes. Listen to check. Where does the stress fall?

Unlike suffixes such as *-ment, -ous, -al*, which usually change word class (for example, *enjoy, enjoyment*), productive suffixes can be used to create brand new words:

Suffix	Definition	Example
___-friendly	helpful or safe	a user-friendly interface
___-conscious	concerned about	a politics-conscious artist
___-oriented	directed at, focused on	a consumer-oriented company
___(-)like	similar to	a lifelike portrait
___-related	connected with	an age-related disease
___worthy	deserving of something	a newsworthy event

1 The book is thoroughly researched and very reader-________ at the same time.
2 Your review of the current literature on dreams is especially praise ________ .
3 Highly competitive, results-________ individuals often have this sort of dream.
4 It really sounds as if your nightmare is stress-________ .
5 I have a recurring dream of being chased through the woods by a tall, ghost-________ figure.
6 The more image-________ we are, the worse it gets.

B In pairs, take turns thinking of an example for each item in column 3. Share opinions.

I think the iPhone has a very user-friendly interface.

I'm not sure. I think Androids are slightly more user-friendly.

C Reword the phrases in italics with a suffix from **A**.

1 *People who are concerned about their health* aren't fun to hang out with.
2 *A leader that you can trust* is almost impossible to find these days.
3 *Teaching that is directed at exams* does students more harm than good.
4 *Entertainment that's safe for the whole family* is almost impossible to find these days.
5 *Programmes connected with school* are a great way for children to develop independence.

D Make it personal Are you set in your ways? What fixed opinions do you have?

1 4.5 **How to say it** Complete the table. Listen to check.

Committing to a point of view	
What they said	What they meant
1 I wouldn't go so ________ as to (call it a masterpiece).	I wouldn't go to the extent of ...
2 The ________ is still out on (whether that's true).	There's no agreement that ...
3 There's no ________ in my mind that (they will).	I'm absolutely sure that ...
4 Oh, yes, without a ________ of a doubt.	I'm positive.
5 We should take (these claims) with a grain of ________.	We should be sceptical of ...

2 Choose two statements from **2C** you feel strongly about. Note down a few ideas under 'I'm convinced that ...'/ 'I'm not entirely convinced that ...'

3 In groups, share your ideas. Use *How to say it* expressions. Any major disagreements?

OK, number 1: 'Health-conscious people aren't fun to hang out with' ... Hmm, I wouldn't go so far as to call them boring, though.

Well, not unless they try to change your eating habits.

3 Language in use

A 4.6 Use the photos and speech bubbles to guess what happened. Listen to check. Then choose the correct option in the heading.

Didn't *The War of the Worlds* begin as a radio show?

Yes, with actor Orson Welles. I think it might have been about ...

B 4.6 Number the events in order (1–5). Listen again to check. Then look in AS 4.6 on p.162. Underline phrases that helped you decide.

- ☐ People tried to escape from their homes.
- ☐ Listeners discovered the truth and relaxed.
- ☐ The radio station learned about the impact of the show.
- ☐ The show was heavily criticised.
- ☐ News of the killer aliens scared listeners.

C 4.7 Match each verb (1–5) with an object (a–e). What does each phrase mean? Listen to check. Which two verbs are used figuratively?

1 throw	a ☐ a sigh of relief
2 clog	b ☐ havoc
3 flee	c ☐ someone into a frenzy
4 breathe	d ☐ the attack
5 wreak	e ☐ the highways

D In pairs, take turns telling the story from memory. Use expressions from C, making sure you know the past forms, too.

E **Make it personal** Have you, or has anyone you know, ever believed a science-fiction story about one of these topics? What happened as the result?

mythical creatures   the end of the world
natural disasters   transport

When I was a child, I believed a dragon could fly through our window. I really thought I might have to flee an attack!

4 **Grammar:** Emphatic inversion

A Read the grammar box and tick (✔) the correct rules.

Emphatic inversion: Inverted subject and verb

Rarely **do we find**	such realistic sound effects.
Little **did they know**	what the show would cause.
Nowhere **could they find**	the cause of the panic.
Only after the scandal had blown over	**was he** asked to direct *Citizen Kane*.
Not since the BBC aired the show,	**has there been** so much excitement.

1 Inversion is used with adverbs and adverbial expressions to ☐ **emphasise** ☐ **de-emphasise** what you are saying. It is especially common in writing.
2 Whether inversion is possible is determined by the ☐ **topic** ☐ **adverb or adverbial expression**.
3 With *only after / when, not since*, etc, inversion is always in the ☐ **first** ☐ **second** clause.
4 The adverbials in italics have a ☐ **positive** ☐ **negative or, in some cases, limiting** meaning.

Common mistakes

Only when ~~did I watch~~ *I watched* the film did I appreciate it.
Not only ~~I watched~~ *did I watch* it six times, but I memorised the script.

Grammar expansion p.144

B Circle the correct answers in column B. Then rephrase the sentences from 3A so they are neutral.

Orson Welles' *Citizen Kane*: What the reviewers have said

A: Neutral	B: Emphatic
1 There'll never be such an excellent script again!	Never again [**will there be / there will be**] such an excellent script.
2 You'll only fully appreciate this film when you watch it.	Only when [**you watch / do you watch**] this film, [**you will / will you**] fully appreciate it.
3 Critics have rarely voted a film 'the greatest film of all time'.	Rarely [**have critics voted / critics have voted**] a film 'the greatest film of all time'.
4 There hasn't been such a critical success since the film came out.	Not since the film [**did come out / came out**] [**has there been / there has been**] such a critical success.

C Rewrite 1–4 starting with the adverbials in brackets. What was your favourite prank?

The most epic April Fools' Day pranks of all time!

2015: A train company announced that it had plans to replace conventional seats with state-of-the-art gym equipment. (1) *Train travel would no longer be sedentary* (no longer)!

1992: Passengers approaching Los Angeles airport were shocked to see a huge banner welcoming them to Chicago! (2) *They only realised it was a prank after the plane had landed.* (only after)

1980: A TV station reported that London's iconic Big Ben was going to be turned into a digital clock. (3) *People were not only shocked, but they were also outraged.* (not only)

1957: A news programme had convinced viewers that spaghetti could grow on trees. (4) *There had not been such a creative prank since the invention of TV.* (not since)

D **Make it personal** Search on 'April Fools' Day pranks' and share your best two in groups. Which one was funniest?

This guy bought coloured post-it notes and covered his friend's car. So not only did she not recognise her own car, but she also thought it was a wedding decoration.

5 Vocabulary: Nouns and adjectives from phrasal verbs

A Read *Synonyms for nouns and adjectives from phrasal verbs*. Then circle five more examples in the headlines below and draw an arrow connecting them to their synonyms.

Synonyms for nouns and adjectives from phrasal verbs

Nouns and adjectives formed from phrasal verbs often have neutral or slightly more formal one-word synonyms:

We've had two burglaries this year. I'm of tired of these **break-ins** (n). We need to beef up security. (= Someone **broke in**.)

Even computers can be disposable. Most companies these days are producing **throwaway** laptops with cheap plastic bodies. (= That we **throw away**.)

Remember: Some words formed from phrasal verbs are hyphenated, and some are one word. The stress is on the first syllable.

Our favourite 'conspiracy headlines' of the past few years

Conspiracy theories are more pervasive than ever before on social media.

	KIND OF CONSPIRACY	TYPICAL HEADLINE
1	Earth's imminent destruction	*Total wipeout of the planet likely due to solar storm in 2023. So far, no precautions taken!*
2	Restriction of our personal freedom	*Sales of surveillance cameras up by 80%: Crackdown on civil liberties 'worse than ever before', study suggests.*
3	Concealment of official information	*The cover-up of the decade: Cure for cancer available at least since 2002.*
4	Control by evil creatures accelerates	*Illuminati takeover enters its final phase.*
5	Confidential warning about dead celebrity sightings	*'English singer David Bowie is alive and well', tip-off reveals.*

B Complete 1–5 with the phrasal verb form of the words you circled in the headlines in A. Then change the sentences, if necessary, so they're true for you.

1 Where I live, if you witness a crime, it's easy to ________ ________ the police anonymously.
2 The police should ________ ________ on graffiti artists. Enough is enough!
3 I suspect the truth behind the side effects of many drugs has been ________ ________ by drug companies.
4 I'm not entirely convinced dinosaurs were ________ ________ by an asteroid.
5 I'm sure tech companies are trying to ________ ________ the world.

I doubt tech companies are trying to take over the world. They're only offering products we want.

C Make it personal In pairs, answer 1–3. Who's more sceptical of conspiracy theories?

1 Which conspiracy theories from 3 are you familiar with? Which are the most outlandish / plausible?
2 Search online for conspiracy theories. Share your favourite ones.
3 Why are some people attracted to these theories?

I think some people are suspicious by nature, and so they love these kinds of theories.

6 Reading

A Read paragraph 1 of the article. How would the author answer question 3 in 5C?

- ☐ Because they have a natural tendency to look for meaning in random events.
- ☐ Because the evidence the theories are based on can be misleading.

Why Do Some People Believe in Conspiracy Theories?

Christopher French, a professor of psychology at Goldsmiths, University of London, explains:

Although conspiracy beliefs can occasionally be based on a rational analysis of the evidence, most of the time they are not. As a species, one of our greatest strengths is our ability to find meaningful patterns in the world around us and to make causal inferences. We sometimes, however, see patterns and causal connections that are not there, especially when we feel that events are beyond our control.

The attractiveness of conspiracy theories may arise from a number of cognitive biases that characterise the way we process information. 'Confirmation bias' is the most pervasive cognitive bias and a powerful driver of belief in conspiracies. We all have a natural inclination to give more weight to evidence that supports what we already believe and ignore evidence that contradicts our beliefs. The real-world events that often become the subject of conspiracy theories tend to be intrinsically complex and unclear. Early reports may contain errors, contradictions and ambiguities, and those wishing to find evidence of a cover-up will focus on such inconsistencies to bolster their claims.

'Proportionality bias', our innate tendency to assume that big events have big causes, may also explain our tendency to accept conspiracies. This is one reason many people were uncomfortable with the idea that President John F Kennedy was the victim of a deranged lone gunman and found it easier to accept the theory that he was the victim of a large-scale conspiracy.

Another relevant cognitive bias is 'projection'. People who endorse conspiracy theories may be more likely to engage in conspiratorial behaviours themselves, such as spreading rumours or tending to be suspicious of others' motives. If you would engage in such behaviour, it may seem natural that other people would as well, making conspiracies appear more plausible and widespread. Furthermore, people who are strongly inclined toward conspiratorial thinking will be more likely to endorse mutually contradictory theories. For example, if you believe that Osama bin Laden was killed many years before the American government officially announced his death, you are also more likely to believe that he is still alive.

None of the above should indicate that all conspiracy theories are false. Some may indeed turn out to be true. The point is that some individuals may have a tendency to find such theories attractive. The crux of the matter is that conspiracists are not really sure what the true explanation of an event is – they are simply certain that the 'official story' is a cover-up.

B 4.8 A *cognitive bias* is a tendency to confuse our subjective perceptions with reality. Listen to and read the article. Match the quotes (1–3) to the types of cognitive bias in the article (a–c).

a confirmation bias   b proportionality bias   c projection

1 ☐ 'I'm sure our politicians are spying on us. If I were in charge, I'm sure I would do the same.'
2 ☐ 'A legend like David Bowie couldn't have died just like that without our knowing he was ill. Something sounds fishy.'
3 ☐ 'I get severe headaches whenever I use my phone a lot. I've always believed in the dangers of radiation.'

C Read *Tentative language*. Underline two examples in each paragraph in the article.

Tentative language

Academic writing is **often** based on hypotheses and interpretation. Therefore, **most** writers **tend** to avoid making generalisations and being too assertive, which **might** put readers off. The words in bold (e.g. modals, adverbs, quantifiers) are examples of how writers use tentative language to show they aren't 100% certain.

D Make it personal What are *your* biases?

1 In groups, read each word in turn and say the very first word that comes to mind.

cooking   fitness   Hollywood   smartphones
Lady Gaga   politics   football   taxi drivers

2 Which words, if any, reveal(s) a hidden bias?

Taxi drivers conjure up images of speeding!

I think that's biased. Some drive very carefully.

7 Language in use

A Look at the eyes and pick the one you're immediately drawn to. Then search on 'eye personality test' and read the results on one of the sites you find. Are they accurate for you?

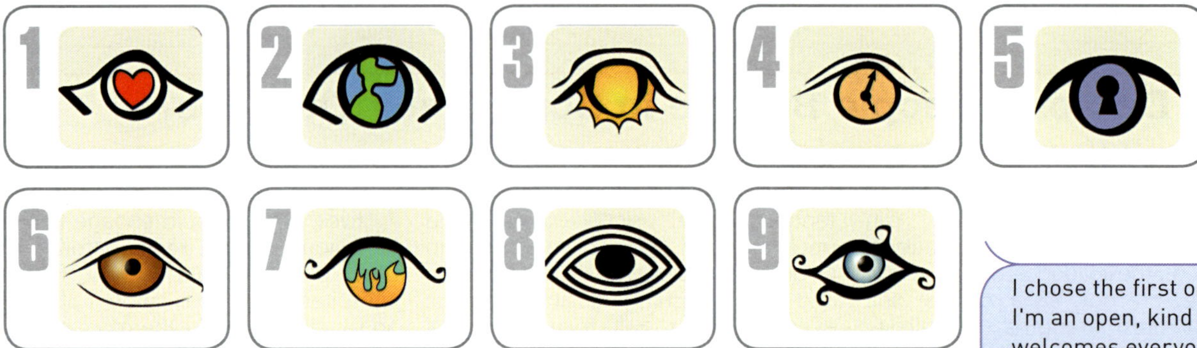

I chose the first one. It says I'm an open, kind spirit who welcomes everyone into my life.

B 4.9 Listen to the start of an interview with a psychologist. How does he feel about the test in A? Do you agree?

C 4.10 Listen to the rest. Why is he sceptical of personality tests? Tick (✔) the points he makes.

1 People's personalities ...
- a ☐ are sometimes contradictory.
- b ☐ are influenced by life events.
- c ☐ can be captured better in interviews than tests.

2 Employee personality tests ...
- a ☐ haven't been updated in years.
- b ☐ may be used inappropriately.
- c ☐ can't predict performance accurately.

D 4.11 Read *Pronouncing the letter s*. Then write /s/ or /z/ next to the highlighted letters in 1–4. Listen to check.

Pronouncing the letter s

The letter *s* is tricky. We say *assume* /s/, but *possess* /z/; *base* /s/, but *phase* /z/. These simple rules will help you. Say ...
- /s/ in the suffix sis: *basis* and in the prefix dis: *disadvantage*.
- /z/ in the suffix sm: *sarcasm*.
- /z/ for a verb (*use* a pen) and /s/ for a noun or adjective (make *use* of it) in homographs.

1 It depends on the kind of research on which the test was based ☐ and on the subsequent data analysis ☐.
2 The web is full of amateur tests, all of which have come in for a lot of criticism ☐ in recent years.
3 These tests provide vague personality descriptions, with which it's hard to disagree ☐.
4 I interviewed over a hundred recruiting managers, some of whom admitted to using test results as an excuse ☐ not to hire or promote someone.

E Make it personal In pairs, how do you feel about ...? Be sure to pronounce the bold words correctly.

fad diets faith-healing fortune-telling horoscopes self-help books telepathy

I (don't) think ... make(s) sense. I can('t) understand people's **scepticism**!
Once I ... and I was(n't) **disappointed**. What happened was ...
Most of my friends would **disagree** with me, but ...
The **hypothesis** that ... sounds ... to me. For one thing ...
I don't think you can **use** ... to ...

Most of my friends would disagree with me, but I don't think you can use the argument that fad diets are better than no diet.

8 Grammar: Formal relative clauses

A Read the grammar box and complete rules 1–3. Then look at 1–4 in 7D and say which nouns *which* and *whom* refer to.

Formal relative clauses with *which* and *whom*

A hundred **people** were surveyed,	**most of whom** regularly take personality tests.
Most tests are based on **theories**	**about which** very little is known.
I'd like to thank **Dr Cooper**,	**without whom** this study wouldn't have been possible.
I prefer to read **books** and **articles**	**from which** I can derive new insights.

In formal relative clauses ...

1 the preposition goes ___________ the relative pronoun.

2 we use the pronoun ___________ for people and ___________ for things.

3 a non-restrictive clause is preceded by a ___________.

Grammar expansion p.144

B Unscramble the bold words in 1–6 using formal relative clauses. There's one extra word in each group.

Common mistake

This is the book ~~(that) the film is based.~~
✓(that) the film is based **on**. (neutral)
✓**on which** the film is based. (more formal)

The "Big 5"

The Five Factor Model is based on the idea that there are five broad domains [1][which / our / can / personalities / that / into / be / classified]:

1 Openness to experience: This describes the extent [2]**[which / to / what / someone / curious / is]**, imaginative, and adventurous. Can he or she 'think outside the box'?

2 Conscientiousness: Reliability, thoroughness, and self-discipline are traits [3]**[whom / with / often / is / conscientiousness / which / associated]**.

3 Extroversion: Extroverts thrive on social interaction and seek the company of people [4]**[who / exchange / can / they / with / ideas / whom]**.

4 Agreeableness: These individuals, [5]**[on / which / we / count / usually / whom / can]** in times of trouble, tend to be kind, cooperative, and sympathetic.

5 Neuroticism: This trait refers to the frequency [6]**[that / with / an / which / experiences / individual]** negative emotions, e.g. anxiety, anger, or depression.

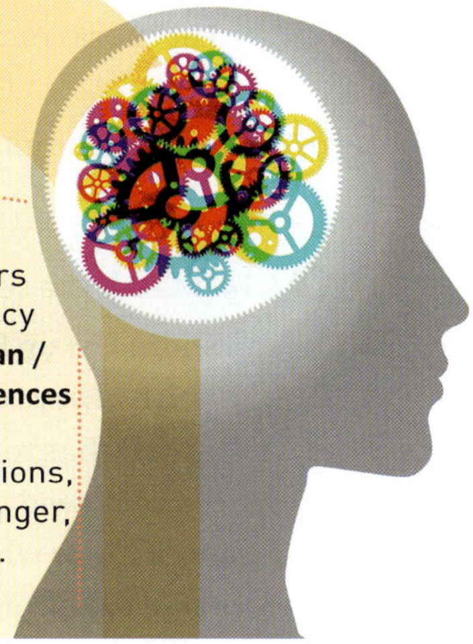

C Complete the survey results with *which*, *whom*, and a preposition. How would *you* personally rank 1–5?

What do you value the most when choosing a boyfriend / girlfriend? Our survey results:	Number 1 for % of responses
1 The kindness _______ _______ they treat pets.	15
2 The creativity _______ _______ they approach their job.	25
3 The friends _______ _______ they surround themselves.	55
4 The sense of ethics _______ _______ they base their lives.	75
5 The people _______ _______ they show empathy.	90

D Make it personal In groups, answer the question and list at least three qualities or characteristics. Use formal relative clauses where possible. Similar opinions?

What do you value the most when choosing a(n) ...?

Doctors? I value the empathy with which they treat their patients.

airline bank doctor / dentist friend language school flatmate holiday destination

9 Listening

A 4.12 In pairs, guess two reasons for 1–2. Then listen to the first part of a conversation between Julie and Seth to check.

Should an employer have a right to know if an applicant has a criminal record?
1 Yes, because ... **2** No, because ...

B 4.13 Listen to the rest. Match topics 1–4 with arguments in favour of censorship a–e. There's one extra argument.

1 sensitive government information

2 Internet sites

3 books

4 history

a ☐ Too many details might erode trust.
b ☐ Too much can make you nervous.
c ☐ The more control, the better.
d ☐ They might be too upsetting.
e ☐ Children lack the maturity to evaluate them.

C In pairs, can you remember Seth's four arguments <u>against</u> censorship? Check in AS 4.13 on p.162 and underline them.

D 4.14 Match the sentence halves. Listen to check. Which of the highlighted expressions did you know?

1 You should **be up front** about
2 **The truth always comes out** when your
3 A company has to hire you
4 We have no need to see
5 I want to know what my government
6 If we **conceal information**,
7 Shouldn't some novels be **banned from**

a ☐ **sensitive** government **documents**.
b ☐ boss starts to wonder why you're secretive.
c ☐ children will be suspicious.
d ☐ **a prior conviction**.
e ☐ with all the information **on the table**.
f ☐ is **up to**.
g ☐ school?

10 Keep talking

A Choose a topic from 9A or B, and decide if you are for or against censorship. Note down at least three arguments to support your position.

B **Make it personal** In groups, present your arguments using the expressions below and in 9D. Whose are the most convincing?

Rarely do we ... That may be, but ... That's my whole point.
There's no such thing as ... I'm 100% opposed to ... At the very least, it can ...

Schools shouldn't censor what students read. Rarely do children suffer from overexposure to ideas!

That may be, but teachers might still have to conceal some information.

11 Writing: A letter to the editor

A Read Julie's letter to the editor. Answer 1–3.

1 Identify the thesis statement in paragraph 1.
2 Identify the opposing argument in paragraph 2.
3 Summarise the main arguments in paragraphs 3–5.

B Read *Write it right!* Look at the highlighted expressions (1–7) in context. Then circle the options in 1–4 below that logically reflect Julie's most likely point of view.

Write it right!

In formal writing, writers support their arguments with fixed expressions that add clarity to their message:

Contrary to popular belief, I strongly believe that a job candidate should never be required to reveal a prior conviction.

There is some debate as to whether a prior conviction is an accurate predictor of job performance.

1 [**Many would argue that / There's certainly no denying that**] 'once a criminal, always a criminal'.
2 [**There is some debate as to whether / I strongly believe that**] personality tests can reveal a criminal mind.
3 [**Irrespective of the seriousness of the crime, / There is some debate as to whether**] criminals often serve a lifelong 'sentence'.
4 [**Despite claims to the contrary, / I believe strongly that**] everyone deserves a second chance.

C Your turn! Choose a topic from 10B and write a five- to six-paragraph letter to the editor in about 280 words.

Before
Decide whether you are for or against, and note down three arguments with supporting details. Also note down an opposing argument.

While
Write the letter, following the model. Include expressions from B to support your argument in three paragraphs. Introduce your thesis in paragraph 1 and summarise it at the end.

After
Post your letter online and read your classmates' work. Whose is most convincing?

Common mistake

~~The unemployment~~ *unemployment* also erodes confidence.

Remember: Non-count and plural nouns used to make generalisations have no article.

By Julie Montague

Many letters in this column have praised the benefits of openness, transparency, and a lack of censorship. However, there's one area where openness is unlikely to have a positive outcome. [1]I strongly believe that a job candidate should never be required to reveal a prior conviction for a crime. In fact, it should be illegal for employers to gain access to information on crimes that occurred more than ten years ago.

[2]Many would argue that employers have a responsibility to their staff, and that safety is of utmost importance. While [3]there is certainly no denying that companies need to keep their employees safe, there are compelling reasons to eliminate background checks.

First, [4]contrary to popular belief, [5]there is some debate as to whether a prior conviction is an accurate predictor of job performance. The conviction may have been for a minor offence and in an area that has no relevance to the job in question. Moreover, background checks do not provide contextual information or information on mitigating circumstances. They do, however, create an image. And nowhere are our imaginations more active than in imagining the flawed characters of those once convicted of crimes. An enormous pool of potential workers, many of whom have long ago served their sentences, are never given an opportunity to prove their worth. In fact, many never even get so far as an interview.

Second, in no way is public safety undermined more than by having large numbers of unemployed people on the streets. Unemployment also erodes confidence, which, in turn, might encourage a return to crime. Facing a lifetime of social and economic disadvantage, those with prior convictions who cannot find work have little motivation not to fall prey to negative influences. In addition, our economy needs workers willing to take entry-level jobs. [6]Irrespective of our personal prejudices, employment for all means improvement in our economy, and a rising standard of living across the board actually improves safety.

Finally, [7]despite claims to the contrary, studies have shown that background checks may contain errors, all of which are a potential tool for discrimination. The information may be out of date, offered by obsolete computer systems. It may not show that an arrest never led to a conviction. And shockingly, even those falsely arrested in cases of mistaken identity may be denied jobs.

For all of the reasons above, I strongly recommend a rethinking of our current policies. Withholding information, as opposed to offering it, may be the best way to offer productive employment to all. Let's not ask a percentage of our population to serve a second, lifetime sentence.

Review 2
Units 3–4

1 Speaking

A Look at the photos on p. 28.

1 Note down three language-learning techniques you think work well, using these words and expressions.

access (n,v) command (n) get by improve by leaps and bounds increase (n,v) out of my depth pick it up progress (n,v) put a lot of effort into rusty

2 In groups, share your reasons. Any original ideas?

Your vocabulary can improve by leaps and bounds if you listen to music more.

Really? Have you ever tried that?

B Make it personal Language-learning problems!

1 Note down two areas where you're still having trouble. Use participle clauses.

When speaking to new people, I often feel very shy.

2 Share your problems with a partner, who will give you advice. Use some of these expressions.

Problem: I can't even begin to imagine I have my doubts about to say the least if you ask me to put it mildly to a certain extent so to speak

Advice: practice makes perfect set yourself impossibly high standards give it a try go to the other extreme hit a middle ground put your mind to it

When speaking to new people, I often feel very shy. I have my doubts about whether I seem interesting.

Perhaps you're setting yourself impossibly high standards.

2 Grammar

A Rewrite Lucille's story about dreams, changing the underlined phrases (1–7) so there is an emphatic inversion using the words in brackets.

When I woke up in a cold sweat during the night, [1]<u>I didn't know</u> (little) I'd had a fairly common dream. [2]<u>When I read an article on the subject, I found out</u> (only when) dreams of being chased were common. [3]<u>And they're not only</u> (not only) common, but they usually mean the person is feeling vulnerable. I was feeling that way because I'd broken up with my boyfriend after five years, and [4]<u>I'd never felt so guilty before</u> (never before). [5]<u>After I learned that guilt could lead to such dreams, I started to relax</u> (only after) little by little. I'm a lot more aware of my dreams now, and [6]<u>I haven't had a similar dream since then</u> (not since). Before this happened, [7]<u>I hardly ever thought</u> (rarely) about the significance of dreams, but now I'm fascinated by the topic.

B Make it personal In pairs, share a story about something you learned about yourself from a dream. Use emphatic inversion and formal relative clauses.

Rarely had I had recurring dreams until I changed schools ...

3 Reading

A Read the article about Martin Luther King, Jr. In pairs, recall three reasons he was a great public speaker.

One of the greatest orators of all time was Martin Luther King, Jr. Only 34 years old when he delivered his famous 'I have a dream' speech in 1963, he changed the course of history. However, rarely have people stopped to consider the qualities that made King such a powerful speaker. Let me point out just a few.

First, really convincing speakers are authentic. They have a message to deliver, which they themselves fully embody, and King's life and words were harmonious. By the time he delivered his famous speech, he had already established himself as a committed civil rights leader.

Listen carefully, and you'll also notice King's tone and cadence. He usually began his speeches slowly before building up to a powerful, more rapid delivery. As he increased his pace and volume, he captivated his listeners. Not only did he create a powerful connection in this way, but he also reinforced his message through repetition. The repetition of the words 'I have a dream' comes through again and again in his speech.

Finally, while King may have improvised his famous speech, delivered without notes, what is less well-known is that not only had he been practising parts of it for years, he also had been preaching about dreams since 1960. Rehearsing his message over and over, King was able to evaluate its impact on smaller audiences to whom he had delivered it. Fully aware that 'practice makes perfect', he honed his talents. It is no wonder that 'I have a dream' was ranked the top speech of the 20th century in a 1999 poll.

B Make it personal Search on 'I have a dream', and read or listen to the speech. What other qualities do you feel make a good public speaker?

He mentions history a lot, so listeners can feel part of something greater.

4 Self-test

Correct the two mistakes in each sentence. Check your answers in Units 3 and 4. What's your score, 1–20?

1 I used to feel really out of the depth at university, even though I could more or less get through.
2 You're putting yourself very high standards and need to hit a middle road.
3 Why do I still have an accent is a mystery, but an article I read recently said speaking makes perfect.
4 How often people uses hashtags differ from one location to another.
5 At first, I couldn't get the word in edgewise, but later on, I was actually at a loss for the words.
6 I wouldn't go too far as to say it's an agerelated illness.
7 Not only I watched the man break in to the flat, but I also tipped up the cops.
8 It's the film which the show is based and about that I wrote a review.
9 So many people suffer from stress-oriented problems, most of who don't know it.
10 I read lots of blogs from that I get ideas, unrespective of the author.

5 Point of view

Choose a topic. Then support your opinion in 100–150 words, and record your answer. Ask a partner for feedback. How can you be more convincing?

a You feel most people have serious hidden biases. OR
You feel only a small percentage do, just like a small percentage believes in conspiracy theories.

b You think parents need to monitor what their children read. OR
You think any kind of censorship is inappropriate and children need to be exposed to the real world.

5 Why do good plans sometimes fail?

1 Listening

A 5.1 In pairs, use the photo and excerpts from a radio show (1–4) about a publicity stunt to guess what happened. Listen to check. How close were you?

1. Snapple sought to break a world record, so it came up with a creative if mad idea: erect the world's largest ice lolly.
2. It was roughly 27 degrees outside.
3. They're usually very thorough when planning big campaigns.
4. Sounds as chaotic as a snowstorm with unploughed side streets!

B 5.1 Listen again. T (true) or F (false)?

1 Snapple had an innovative campaign.
2 The ice lolly completely collapsed.
3 The company narrowly avoided a problem on the nearby streets.
4 Snapple managed to finish their promotional event.
5 There was fear the problem might get out of control.

C 5.2 Listen to the next part of the programme. Tick (✔) the hypotheses suggested (1–6). What do *you* think happened?

1 ☐ lack of planning
2 ☐ a computer bug
3 ☐ transport
4 ☐ unusual weather
5 ☐ sabotage
6 ☐ no direct cause

2 Pronunciation: Words ending in *-ough*

A 5.3 and 5.4 Read and listen to the pronunciation of *-ough* words. Then listen to the sentences in 1A and write the words next to the sounds.

Some of the hardest words to pronounce in English are those ending in *-ough*, as they can be pronounced in many different ways, and there are no rules to help you. For example, *cough* is pronounced /ɒf/, whereas *tough* is pronounced /ʌf/, and *through* is pronounced /u:/.

a /əʊ/ (al)though ____________ c /ʌf/ enough ____________
b /ɔ:/ thought ____________ d /aʊ/ drought ____________

B **Make it personal** Search online for other 'publicity disasters'. In groups, share the most interesting stories. Use the sentences below. Pronounce the underlined words correctly.

[Company] sought to ____________, but it didn't work.
They must have ____________ thoroughly, but it was a fiasco.
Things got a bit (really) rough when ____________.
It must have been tough for them (not) to ____________.

Here's one. A US company sought to prove it offered identity-theft protection and posted the CEO's personal information. Can you believe it?

Was he hacked?

He certainly was! And things got really rough when he was also fined for deceptive advertising!

3 Vocabulary: Failed plans

A 5.5 Match the two sentence halves. Listen to check.

1 They were **on the verge of** something big,
2 Their plans **fell through** and the whole thing
3 The company decided to **call** the whole thing **off**
4 But was it an **oversight**?
5 It was a **high-stakes** operation, meaning that
6 It might have been a **glitch** or something, maybe

a ☐ and stopped raising the ice lolly.
b ☐ but the campaign never materialised.
c ☐ if it failed, it would be a disaster.
d ☐ ended in a sticky mess.
e ☐ I mean, didn't they see it coming?
f ☐ software related.

B Choose the most likely meaning (a or b) for the **highlighted** expressions (1–6) in **A**.

1 a ☐ about to experience something — b ☐ at the end of a difficult process
2 a ☐ took a long time to succeed — b ☐ failed
3 a ☐ cancel — b ☐ delay
4 a ☐ a deliberate mistake — b ☐ an unanticipated mistake
5 a ☐ important and risky — b ☐ important and relatively risk-free
6 a ☐ an unexpected, but minor problem — b ☐ a lack of attention to detail

C In pairs, role-play retelling the ice lolly fiasco as: 1) a journalist reporting it on TV or 2) the owner of Snapple talking to the campaign planner. Use the new expressions in **A**.

> Snapple planned a really high-stakes promotion event, and …

D 5.6 Listen to the DJ's story and take notes. Then summarise it using expressions from **A**.

E **Make it personal** Can you remember a plan or goal that fell through?

1 5.7 **How to say it** Complete the table. Listen to check.

Talking about disappointments

What they said	What they meant
1 I fell flat on my ________.	I failed completely.
2 Things got out of ________.	Things got out of control.
3 It took me a while to ________ myself together.	It took me a while to recover.
4 It was ________ to square one!	I had to start from scratch.
5 I came this ________ to (having a nervous breakdown)!	I almost (had a nervous breakdown).

2 Choose a topic and note down a few details. Ask yourself:
What / When / Where / Why / How …?

a date a do-it-yourself project a job application a party travel plans

3 In pairs, share your stories. Use expressions from **A** and **E**. Any comic moments?

> I once invited 20 people to a party and at the last minute, I dropped all the food on the floor.

> You're joking!

> I came this close to having a nervous breakdown. I wasn't sure whether to call the whole thing off …

Common mistake

I came close to ~~lose~~ *losing* my job.

4 Language in use

A 5.8 Listen to the start of a documentary about New Year's resolutions. Which of the man's resolutions isn't mentioned? How many other resolutions can you list in one minute?

B 5.8 Match the two columns. Listen again to check. How would you answer the last question the reporter asks?

Making resolutions		Keeping resolutions	
1 make	☐ anew	4 get	☐ with your (plans)
2 start	☐ a fresh start	5 follow through	☐ your act together
3 turn	☐ the page	6 stick to	☐ your (resolutions)

I think the reason is that we have too many temptations.

C 5.9 Listen to the second part. Choose the answer (a or b) that matches the doctor's opinion. Any surprising information?

1 'Given what we know about the nature of the human psyche, this shouldn't come as a surprise.'
Why not?
a ☐ Our habits may have emotional origins. b ☐ Willpower is a relatively rare quality.

2 'With a view to better understanding the problem, a number of researchers have looked at the success rates of peoples resolutions.'
What were the results?
a ☐ They tend to reveal a recurring pattern. b ☐ They vary widely from person to person.

3 'So you're saying some people sabotage themselves so as not to succeed?'
How do they do that?
a ☐ By making too many resolutions. b ☐ By setting the bar too high.

4 'But in view of what we know about recent motivational theories, this rarely works.'
What are they talking about?
a ☐ Focusing on small steps. b ☐ Focusing on the end result.

D Make it personal Look at your list of New Year's Resolutions from A. Answer 1–4 using expressions from B. Which resolutions (if any) ...

1 have you made in recent years?
2 were you / would you be able to stick to? For how long?
3 would you consider making this coming 31st December?
4 might have / have had the biggest impact on your life?

I had terrible eating habits, so last year, I decided to get my act together.

Good for you! Were you able to stick to your new plan?

5 Grammar: Formal conjunctions and prepositions

A Read the grammar box and complete rules 1–3. Then rephrase the quotes in 4C using *to* or *because of*.

Formal conjunctions and prepositions for reason and purpose

In view of **Given** **Thanks to**	the increase in stress levels, the fact that life is so busy, good promotion,	more and more people are doing yoga.
With the aim of **With a view to**	studying people's resolutions,	a number of studies were conducted.
So as to **In an effort to**	save money,	I moved back in with my parents.

1 ________ , ________ , and ________ mean 'because of'.
2 ________ , ________ , ________ , and ________ mean '(in order) to'.
3 *With a view to* is followed by the ________ form. *So as to* is followed by the ________ form.

» Grammar expansion p.146

B Read the blog post and circle the correct alternatives (1–5).

Resolutions, goals, deadlines ...

[1][**Given / With a view to**] our hectic lifestyles, our days sometimes pass us by while our minds are elsewhere, either dwelling in the past or making plans. I work for a major finance company and [2][**with the aim of / in view of**] the long hours I had to work, I kept trying new relaxation techniques [3][**so as to / with a view to**] reduce the toll on my physical and mental well-being. That was when a friend suggested mindfulness, and it's changed my life. Mindfulness means being aware of your senses, actions, and thoughts. It's living in the present moment [4][**with the aim of / thanks to**] feeling more relaxed and fulfilled. I started to practise it throughout the day [5][**with a view to / in an effort to**] defeat anxiety, and I couldn't be happier.

C Rephrase 1–5 using the words in brackets.

So ... Why do we live in the future? [1]We live in the future because it offers endless possibilities. (in view of) [2]We feel dissatisfied in the present, so we take refuge in the future. (given) [3]We fantasise about our future successes because we want to escape our current misery. (in an effort to) How can we live in the present moment? [4]Accept the fact that there are things you can't control if you want to find peace. (so as to) [5]Learn how to do one thing at a time so that you can give it your full attention. (with a view to)

Common mistake

I decided to resign ~~in view of~~ *in view of the fact that / given (the fact that)* there were no fringe benefits.

'the fact that' is optional after *given*, but obligatory after *in view of*.

D Make it personal Are we in control of our destiny?

1 Explain the idea behind each quote (a–f). Use some of the formal conjunctions and prepositions in A.

a 'Life is what happens to you while you're busy making other plans.' (performed by John Lennon; attributed to Allen Saunders)
b 'There's so much to be said for challenging fate instead of ducking behind it.' (Diana Trilling)
c 'Maybe our mistakes are what make our fate.' (Sarah Jessica Parker)
d 'I think in terms of the day's resolutions, not the year's.' (Henry Moore)
e 'Our history is not our destiny.' (Alan Cohen)
f 'I think destiny is just a fancy word for a psychological problem.' (Jodie Foster)

2 Choose your favourite one. Why do you like it?

I think the last one means that given that people keep repeating the same patterns, their destiny may actually be some sort of emotional problem.

6 Reading

A Read the introduction. In one minute, list all the parts of life people commonly fail at that you can think of. Then in pairs, suggest an answer for the last question.

Well, for one thing, most people fail in their relationships from time to time ...

Coming to terms with failure

Can you think of even one person who doesn't dread failure and go to great lengths to avoid it? Who in their right mind would want to experience all the negative emotions that come from failing to accomplish an important goal? Obviously the answer is no one. However, failure is an inherent part of life, so our best bet is to keep it in perspective. Why is that so very difficult?

"Well, there's nowhere to go but up."

Below are five strategies designed to help you make it through unscathed:

1 **Be upset!** Yes, that's right. Give in to your emotions. Simultaneously, reject the temptation to take failure personally. Even though your relationship or job didn't pan out, you are still a successful person. Separate your failure from your self-esteem. You'll go far. And the proof: Lady Gaga was fired from her record label after only three months. Ang Lee failed Taiwan's college entrance examinations and couldn't get into acting because his English 'wasn't good enough'. Look where they are today. Lady Gaga may have 'cried so hard she couldn't talk', but we know she succeeded in putting her failure behind her.

2 **Snap out of it!** After you've had a good cry, then it's time to move on. The longer you dwell on your failure, the more miserable you'll be. The Irish writer Oscar Wilde died young and faced many obstacles in his lifetime. But you'd do well to heed his advice, 'Life is too important a thing ever to talk seriously about'. It's critical not to obsess about what might have been because you'll only sink deeper into depression.

3 **Make a right turn.** Think of your failure as you would a road blocked by construction and evaluate it logically. First you take stock of the situation, and then you act. And fairly quickly. The same can be said for failure. You need to keep moving, but just in a slightly different direction. Oh, 'come on'. you might say. That analogy doesn't hold water. The evidence, however, shows it does. A case in point is Theodore Seuss Geisel, known as Dr Seuss – author of *The Cat in the Hat* and many other children's books that have delighted young readers the world over. He had his first book rejected by 27 publishers! Just as he was on the verge of burning the manuscript, he ran into an old classmate who helped him get it published at Vanguard Press. You may not know that until this point, Geisel had supported himself entirely through drawing cartoons.

4 **Reject others' opinions.** If you hold on to someone else's negative opinion of you, it will be hard to move forward, so be careful to avoid that trap! Never forget that what someone thinks is true about you may actually be false. Terry Gross of National Public Radio felt she 'couldn't do anything' when she failed at her first teaching job and was fired after only six weeks. That was before she discovered radio. Her programme 'Fresh Air' now reaches over five million listeners.

5 **Focus on the positive!** It may seem obvious, but your attitude may be the only thing separating you from those who have achieved greatness. It's so tempting to let a negative voice take over, and give way to anger and despair. However, Confucius certainly had it right when he proclaimed, 'Our greatest glory is not in never falling, but in rising every time we fall'.

B ▶ 5.10 Listen to and read the whole article. In pairs, complete each sentence so that it captures the essence of each section in the article.

1 Even if you've failed, it's OK to be upset, but important not to *take failure personally*.
2 Stop **obsessing** about your failure because ______________.
3 Look at **failure** analytically, which means ______________.
4 It's dangerous to give too much power to others' opinions because ______________.
5 It's important to think positively and ______________.

C Find the underlined words in the article. Circle the word or expression with the same meaning in context.

1 dread: [**feel afraid of / feel reluctant about**] failure
2 unscathed: [**uninjured physically / unharmed emotionally**]
3 give in to: [**accept / hand over**]
4 pan out: [**succeed / take place**]
5 heed: [**read / pay attention to**]
6 hold water: [**seem factual / seem logical**]

D **Make it personal** Choose a statement from **B** you agree with. Do you have a story to back it up?

> I definitely agree with number 1. Let me tell you about what happened to me at my old school ...

7 Vocabulary: Evaluating success

A Complete 1–6 with six of the highlighted expressions from the article. What's your favourite tip? Can you think of any others?

Success: Don't let it go to your head!

Some people [1] ________ to achieve success in life, but don't always know what to do with it. Here are four tips to help you [2] ________ fame and fortune ________.

– Keep your feet on the ground. Before making major decisions, stop and [3] ________ of your values, goals, and interests.
– Fame doesn't erase your own failures, so be empathetic! You've just [4] ________ them ________ you successfully and moved on.
– Keep in mind that success may not last forever, however hard you may try to [5] ________ it.
– If you find your new-found fortune slips away, there's no point [6] ________ what might have been. Remember, you're still you!

B **Make it personal** In pairs, discuss 1–2.

1 Do you know anyone who changed after he / she got ...

a new job famous into university married promoted rich

2 What happened? Use expressions from **A**.

> My brother went to great lengths to find a new job. But then ...

8 Language in use

A 5.11 Listen and match six conversations to pictures a–f. In pairs, what character trait was the surprise in each case?

a 
b 
c 
d 
e 
f 

In the first one, the man was actually irresponsible.

B 5.12 Read the conversation excerpts and guess whether the speakers are those in A or new people. Listen to check.

1 I resent him expecting me to do everything! I thought I could **count on** his help, but I can't. It looks as if I'll have to **team up with** someone else.

2 I heard about you breaking up and that you couldn't **work** things **out**. I can see why you didn't want to stay with him!

3 Bill and I have some legitimate concerns about your not **sticking to** the deadline. I know that might strike you as heartless.

4 The principal is appalled at the boy's cheating and plans to **take** the matter **up** with his parents.

5 She appreciated us inviting her, even though it didn't **come off** that way ... We might **wind up** being good friends.

6 The police officer insisted on our coming to the station. At first, I thought he'd **let** us **off**.

C 5.12 Listen again. Complete the misleading behaviours. Which one is the worst?

1 Roger misled Barbara by taking ________ and asking ________.
2 At first John would ask about Ann's ________ and cook a wonderful ________ .
3 Bill used to stop by Susan's ________ often and ask about her ________ .
4 Simon would talk about ________ and ________ in classes on social issues.
5 Georgina didn't know Amy was ________ because she always offered to give ________ .
6 The officer had good ________ and a ________ accent.

Common mistake

I'm really counting ~~with~~ *on* you.

D Write the **highlighted** phrasal verbs in B next to their meanings in context.

1 ________ solve
2 ________ depend on
3 ________ not punish
4 ________ work with
5 ________ stay with
6 ________ end up
7 ________ discuss
8 ________ seem, appear

E **Make it personal** Has your first impression of anyone ever been really wrong? How did you find out? Share your stories in groups, using phrasal verbs from C. Whose was the most unusual?

I had a neighbour who came off as really easygoing at first. He smiled a lot and told jokes. But then one day, he showed his true colours!

9 Grammar: Nouns, object pronouns, and possessive adjectives + *-ing* form

A Read the grammar box and tick (✔) the correct rules.

Levels of formality in nouns, object pronouns, and possessive adjectives + *-ing* form

Informal	I'm sick of	**my mum**	shouting at me.
	Roger was counting on	**me**	helping him with the project.
	I resent	**you**	not doing your fair share.
	The officer insisted on	**them**	going to the station.
Neutral to formal	I'm against	**our school's**	giving so many exams.
	My boss showed concern about	**my**	not turning in the report.
	He wasn't very supportive of	**your**	being ill.
	I'm uncomfortable with	**their**	not giving me an honest answer.

1 Informal sentences have a(n) ☐ **object pronoun** ☐ **possessive adjective** before the verb, and more formal sentences have a(n) ☐ **object pronoun** ☐ **possessive adjective.**

2 Therefore, when talking to your boss, say 'I appreciate ☐ **him** ☐ **his** phoning me' because it is ☐ **more** ☐ **less** formal.

3 The form of the verb is ☐ **sometimes** ☐ **always** an *-ing* form, and the form of the negative is ☐ **sometimes** ☐ **always** *not*.

4 When there is a noun before a verb, the more formal form is ☐ **possessive** ☐ **plural**.

B Find the six underlined examples in 8B of nouns, pronouns, or possessive adjectives before *-ing* forms. Write *I* next to the informal forms and *N* next to the neutral to formal ones.

» **Grammar expansion p.146**

C Rewrite 1–7 informally with nouns or object pronouns. Do you identify with any of the complaints? Can you think of any others?

Top seven relationship complaints

1 'She's constantly criticising me. I'm tired of that.'
2 'His parents drop by unexpectedly. I'm not comfortable with that.'
3 'You snore. I'm tired of that.'
4 'Jim is Facebook friends with his ex. I resent that.'
5 'He gives me the silent treatment when he's angry. I'll never get used to that.'
6 'I take a long time to answer his texts. He can't stand that.'
7 'We want different things. I'm not happy with that.'

I'm tired of her constantly criticising me.

D Make it personal Do you approve? In groups, read the headlines and share your reactions. Use nouns or object pronouns before *-ing* forms, where possible. Any big differences?

I'm (not) in favour of ...	I'm against ...	I'm concerned about ...	I'm sceptical of ...

1 **A bittersweet ending: Japanese train station closes after lone passenger, picked up every day at 7.04am and brought back at 5.08pm, finished secondary school**
2 **Undercover officer dressed as homeless man catches drivers using phones**
3 **Deputy headteacher greets students with singing, dancing every morning**
4 **Table manners rewarded: restaurant offers diners 5% off to drop their devices**

I'm not in favour of trains operating with just one passenger. What a waste of money!

I disagree. This station stayed open to support education.

10 Listening

A 5.13 Listen to a conversation between Monica and Ed about bad drivers. In pairs, answer 1–2.

1 What dangers do pedestrians face in their city?
2 What does Ed think can be done about it?

B 5.14 Listen to a second conversation. Note down ...

1 two problems with Ed's proposal for a test based on the London exam.
2 one problem with Monica's proposal for speed bumps.

C 5.15 Listen to a third conversation. Tick (✔) the aspects of driver psychology mentioned.

1 ☐ future ability to stay focused 2 ☐ driver sociability 3 ☐ current degree of concentration

D **Make it personal** In pairs, would Monica and Ed's proposal work in your city? Is the revised proposal an improvement?

> I think it's still impractical. What if a driver can only afford one driving test?

11 Keep talking

A 5.16 Read *Proposal language*. Then complete 1–5 using a form of the words or expressions in the box. There's one extra. Listen to check.

Proposal language

Specific expressions are used to talk about proposals. For example, we *make* or *put together* a proposal, and a proposal has a *rationale* behind it, or central reason for existing.

airtight	entail	put together	rationale	redo	spell out	steps	turn down

1 I'm going to ________ a proposal anyway. And maybe I can submit it next week.
2 They ________ my proposal. Guess it's back to square 1.
3 What did your proposal ________ ? What was the general idea?
4 The ________ was that there would be a special exam for city drivers.
5 It [the proposal]'s got to be ________ this time. It has to ________ all the different ________ and show how to get from point A to point B.

B In groups, choose a topic below and develop a proposal. Make certain it has a clear rationale and list at least four features as bullet points. Use proposal language from A and the expressions below. Share it with the class. Whose is most convincing?

How to ...

evaluate students who aren't good at exams
make your neighbourhood cleaner or safer
earn money if you can't find a good job
develop new parking rules in your city
offer scholarships to needy students

I think you're on to something.	Why not focus on ...?	Suppose you only ...	You've got a point.

> OK, exams. My proposal is to eliminate the final exam.

> I think you're on to something. First, let's go over the rationale.

12 Writing: A proposal

A Read the proposal and find ...

1 the purpose of the email.
2 one supporting argument for each of the goals in paragraphs 4, 5, and 6.
3 the next step in the proposal.

B Read *Write it right!* Then read 1–4 and choose the most logical answers.

Write it right!

In many kinds of writing, adverbs and adverbial expressions not only help to link ideas, but they also signal what the sentence or next point will be about:

Admittedly [= I concede it's true that] our university is not a charity.

1 [**Admittedly / Incidentally**] we have an ambitious plan, but we still think there are ways to achieve it.
2 [**Frankly / Essentially**], our proposal can be summarised in one sentence.
3 [**Apparently / Obviously**], it seems two other universities have tried something similar from what I've heard.
4 [**Obviously / Broadly speaking**], our proposal has three parts.

C Read *Formulaic expressions (1)*. Circle five more fixed expressions in the underlined sentences in the proposal.

Formulaic expressions (1)

Formal letters and emails often contain formulaic expressions, where the wording is fixed. They facilitate written communication by offering standard openings, closings, and other useful language.

Thank you (very much) for your response to our proposal of 15th February (date).

D Your turn! Choose a proposal you discussed in 11B and write a formal email to present it in about 280 words.

Before

Plan three arguments for your proposal and note down supporting details.

While

Write five to six paragraphs to support your proposal, following the model in A. Use a variety of adverbs and at least one formulaic sentence.

After

Post your essay online and read your classmates' work. Whose proposal is most convincing?

Dear Ms Harbinger:

Thank you very much for your response to our proposal of 15th February. We were quite disappointed that our project wasn't accepted, as I'm sure you can understand. However, we understand that the budget was insufficient. With the aim of finding an acceptable solution, we've rethought some aspects of our strategy. I'd now like to propose the following in an effort to submit a plan that is more practical:

1. Our university would offer a scholarship each semester to 50 qualifying students, rather than a full scholarship.
2. The remaining tuition costs would be covered in three potential ways:
   a) Through work-study programmes at our university.
   b) By offering loans, which would be repaid within ten years of leaving university.
   c) By offering part-time degree programmes, thereby allowing students to pay half tuition and take jobs in the community.

Broadly speaking, we have three goals: (1) to give needy students a chance at upward mobility, (2) to expand our student base and make it more diverse, and most importantly, (3) to reward academic effort and achievement. The importance of these objectives cannot be overemphasised, so please allow me to elaborate.

Admittedly, our university is not a charity. Nevertheless, our long-term goal should be a more egalitarian society with opportunities for all. Frankly, in the 21st century, with the acute needs of our global economy at stake, we simply cannot afford to have segments of society who are left without access to continuing education. Upward mobility must be a dream within the reach of all of us.

Exposing students to diversity is also important if we hope to create a society free of conflict, and essentially, our university has attracted students from only one social and economic background. Apparently, as we've learned from a survey we conducted in one of the communities we have in mind, promotion is not reaching students from across the city. In view of this, we feel we need to try harder. We owe it to our students to enable them to experience the richness of different cultures and sub-cultures. Incidentally, a brief survey here at Fourth District University shows that our own students find this goal important, as well.

Clearly, in a just society, academic achievement must be rewarded also. Poor students, quite obviously, face enough obstacles and prejudice. This last goal doesn't seem to require amplification.

I hope I have managed to provide a convincing rationale. Regarding our next step, we would be happy to meet with you at your convenience to discuss the specifics. We will do our best to answer any questions you may have.

Sincerely,
Ricardo Ortega

Student Union President

6 »

Do you still read paper books?

1 Listening

A 6.1 Listen to the start of an interview with Dr Soars. Then in pairs, look at photos 1–2 and compare your understanding of 'the digital apocalypse never came'.

B 6.2 Guess whether the features (1–6) are E (e-book), P (paper book), or NI (no information)? Listen to the next part to check.

1 convenient
2 affordable
3 prone to damage
4 environmentally friendly
5 sensory-rich
6 reader friendly

C 6.2 Listen again. Match the opinions (1–6) to their responses (a–e). Then give your own responses.

1 Paper books aren't going anywhere in the foreseeable future.
2 Reading is essentially an abstract activity, right?
3 You see, reading involves a certain degree of physicality.
4 So ... e-books fail to recreate this sort of hands-on experience?
5 Some people find it easier to take notes using a pen or pencil.

a ☐ 'You've lost me there.'
b ☐ 'But how can that be?'
c ☐ 'Well, guilty as charged.'
d ☐ 'Well, yes and no.'
e ☐ 'To some extent, yes.'

Paper books aren't going anywhere in the foreseeable future.

I completely disagree. Actually, I just read today that ...

D 6.3 Listen to the end of the interview. How does Dr Soars feel about phone reading? Do you agree?

E 6.3 Match the two columns. Listen again to check. Which phrases do you associate with fast reading?

1 skip	a ☐ it past the first paragraph
2 (not) make	b ☐ your eyes over a text
3 run	c ☐ over whole sentences

4 get	a ☐ over a challenging text
5 pore	b ☐ the gist of a text
6 read	c ☐ between the lines

F **Make it personal** In groups, discuss 1–2.

1 Do you think paper books will have a future similar to CDs? Why (not)?
2 How do you usually read these items? Use expressions from E.

books by (Stephen King) (Facebook) posts (computer) instruction manuals
news about (politics) (physics) textbooks (rental) contracts

I almost always read Facebook posts on my phone. They're usually short, so I can get the gist right away.

I like to read them on my laptop so I don't just skip over the comments.

2 Vocabulary: Phrasal verbs with *out*

A ▶ 6.4 Complete 1–6 with the nouns in the box. Listen to check.

e-books	meaning	nature	sentences	studies	titles

1 It's so much easier to browse an online store, **pick out** (= select from a group) your favourite ________ and download them.
2 You can't **wear out** (= damage from too much use) or accidentally tear ________ .
3 A paper book has an easily identifiable size, shape, and weight, which **brings out** (= reveals) its more concrete ________.
4 Some people find it easier to take notes, highlight, or even **cross out** (= draw a line through) ________ in a paper book.
5 Some ________ **point out** (= mention) that people reading on their phones take lots of shortcuts.
6 They're also more likely to ignore unknown words rather than **work out** (= try to discover) their ________ in context or look them up.

B Complete the mind maps with **highlighted** phrasal verbs from **A**. Then, in pairs, use the prompts to find out more about each other.

1 ________
- your new (shoes)
- (the battery) through overuse
- your (welcome) at someone's house

2 ________
- your inner (beauty)
- the best (worst) in me
- the flavour of (the meat)

3 ________
- a solution to (a problem)
- the answers to (a question)
- a new way of (saving money)

Do / Have you ever ...? When did you last ...? Who in your (family) ...? What do you do to / when ...? What's the best way to ...? What would you do if ...?

> Have you ever ... your welcome at someone's house?

> Not as far as I know! I hope not.

C Make it personal How do you feel about reading?

1 Choose your three favourite quotes from those below. In pairs, explain what they mean.

a '"Classic" — a book which people praise and don't read.' (Mark Twain)
b 'Think before you speak. Read before you think.' (Fran Lebowitz)
c 'Books are no more threatened by Kindle than stairs by lifts.' (Stephen Fry)
d 'School made us "literate" but did not teach us to read for pleasure.' (Ambeth R. Ocampo)
e 'No two persons ever read the same book.' (Edmund Wilson)
f 'Today a reader, tomorrow a leader.' (Margaret Fuller)
g 'Read a thousand books, and your words will flow like a river.' (Lisa See)
h 'If you don't like to read, you haven't found the right book.' (JK Rowling)

> I really like b. The first part is quite obvious. But the second part means that books help us think in new ways. They bring out our creativity.

2 Do the quotes remind you of anyone or anything? Share your ideas, using phrasal verbs from **A** where possible.

3 Language in use

A 6.5 Listen to two friends, Grace and Noah, talking about the film *La Vie en Rose*. Complete 1–5 with short phrases.

1 Grace really enjoyed watching the film, while Noah ________ .
2 He's not used to ________ .
3 In Germany, most TV shows and film ________ .
4 Grace seems surprised, given ________ .
5 Countries that avoid subtitles include ________ .

B 6.6 Guess the speaker's main arguments. Then listen to check. Can you think of any others?

Noah doesn't like subtitles because ...
1 he misses ________ .
2 it's hard for him not to ________ .

Grace doesn't like dubbed films because ...
3 the voices don't ________ .
4 actors can't ________ as well.

C 6.7 Read *Using out of*. Then write the use of *out of* (1–4) next to the bold phrases below. Listen to check. Notice the /ə/ sound in *of*.

Using *out of*

Out of is a very common prepositional phrase. Here are four uses:
1 movement from within outwards: *We walked* ***out of the room****.*
2 caused or motivated by: *I watched the Oscars last night, more* ***out of curiosity*** *than interest.*
3 not having: *The theatre company is* ***out of money*** *and can't produce a new play this year. Lots of record shops went* ***out of business*** *in the 2010s.*
4 selection from a group: *Ask anyone who the greatest American actress is, and at least* ***three out of five*** *people will say Meryl Streep.*

1 In Germany, nearly every foreign TV store is dubbed. I mean, like **8 out of 10** ☐, unless it's pay per view or something.
2 I end up reading the subtitles whether or not I understand what's being said. I guess I do it **out of** sheer **habit** ☐ – just in case I might have missed something.
3 It annoys me how the actors' lips and their voices are always a bit **out of sync** ☐, even if the dubbing is done well.
4 Sometimes I just feel like getting up and walking **out of the cinema** ☐.
5 I don't mind the occasional subtitle as long as there's not too much text to process. Otherwise, I find I'm **out of patience** ☐ quite quickly.

D **Make it personal** In groups, answer 1–3.

1 Modify 1–5 in C so that they're true for you.
2 Are most foreign films dubbed or subtitled where you live?
3 Search on a recent film in English that you've seen or would like to see and watch the original trailer (name of film + 'original trailer'). Then search again for a dubbed trailer in your own language (name of film in your language + 'trailer' + name of language) and compare.

I just watched the trailer for the film *Brooklyn* in English and Spanish. I couldn't stand the dubbed version!

What was wrong with it?

Well, for one thing, the accents, one of the most appealing parts of the film, were completely lost. The Irish accent, the Italian-American accent: they're all gone!

4 Grammar: Adverb clauses of condition

A Read the grammar box and tick (✔) the correct rules (1–2). Do 1–5 below mean the same as a–e? Write S (same) or D (different).

Adverb clauses of condition: *as long as*, *whether or not*, *in case*, *unless*, and *even if*	
a I don't mind dubbed films	**as long as** the voices are good.
b **Whether or not** you speak Spanish,	you should try to watch the original versions.
c I think I should turn on the subtitles	**in case** I miss something.
d **Unless** I stop watching dubbed films,	my listening won't improve.
e I don't miss a single episode of *The Simpsons*	**even if** it's the dubbed version.

1 In the clause expressing condition, the verb is always in the ☐ **present** ☐ **future**.
2 We ☐ **use** ☐ **don't use** a comma when the main clause comes first.

Remember: *Even though* expresses contrast, not condition:
Even though I don't like Quentin Tarantino that much, I enjoyed his latest film.
I rarely watch Hollywood blockbusters, **even if** the reviews are good.

Grammar expansion p.148

1 I don't object to dubbed films, but only if the voices are good.
2 You should try to watch the original versions, especially if you speak Spanish.
3 There's a chance I might miss something. I think I ought to turn on the subtitles.
4 My listening won't get better if I don't stop watching dubbed films.
5 I don't watch *The Simpsons* if it's dubbed.

Common mistake

We're going away for the weekend ~~even though~~ *even if* it rains. Nothing's going to stop us!

B Circle the correct answers. Can you think of any other reasons?

Three reasons people aren't going to the cinema anymore

1 Ticket prices
Ticket prices are on the rise, especially now with IMAX and 3D. This might put some viewers off, [1][**as long as** / **unless**] they have the extra money to spare, of course. Not to mention the popcorn, which we're mysteriously compelled to buy, [2][**even if** / **whether or not**] we're actually hungry!

2 Streaming
Who needs to leave home on Saturday night when there's Netflix? [3][**As long as** / **Even if**] you have an Internet connection – [4][**even if** / **even though**] it's a relatively slow one – you can watch thousands of films from the comfort of your sofa.

3 Better quality TV
[5][**In case** / **Unless**] you haven't noticed, we might be experiencing the golden age of television. Because of shows such as *Game of Thrones*, people don't need to go to the cinema anymore.

C Make it personal In groups, discuss which trends are popular.

1 Among people your age, are more or fewer people doing these things compared to five years ago? Write M (more) or F (fewer).

Arts, news, and entertainment	Shopping	Relationships
reading paper newspapers	buying bigger cars	sticking to relationships
going to museums / galleries	avoiding brand names	interacting face to face
downloading / streaming music	choosing more casual clothes	breaking up by text message

2 Choose two trends. Give three reasons that might explain each one. Use expressions from A and 3C.

More people my age are definitely breaking up by text message unless they were very serious.

How awful! Why do you think that is?

5 Reading

A Roald Dahl (1916–1990) was a British writer. His short story *The Way Up to Heaven* was published in 1954. Read the first two paragraphs of the excerpt. What is unusual about Mrs Foster?

B Read the rest. Underline a sentence that shows ...

1 Mrs Foster was probably a traditional wife. 2 the Fosters were most likely wealthy.

The Way Up to Heaven

By Roald Dahl

All her life, Mrs Foster had had an almost pathological fear of missing a train, a plane, a boat, or even a theatre curtain. In other respects, she was not a particularly nervous woman, but the mere thought of being late on occasions like these would throw her into such a state of nerves that she would begin to twitch.

It was really extraordinary how in certain people a simple apprehension about a thing like catching a train can grow into a serious obsession. At least half an hour before it was time to leave the house for the station, Mrs Foster would step out of the elevator all ready to go, with hat and coat and gloves, and then, being quite unable to sit down, she would flutter and fidget about from room to room until her husband, who must have been well aware of her state, finally emerged from his privacy and suggested in a cool dry voice that perhaps they had better be going now, had they not? Mr Foster may possibly have had a right to be irritated by this foolishness of his wife's, but he could have had no excuse for increasing her misery by keeping her waiting unnecessarily.

Mind you, it is by no means certain that this is what he did, yet whenever they were to go somewhere, his timing was so accurate – just a minute or two late, you understand – and his manner so bland that it was hard to believe he wasn't purposely inflicting a nasty private little torture of his own on the unhappy lady. And one thing he must have known – that she would never dare to call out and tell him to hurry. He had disciplined her too well for that. He must also have known that if he was prepared to wait even beyond the last moment of safety, he could drive her nearly into hysterics. On one or two special occasions in the later years of their married life, it seemed almost as though he had wanted to miss the train simply in order to intensify the poor woman's suffering.

Assuming (though one cannot be sure) that the husband was guilty, what made his attitude doubly unreasonable was the fact that, with the exception of this one small irrepressible foible, Mrs Foster was and always had been a good and loving wife. For over thirty years, she had served him loyally and well. There was no doubt about this. Even she, a very modest woman, was aware of it, and although she had for years refused to let herself believe that Mr Foster would ever consciously torment her, there had been times recently when she had caught herself beginning to wonder.

Mr Eugene Foster, who was nearly seventy years old, lived with his wife in a large six-storey house in New York City, on East Sixty-second Street, and they had four servants. It was a gloomy place, and few people came to visit them. But on this particular morning in January, the house had come alive and there was a great deal of bustling about. One maid was distributing bundles of dust sheets to every room, while another was draping them over the furniture. The butler was bringing down suitcases and putting them in the hall. The cook kept popping up from the kitchen to have a word with the butler, and Mrs Foster herself, in an old-fashioned fur coat and with a black hat on the top of her head, was flying from room to room and pretending to supervise these operations. Actually, she was thinking of nothing at all except that she was going to miss her plane if her husband didn't come out of his study soon and get ready.

'Walker, what time is it?' 'Twenty-two minutes past, Madam.'

As he spoke, a door opened and Mr Foster came into the hall.

'Well,' he said, 'I suppose perhaps we'd better get going fairly soon if you want to catch that plane.'

'Yes, dear – yes! Everything's ready. The car's waiting.' 'That's good,' he said.

With his head over to one side, he was watching her closely. He had a peculiar way of cocking the head and then moving it in a series of small, rapid jerks. Because of this and because he was clasping his hands up high in front of him, near the chest, he was somehow like a squirrel standing there – a quick clever old squirrel from the Park.

'Here's Walker with your coat, dear. Put it on.'

'I'll be with you in a moment,' he said. 'I'm just going to wash my hands.' She waited for him, and the tall butler stood beside her, holding the coat and the hat. 'Walker, will I miss it?' 'No, Madam,' the butler said. 'I think you'll make it all right.'

Then Mr Foster appeared again, and the butler helped him on with his coat. Mrs Foster hurried outside and got into the hired Cadillac. Her husband came after her, but he walked down the steps of the house slowly, pausing halfway to observe the sky and to sniff the cold morning air.

'It looks a bit foggy,' he said as he sat down beside her in the car. 'And it's always worse out there at the airport. I shouldn't be surprised if the flight's cancelled already.'

'Don't say that, dear – please.' They didn't speak again until the car had crossed over the river to Long Island.

C 6.8 Listen to and re-read the excerpt. T (true) or F (false)?

1 In many areas of her life, Mrs Foster wasn't a calm person.
2 Mr Foster may have enjoyed seeing Mrs Foster suffer.
3 Mrs Foster was sure Mr Foster could be deliberately cruel.
4 The writer feels Mr Foster is controlling and potentially mean.

D Make it personal In groups, discuss 1–3.

1 Why were(n't) the Fosters probably a happy couple?
2 How typical are the Fosters of couples who have been married for decades? Are things the same / different today?
3 Guess how the story will end. Then search on '*The Way Up to Heaven*' and find a plot summary. How surprised are you by the ending?

6 Vocabulary: Evocative language

A Read *Evocative language*. Then complete the sentences (1–6) with a form of the highlighted words in the excerpt. There's one extra.

Evocative language

Meaning can often be guessed from context. Writers often use vivid verbs to create an image, whose rough meaning you can guess if you try to visualise the situation:

Her husband *sniffed* the cold morning air. (= smelled)

1 Her eye ________ when she was anxious.
2 Her eyelashes ________ when he looked at her.
3 My dog ________ his head to one side whenever I open the door.
4 She ________ her hands behind her back.
5 In the market, tons of workers were ________ .
6 My children are always ________ and can't sit still.

B Make it personal How nervous do you get when you think you might be late to class or for an important appointment? Do you know anyone with nervous habits like Mrs Foster? Use words from **A**.

I look at my watch constantly, and my eye sometimes starts twitching …

7 Language in use

A 6.9 Look at the photos. Do you know which countries the artists are from? Listen to two friends, Donna and Jason, to check.

Maya Hayuk

Os Gêmeos

Olek

El Bocho

Inti

Kashink

B 6.9 Match the extracts with the photos Donna and Jason were talking about at the time. Listen again to check.

1 It does look original, doesn't it? I wish I could buy one!	3 I have seen some women graffiti artists.	5 But his name does sound Mexican. Let me look it up.
2 I did like it. It's just that I really like graffiti with a message.	4 I had realised. But still, I always thought graffiti was mainly done on buildings.	6 The mural does seem very South American, doesn't it?

C 6.10 and 6.11 Listen and read about falling intonation on question tags. Then listen to 1–4 and mark the intonation ↗ or ↘.

Sometimes tag questions are not true questions, but are opinions. In that case the intonation falls, rather than rises. Compare:

The mural seems South American, doesn't it? ↗ It looks original, doesn't it? ↘

1 You can't call that art, can you?
2 You liked this painting, didn't you?
3 She really has talent, doesn't she?
4 He's really awful, isn't he?

D Make it personal In pairs, which is your favourite piece of graffiti in A? Your least favourite? Use some of these words and tag questions to give opinions. Then take a class vote.

amazing bizarre colourful creative dull (un)imaginative (un)inspiring (un)original thought-provoking vibrant

The Os Gêmeos piece is amazing.

Yes, it's so original, isn't it? I can't take my eyes off it!

8 Grammar: Using auxiliaries as rejoinders

A 6.12 Read and listen to the sentences in the grammar box and circle the word with the main stress. Then tick (✔) the correct rules (1–4).

Using auxiliaries to express emotions and emphasis

I	**am**	open to appreciating graffiti.
It	**does seem**	kind of dull, doesn't it?
I really	**did like**	the play, even though the acting was bad.
I	**have been**	listening to you!
I	**haven't been**	looking at my phone!
I	**do not have**	other priorities!

1 To express emphasis or emotion, stress the ☐ **auxiliary** ☐ **main verb** and, in affirmative sentences, ☐ **contract** ☐ **don't contract** the auxiliary.
2 Add a form of ☐ **do** ☐ **have** before an affirmative verb in the present simple.
3 When a negative sentence isn't contracted, the stress is on ☐ **the auxiliary** ☐ ***not***.
4 Tag questions ☐ **can** ☐ **can't** be used in sentences where an auxiliary expresses emotion or emphasis.

» Grammar expansion p.148

B Look at AS 6.9 on p. 163. Circle six examples of auxiliaries for emotion or emphasis. Then underline the six sentences that the examples are in response to.

C Complete the conversations (1–4) about the artists from 7A with appropriate auxiliaries and verbs to express emotion or emphasis. How many opinions matched yours?

1 A: You didn't like the yellow head in the Os Gêmeos piece, did you?
B: I ____________ it! It's actually sweet.

2 A: You haven't looked at the El Bocho piece yet.
B: I ____________ it! I just didn't like it. In fact, it leaves me cold!

3 A: You don't see what's so unusual about Inti.
B: I ____________ what's unusual! Just look at the expression. She represents all of us.

4 A: Maya Hayuk, Kashin, and Olek all use vibrant colours.
B: Olek ____________ vibrant colours. That's just typical crochet yarn!

D Complete the conversations again in a different way, this time avoiding auxiliaries for emphasis.

> You didn't like the yellow head in the Os Gêmeos piece, did you?

> I never said I didn't like it! It's actually sweet.

E **Make it personal** In groups, discuss 1–3.

1 Does graffiti always need to have a message? Which in 7A have one?
2 How effective is graffiti in influencing people's ideas?
3 Should the government encourage graffiti as a means of expression?

> Graffiti should have a message. The Olek bicycle is colourful, but it doesn't say anything.

> It does say something. To me the message is that even everyday objects have beauty.

6.5 Are musicals popular where you live?

9 Listening

A Look at the photos. In pairs, discuss 1–2.

1 Do you ever go to musicals? What do(n't) you like about them?

2 Are you familiar with any of these musicals? Which others do you know?

B 6.13 Listen to the first part of a conversation between two friends, Stan and Kenna. T (true), F (false), or NI (no information)? Correct the false statements.

1 The name of the book is *The Secret Life of the American Musical: How Broadway Shows its Guilt* .

2 The book is written for the general public.

3 One of the musicals talked about is *Mamma Mia*.

4 The book compares different musicals, which can be boring for more knowledgeable readers.

5 Millennials may not know that much about musicals.

C 6.14 Listen to the second part. Tick (✔) the best description (1–3) for the first part of the book.

1 ☐ From *Oklahoma* to *Hamilton*: a complete chronology of the American musical

2 ☐ A common core and then 'an eleven o'clock number': how the typical musical is structured

3 ☐ An experience for all, even those with limited English

D 6.15 Listen to the third part. Does Stan imply the book fully covers the musical of the future? Is it important for the book to cover this topic?

10 Keep talking

A 6.16 **How to say it** Complete the table. Listen to check.

Recommending books	
What they said	What they meant
1 (This book is) a really good ________.	I really liked it.
2 It's written with a ________ audience in mind.	It's written for all audiences.
3 This book will ________ you ________ on lots of interesting facts.	This book will explain lots of interesting facts.
4 So what else does this book ________ ________?	So what else does this book cover?
5 What's really ________ about the book is that it (captures what musicals have in common).	What's special and noteworthy about this book is that it ...

B Choose a book you've recently read or research one you'd like to recommend.

1 If it's fiction, note down the setting, characters, and plot, but not the ending!

2 If it's non-fiction, note down the organisation, main themes, and at least three details.

C In pairs, make your recommendation! Use *How to say it* expressions.

1 Convince your partner to read the book. Make sure your reasons are persuasive.

2 Add in any criticisms you can think of, but make it clear you still feel the book is worthwhile.

11 Writing: A book review

A Read the review about a work of fiction and find the paragraph(s) where …

1 the character's personality and a conflict are introduced.
2 something unusual about the book is first mentioned.
3 a recommendation is given.
4 the plot and main character are first introduced.

B Read *Write it right!* Then match each point to the underlined examples in the review (1–4).

Write it right!

A good book review maintains interest throughout the review. Some common techniques are:

- praising the author.
- using descriptive adjectives.
- contrasting the book with others like it.
- offering plot details.

C Book reviews also contain many other specific expressions that capture the reader's attention. Test your memory. What are the missing words? Then check in the review.

1 As the story ________, we learn (what a complicated decision that is).
2 We're left with the ________ that she doesn't really wish to leave.
3 I wouldn't want to ________ the pleasure of reading this (absorbing narrative).
4 I couldn't put this book ________. It was a real page-________.
5 I ________ recommend *Brooklyn*.

D Your turn! Choose a book you discussed in 10B and write a book review in about 280 words.

Before

Note down the setting, plot, and characters if your book is fiction, and the organisation and main themes if it is non-fiction. Then decide your recommendation.

While

Organise your book review in five to six paragraphs, following the model. Use *Write it right!* techniques from B and expressions from C.

After

Post your review online and read your classmates' work. Which book would you most like to read?

Brooklyn
– Colm Tóibín

1 [1]So many books have been written about the immigrant experience in the United States that it would be hard to imagine that anything new could possibly be said. Yet Colm Tóibín's novel *Brooklyn* delivers something very special and unique – a calm, measured depiction of two ways of life, along with the feelings and motivations of the characters that inhabit both.

2 [2]The plot centres around Eilis Lacey, a young woman unable to find work in her native Ireland in the early 1950s. Her well-meaning older sister, Rose, arranges a visit for her with a local priest, who's just returned from a trip to New York City. Dazzled by his description of the employment and social opportunities that await her, she decides to emigrate from her home in Enniscorthy, the same Irish town the author is from. As the story unfolds, we learn what a complicated decision that is.

3 Before Eilis's departure, we're left with the impression that she doesn't really wish to leave her hometown and has no reason but the practical for doing so. Nevertheless, she is eager to please her mother and sister. The protagonist, like the members of her family, is somehow unable to express her emotions openly, but [3]Tóibín is a master at capturing his character's underlying feelings. Yet perhaps because she is young, or simply passive by nature, Eilis boards the ship as planned, without ever expressing regret, on her way to a new destiny.

4 [4]The book contains vivid, unforgettable images of Eilis's passage. As readers, we absorb her mood and feelings as she is seasick on the ship and first takes in the sparse Brooklyn boardinghouse where she will live. We are drawn into her loneliness and homesickness as she goes to her job in the upmarket department store that has hired her, and then returns alone in the evening. And we follow her avidly as she meets a young Italian-American man and slowly falls in love.

5 Eilis is called back to Ireland as the result of unforeseen family events. I wouldn't want to spoil the pleasure of reading this absorbing narrative by saying more. What I can add is that I couldn't put this book down as I read about her changing perceptions and took in her new maturity. It was a real page-turner, and more than a few surprises await you.

6 I highly recommend *Brooklyn* to anyone looking to understand not only a quintessential American experience, but also the individuality of those who undertook the journey. You won't be disappointed.

Review 3
Units 5–6

1 Listening

A R3.1 Listen to a museum guide discussing the graffiti artists Os Gêmeos. Complete 1–5.

1 Os Gêmeos are known not only in Brazil, but also ________ .
2 Their work includes family, social, and political ________ , and is influenced by Brazilian ________ .
3 Their early influences came from ________ culture, and they started out as ________ .
4 The Brazilian government has commissioned them to paint large ________ and also some ________ .
5 They've become so popular because of their success in appealing to our ________ .

B Make it personal In pairs, share opinions about these Os Gêmeos paintings. Use falling intonation tag questions and some words from the box.

amazing bizarre bring out colourful creative dull (un)imaginative (un)inspiring (un)original point out thought-provoking vibrant

This one's really bizarre, isn't it!

Actually, I think it's ... . As the guide said, Os Gêmeos ...

2 Grammar

A Read the paragraph. Circle the correct answers.

I'm really sick and tired of [1][**my neighbours not taking out / that my neighbours don't take out**] their rubbish. [2][**With the aim of / In an effort to**] improve the situation, I decided to talk to them. [3][**Given the fact that / Thanks to**] they are elderly, I tried to be understanding. The man wasn't very nice, though, and I really didn't like [4][**that he yells / his yelling**] at me. [5][**With a view to / In view of**] finding a solution, I explained that I could smell rotting food in my flat, and that I was very uncomfortable about [6][**that they don't take / their not taking**] the situation seriously. [7][**With a view to / So as to**] lower the tension, I said I'd give them one more week before I speak to the building management.

B Make it personal Complete the online blog about two disappointing people, using more formal structures where possible. Then add a sentence with an expression from the box to explain what you've done to improve the situation. Share your information with a partner.

Given	In view of	So as to	With a view to	In an effort to	Thanks to	With the aim of

1 I can't accept ______________ . ______________ , I ______________ .

2 ______________ isn't very supportive of ______________ , I ______________ .

OK, listen to what I wrote: 'I can't accept my manager's making me work overtime. Given that I have so little free time, I've decided to find a new job.'

That does seem like a good solution!

3 Writing

Write a paragraph about something that hasn't gone well or that you feel you haven't been successful at.

1 Start with an expression in the box and use possessive adjectives + *-ing* forms.

I haven't been happy about ...	I haven't been comfortable with ...
I really haven't enjoyed ...	I'm very tired of ...

2 Use formal conjunctions and prepositions from 2B to suggest a solution.

4 Self-test

Correct the two mistakes in each sentence. Check your answers in Units 5 and 6. What's your score, 1–20?

1 Because of the terrible weather, our plans fell and as a result, our hike was called.
2 I fell flat on my head, and I came close to have a nervous breakdown!
3 In view of I didn't get a bonus, I started staying home at weekends so to save money.
4 I heard about that Bob and Sue broke up last month, but I still hoped they could work things over.
5 I'm going to put a proposal to improve our classroom and try to spell all the steps clearly.
6 Three of five people say you can get used to subtitles as long as you will be open to them.
7 Even though it rains this weekend, I plan to go camping whether anyone else goes.
8 Jim says he really do like the film because it comes into so many interesting themes.
9 Unless you haven't noticed, our Internet connection is dead, as long as the power is on elsewhere.
10 A good dubbing brings through the personality of the original actors, even if the voices and lips are off of sync.

5 Point of view

Choose a topic. Then support your opinion in 100–150 words, and record your answer. Ask a partner for feedback. How can you be more convincing?

a It's essential to fail in order to succeed. OR
Failure is a devastating experience and should be avoided at all costs.

b Dubbed films really spoil the experience of going to a cinema. OR
Some films can be dubbed very successfully and have advantages.

c Graffiti isn't real art even if it's creative. OR
Graffiti is a serious art form and should be given even more attention.

7 What are our most important years?

1 Listening

A 7.1 In pairs, look at the photos and answer the lesson title. Then listen to the start of an interview. Did you agree with Dr Castro?

childhood

adolescence

your 20s

your 30s and beyond

B 7.2 Note down two reasons Dr Castro might give to support her opinion. Listen to check. Were any of your ideas mentioned?

C 7.2 Listen again. Tick (✔) the statements she agrees with.

1 ☐ Society is more forgiving of mistakes you make in your teens.
2 ☐ Your 20s should be a sort of rehearsal for adult life.
3 ☐ It's harder to reinvent yourself in your 30s and 40s.
4 ☐ These days it's relatively easy to succeed in your 20s.

D 7.3 Read *Animal idioms*. Then look at the pictures on the right and guess the missing words. Listen to check.

Animal idioms

There are dozens of common English expressions based on animals:

Who **let the cat out of the bag** (= accidentally revealed a secret) about the surprise party?

I know this is true! I heard it **straight from the horse's mouth** (= from a reliable source).

I was planning to go skydiving, but I **chickened out** (= decided not to do it out of fear) at the last minute.

1 ________ a can of worms (= do something that will lead to problems)

2 take the bull by the ________ (= deal with a difficult situation)

3 You can't teach an old dog new ________ (= It's hard to abandon old habits.)

4 get out of the rat ________ (= abandon a competitive lifestyle)

E Make it personal In groups, discuss 1–3.

1 Look at the lesson title again. Did you change your mind after the interview? Why (not)?
2 Which of the idioms from **D** do you associate with people your age? Your parents' or children's ages? Why?
3 Choose a statement from **C** you (dis)agree with. Support your opinion with a story about yourself.

I agree with number 3. You can't teach an old dog new tricks, as they say!

I totally disagree. My mum went back to university and started a whole new career.

2 Vocabulary: Milestones

A 7.4 Using context, complete 1–6 with a form of the expressions in the box. Listen to check. Which expression always has a negative meaning?

come to terms with	come of age	make it through	the stakes are higher	get off track	take charge

1 Yes, but I would argue that when we ______ (= reach adulthood), we make the decisions that have the greatest impact on our future.
2 Because that's when our lives either take off or ______ (= start to go in the wrong direction).
3 But when you're in your 20s, ______ (= there's more at risk).
4 I ______ (= survived) my 20s, and even the rough times, but I wish I'd been more focused.
5 We need to ______ (= accept) the fact that most of the choices we make in our 20s have life-long consequences.
6 So it's really in your 20s that you need to ______ (= assume control) and determine your destiny.

B In pairs, choose a situation for sentences 1–4. Then role-play a short conversation.

1 'It started well, but it *got off track* halfway through. I nearly fell asleep towards the end.'
2 'It's been a year, but I still haven't *come to terms with* the idea that she's left me.'
3 'I don't know how I *made* it *through* the first week. But then I got used to it.'
4 'I think he really needs to *take charge* of the situation and try to fix it.'

So, how was the lecture? Did I miss anything important?

Well, it started well, but it got off track halfway through. I nearly ...

C Complete 1–6 with the expressions in **A**. Which opinion(s) do you agree with?

WHAT'S THE RIGHT AGE TO GET MARRIED?

→ Not until you're in your 30s. If things don't work out, [1]______, especially if there are children involved.

→ When a relationship [2]______, couples need to stick together so they can [3]______ the bad times, and that takes a lot of maturity. So I'd say wait until you're in your mid-20s at least.

→ There's no such thing as 'the right age'. Once you've [4]______ and feel you're mature enough to [5]______ of your own life without depending on other people, I'd say go for it!

→ I got divorced last year, and I'm still [6]______ being on my own again. So, at the moment, I'm the last person you should ask!

D **Make it personal** In groups, decide on the best ages for these activities. Use expressions from **A**.

get your child a mobile phone · let your child start dating · start learning a foreign language · travel on your own for the first time · have a baby · become a boss · start your own business

You should be at least 40 before you start your own business.

Yes, the stakes are much higher when the company is yours!

Common mistakes

People ~~at / in / of~~ (who are) my age aren't mature enough to have a baby!

Couples who ~~have~~ (are) the same age get on best.

3 Language in use

A 7.5 Listen to a sociology professor discuss changing attitudes toward older people. In pairs, answer 1–2.

1 How does he define 'ageism'?
2 Is he optimistic or pessimistic about the future?

B 7.5 Listen again without looking at the statements below. Then tick (✔) the ones you remember Dr Suárez making to support his prediction of a changing workplace.

1 ☐ By 2050, most of you will have been working for several decades, and you will have developed many valuable skills by that time. You won't be ready to stop.
2 ☐ Nevertheless, some of you will have decided you'd like to spend more time with family.
3 ☐ Many more people will have discovered they can reinvent themselves. The majority of the population will have accepted 60 is the new 40.
4 ☐ The proportion of older workers will have changed because the number of new workers will have slowed considerably.
5 ☐ Society will have been gradually accepting this demographic change, and older workers won't have been fired prematurely.
6 ☐ Older workers also won't have developed the physical limitations they have today.

C In pairs, which statements from **B** do you agree with? Why (not)? Can you add one more of your own?

I agree with number 6. Look how far medicine has advanced in the last 50 years.

Yes, but isn't that wishful thinking? There are limits to how much the aging process can be delayed.

D Make it personal What age-related behaviours might be more / less common by 2050?

1 Look at the photos. Do any of today's age-related behaviours surprise you? Make notes.

2 Read *Clarifying opinions*. Then in groups, share your reactions to the photos. Be sure to clarify any ideas your classmates don't seem to understand.

Clarifying opinions

You may use expressions such as *What I mean(t) is that …*, *What I was trying to say is that …*, and *Let me put it another way* to clarify opinions you realise were too broad or weren't clear:

Sexism will have disappeared. [very broad]

What I mean is that people will have more open attitudes. [more specific]

I think many older women will be dating younger men. For one thing, sexism will have disappeared.

You're joking! But I do think people won't be aging as quickly, and of course, women will still live longer on average.

Well, what I mean is that people will have more open attitudes and abandon the old stereotype that the man must be older.

4 Grammar: Future perfect and future perfect continuous

A Read the grammar box and tick (✔) the correct rules (1–3).

Future perfect and future perfect continuous: active and passive

We	will / won't	have	**worked**	since our twenties.
			been working	for 50 years by the time we retire.
I / People			**seen**	many social changes by then.
These changes			**been accepted**	by the vast majority of people.
Older people			**been forced**	out of the workplace prematurely.

1 The future perfect and continuous ☐ **sometimes** ☐ **never** have the same meaning.
2 When a future event will have ended by the time referred to, use the ☐ **future perfect** ☐ **future perfect continuous**.
3 In passive sentences, use ☐ **either form** ☐ **only the future perfect**.

Grammar expansion p.150

B Underline examples of the future perfect and future perfect continuous in 3B. Next to each one, write rule numbers 1, 2, or 3.

Common mistake

Even when I'm 90, I won't have ~~been forgetting~~ *forgotten* my English.

C Circle the correct options (1–7). In which two are both choices correct? Which do you agree with?

→ By 2050, every two out of nine people [1][**will have reached** / **will have been reaching**] the age of 60, and life expectancy [2][**will have exceeded** / **will have been exceeding**] 76 years.
→ The majority of people [3][**will have lived** / **will have been living**] in urban areas for some time.
→ While we [4][**won't have stopped** / **won't have been stopping**] aging, health care [5][**will have been improving** / **will have been improved**] significantly by then and will be linked to happiness.
→ And, of course, by then, we [6][**will have been using** / **will have used**] technology for over 50 years, and our proficiency [7][**will have become** / **will have been becoming**] impressive.

5 Pronunciation: Reduction of future forms in informal speech

A 7.6 and 7.7 Read and listen to the rules. Then listen to and repeat 1–3.

In rapid, informal speech, future perfect forms are often reduced:
will have been = *will /ə/ been*   won't have been = *won't /ə/ been*
In more formal speech, and when a vowel follows, say *will've* and *won('t)'ve*:
will have exceeded = *will /əv/ exceeded*   won't have exceeded = *won't /əv/ exceeded*

1 I will have been working for 50 years and won't have been bored at all.
2 We will have been exposed to many new things.
3 Employers won't have expected people to retire early.

B Make it personal The sentences in 4C are all positive changes. What negative changes can you imagine might take place in the same areas? Use reduced future forms where possible.

life expectancy   cities   health care   social problems   technology

I predict our online security will have been compromised.

Yes, the government will have been accessing our personal data for some time.

6 Reading

A Read the first two paragraphs and cover the rest. In pairs, guess the things babies might be capable of.

Five Things You Didn't Know Babies Could Do

Himanshu Sharma

There's simply no better way to put it: babies are essentially vegetables. Sure, they're cute and everything, but at the end of the day, [1]we all know that they're primitive organisms who are yet to develop the basic functions to qualify as cognitive human beings. As the babies grow, they will slowly develop various functions necessary to survive in the world.

But as research is gradually finding out, [2]babies are capable of much more than we usually give them credit for.

5 Distinguishing faces, even of other species

If you've ever spent time with a baby, you'll know that they're not so great at recognising people by their faces. They don't seem to behave in a particularly different way when they see someone they have met earlier, unless it's their mother or someone they spend a lot of time with. The ability to tell faces apart from each other is something they acquire much later in their lives. [3]Or that's what the babies would rather have you believe, anyway.

Babies are actually pretty good at identifying faces, even when it comes to creatures of different species. In an experiment conducted by researchers at the University of Sheffield and University of London, six-month-old babies were found to be as good as adults at recognising human faces that they had seen earlier. But, shockingly, they were actually better at recognising monkey faces than the adults. How many of us can tell monkeys apart by their faces? We bet it's not a lot. Yet, apparently, six-month-old babies can do just that. We lose the ability to recognise the faces of different species and races as we grow older, because an adult's facial recognition is based more on familiarity than absolute facial indicators, but babies still carry this vestigial ability up to a certain age.

4 Judging character

[4]The ability to judge how likely someone is to help you comes built in as an evolutionary trait. It's a social skill that's essential to operating in a society as well as to survival. This was especially true during the hunter-gatherer times, when knowing if someone was likely to kill you and steal your belongings was pretty helpful. It's a crucial ability, and – surprisingly enough – one that comes with the package at birth instead of being developed over years of social communication, as we're generally inclined to assume.

Researchers set up an experiment and made some babies watch a puppet show. One puppet was shown to be climbing a mountain, while the second and third puppet would either help the climber up or throw him back down, respectively. When the babies were offered the last two puppets, 14 out of 16 ten-month-olds and all 12 six-month-olds preferred the helper over the hinderer. While researchers still don't know whether it's an informed decision, [5]drooling infants seemingly staring blankly at things sure register far more information than we knew.

3 Learning language in the womb

Learning a whole new language is a process that takes a long time to perfect, especially when it comes to conversing in a social environment. The verbal cues, gestures, subtle winks, and other aspects of communicating take years to master. While it is something that we get better at as we grow older, this development starts much earlier than you'd think: before you're even born.

Babies apparently learn their native language from their mothers in the womb and can identify their mother tongue when they're barely hours old. Researchers recorded the vowel sounds in the native tongues of some 30-hour-old babies and studied their reactions to see if they recognised the sounds. The researchers plugged a pacifier into a computer and made the babies suck on it. Sucking for a shorter period of time meant that the sound was familiar, and vice versa. As it turned out, the babies appeared to recognise the sounds played in their mother tongue, indicating that we're born with at least a rudimentary sense of what our native language sounds like.

2 Understanding social interactions

In our daily lives, we often need to know the context of a social interaction to respond accordingly. The mind can collate data on what's going on around you and suggest the best course of action based on that information. Of course, babies can't do that, but they do know the basics of social communication.

Researchers studied babies between 24 and 120 hours of age. They employed a technique known as near-infrared spectroscopy to monitor the part of the brain responsible for social interactions. What they found was that this section of the brain lit up in response to a real social interaction – facial expressions, social gestures, and so on – but did not respond to, say, an arm manipulating a random object. [6]This suggests that babies are wired to recognise social clues from birth.

There had been similar studies on older babies before, but this was the first time social interactions were studied in babies as young as 24 hours. Interestingly, the older babies were better at successfully differentiating the various types of communication, suggesting that this ability rapidly develops in the early stages of life.

1 Fairness

Our sense of fairness is something that probably helps us save a ton of money by not getting ripped off all the time. It's no surprise that we have it; it's an evolved mechanism that lets us function in a social environment. But what is a surprise is how early we develop this crucial ability. According to science, babies as young as 15 months are able to distinguish a fair deal from an unfair one.

Babies were made to sit on their parents' laps and look at a video of someone distributing food to two people. This was done twice. The first time, the food was distributed equally. The second time, one recipient got more food than the other. The babies were more surprised and hence stared longer at the unfair transaction compared to when the food was divided equally. [7]Even if a baby's basic sense of fairness isn't much use for either the baby or anyone else, it's surprising that this ability starts developing way before it's actually needed in life.

B 7.8 Read and listen to the article. In pairs, recall the explanation for each skill babies have. Were you surprised?

> It seems logical babies would be better at recognising faces.

C Re-read and, in pairs, explain the author's opinions in the numbered sentences 1–7. Replace the blue highlighted expressions with a similar meaning.

> In sentence 1, he's saying that everyone thinks babies still haven't developed cognitive functions.

D **Make it personal** Search on 'Things babies can do'. What other surprising things did you discover?

> Did you know babies can yell at birth, but not cry? Tears can't be formed until they're about three weeks old.

7 Vocabulary: Adjective-noun collocations in writing and speech

A Read *Finding common adjective-noun collocations*. Find the underlined collocations with *social* in context. Which are you familiar with?

Finding common adjective-noun collocations

News sources often use adjective-noun collocations that are common in conversation. For example:

It's a *social skill* that's essential.

B **Make it personal** Have you ever felt you weren't treated appropriately for your age? Look at the highlighted adjective-noun collocations in the article. Then use them and the collocations from A to share stories in groups.

> My parents didn't even have a rudimentary sense of how teenagers think. For example, when it came to social interactions, they didn't seem to remember peer pressure.

8 Language in use

A 7.9 Listen to the start of a community lecture. Complete the notes.

- *Nature vs nurture: the influence of* [1]________ *vs* [2]________.
- *Stage theorists vs others: development is* [3]________ *vs it's affected by* [4]________.

B 7.10 Read the quotes from the street interviews. Then listen to the rest of the lecture. Match the people in the order you hear them (1–6) to their photos.

WHAT IS 'AGE-APPROPRIATE' BEHAVIOUR?

☐☐ It's my grandmother who walks two miles a day. And she's pushing 90!

☐☐ It's my younger brother who's more mature. He's wise beyond his years.

☐☐ We're not the ones who will reform society. We seem to have run out of ideas and just conform to expectations.

☐☐ Act my age? No way! It's a crazy situation I find myself in now. I'm the one who puts food on the table.

1 ☐ My teacher is in her early 70s, and she's really young at heart. It's my classmates who seem old-fashioned.

☐☐ It's not old people who are boring. They have so much insight and first-hand experience. It's us!

C 7.10 Listen again. Match opinions a–d to the six people in B. Did anyone surprise you?

a Nature is more important than nurture.
b Nurture is more important than nature.
c Stage theory is usually accurate.
d People simply don't fit into neat stages.

D In pairs, explain the meaning of the highlighted expressions in context.

> I think to be pushing 90 means 'she's almost 90'. If you think about the meaning of *push*, it makes sense!

E **Make it personal** What are your views on human development?

1 In groups, choose opinions from B. Note down examples from your life or the lives of others.
2 Share a story about yourself or someone you know to illustrate your views. Use expressions from A.

> I'd say life stages are unpredictable, and I have first-hand experience, too! People my age might be at university, but I dropped out to become a singer.

> What convinced you to do it?

9 Grammar: Cleft sentences

A Read the grammar box. Write S (subject) or O (object) next to each sentence. What clue gave you the answer? Then find five cleft sentences in 8B. Write S or O next to each.

Cleft sentences: subject and object focus

It's	older people	**who / that**	have a perspective on life. [1] ☐
	your attitude	**that / which**	must change. [2] ☐
	not how long you live		always determines your savings. [3] ☐
	saving now		will pay off later. [4] ☐
	an unusual phase of life	**(that)**	we find ourselves in. [5] ☐
	a tough situation		we have to face. [6] ☐
	a way of dealing with the future		he's looking for. [7] ☐

A cleft sentence can focus on a subject or object:
Subject: *Your attitude* must change. → It's your attitude that must change.
Object: We must face *a tough situation*. → It's a tough situation (that) we must face.

» Grammar expansion p.150

B Rewrite the underlined parts of Leo's responses (1–6) as cleft sentences.

Does anything tend to bother you, Leo?

Yes, when I see people not acting their age, it really bothers me. [1]I'm not bothered by their behaviour, as such. But [2]my expectations aren't being met. For example, if I see an 80-year-old on a skateboard, [3]the complete surprise leaves me speechless. I guess you could say, [4]I just haven't expected a sight [like that]. As for what bothers me, [5]I think I feel envy. If I can't skateboard now, how will I skateboard at 80? [6]My own fears are getting in the way of positive thoughts!

1 It's not their behaviour, as such, that bothers me.

C Read *Alternatives to cleft sentences*. Find two alternatives in 8B.

Alternatives to cleft sentences

Cleft sentences with pronouns may sound unnatural and, at times, even ungrammatical when the pronoun is a subject. Instead, use *the one(s)*:

~~It's not him~~ who wants to change jobs. → He's not the one who wants to change jobs.

D Change the underlined responses (1–4) using alternatives to cleft sentences.

A: Why did you borrow money from your parents?
B: [1]I didn't borrow money.
A: What do you mean?
B: [2]They borrowed £200 from me. They're really not acting their age!
A: What's it got to do with age? And besides, aren't they out of work?
B: [3]I need the money. I want to buy a car.
A: [4]Maybe you're not acting your age. You're only 17!

E **Make it personal** In pairs, discuss 1–3. Use cleft sentences (and alternatives) where possible.

1 Do you agree with the opinions in 8C?
2 Do you know any adults who don't act their age?
3 Do you think parents are at fault when children don't act their age?

Are parents at fault when children don't act their age?

Yes, because it's their parents that don't set expectations.

10 Listening

A 7.11 Listen to Mia talking to her friend Jack about having a younger boss. Complete the missing words (1–5) in Jack's suggestions.

1 Maybe it's time for some new ________.
2 It's your age you have to take out of the ________.
3 Just relax, be yourself, but still show ________.
4 He also might appreciate your ________ information with him.
5 You're the one who has the most to ________ if you help him solve his problems.

B In pairs, what do these expressions from A mean?

1 'take [something] out of the ________'
2 '[you] have the most to ________'

C 7.12 Listen to the next part of the conversation. Complete the table.

	Mia	Her boss, Tim
Character traits	1	4
Qualifications	2	5
Experience	3	6

7.13 Listen to Mia and her boss. Tick (✔) 1, 2, or 3. Do you think Jack's advice made a difference?

Tim becomes interested in what Mia is saying because ...

1 ☐ she asks his advice. 2 ☐ she presents a solution. 3 ☐ both 1 and 2.

11 Keep talking

A In pairs, brainstorm jobs you feel you're ideally suited for, but where you might be seen as too young (or old).

1 Plan two reasons for each category: character traits, qualifications, and experience.
2 Counter the argument about your age with reasons from 1.

B 7.14 **How to say it** Complete the table. Listen to check.

Formal requests

What they said	What they meant
1 I hope I'm not ________.	You might be busy.
2 I had an idea for the report I wanted to ________ by you.	I want to know what you think.
3 ________ it be OK if I went ahead?	Can I go ahead?
4 I wonder if I could ________ work at home tomorrow.	I'd like to work at home tomorrow.
5 Would you be so ________ as to close the door?	Please close the door.

C Imagine you got the job in A. Role-play a conversation with your boss and ask to work on an important project. Use *How to say it* expressions.

May I come in for a minute? I hope I'm not ...

Yes, by all means.

I had an idea I wanted to ... by you. I wonder if I could ... work on the ... project? You know I'm very ... so I thought I'd be perfect for it.

12 Writing: A job-application letter

A Read the letter. Then identify ...

1 five positive character traits the writer mentions.
2 two qualifications for the job.
3 one example of her past experience.
4 three specific responsibilities she's had.

General Director, Meliá Hotels
12th April, 2017

Dear Sir or Madam,

1 [1]____________ your online advert of March 31, where you posted an opening for an entry-level receptionist in your hotel chain. [2]____________ the position, and am attaching my CV.

2 Having received a BA in Hotel Management from Anhembi Morumbi University in São Paulo, I am eager to put my skills to use. [3]____________ my CV, I speak four languages fluently: English (my native language), Portuguese, Spanish, and German. Therefore, I believe my profile [4]____________ in one of the São Paulo branches of the Meliá Hotels group. However, I'm open to opportunities in Rio de Janeiro, as well.

3 Working in your prestigious hotel chain would be rewarding work for me. I have excellent communication skills and am attentive to detail. In addition, I enjoy interacting with customers and serving their needs. In several summer jobs where I've worked as an assistant in reception, I have been praised as dynamic and pro-active. My past responsibilities have included problem-solving room assignments, checking in customers, and answering routine questions. [5]____________, I have learned to interact with a wide variety of people from many backgrounds and nationalities. Helping customers has strengthened my desire to have a future career in hotel management.

4 While I am aware this would be my first full-time hotel assignment, I consider myself a quick learner. My academic background has familiarised me with many aspects of the hotel industry. On-the-job experience would allow me to translate the theoretical to the practical.

5 [6]____________. Thank you very much in advance.

Sincerely,
Linda Baker

Common mistake

Working there would be ~~a rewarding~~ *rewarding* work for me.

B Read *Formulaic expressions (2)*. Then complete 1–6 in the letter with the expressions given.

Formulaic expressions (2)

Formulaic expressions like these are commonly used in job-application letters.
I believe I am highly suited to (this sort of assignment).
As you will see on (p.2) / in (the attached sample) ...
In this capacity, (I answered phones).
I am writing in response to (your job opening).
I hope you will give my (CV) careful consideration.
(I) would be a perfect fit for (this job).

C Read *Write it right!* In paragraphs 3 and 4, underline two more examples of sentences beginning with noun phrases and one of a sentence beginning with an *-ing* form.

Write it right!

Job-application letters are fairly short and often include sentences beginning with ...

1 noun phrases as subjects:
My past responsibilities have included problem-solving ...

2 *-ing* forms used as nouns, as opposed to sentences beginning with *it*, which take longer to get to the point:
Working in your prestigious hotel would be rewarding work for me.

D Change 1–4 into sentences beginning with an *-ing* form. What kind of job might each person be applying for?

1 It would be fulfilling to use my writing skills.
2 It was responding to emergencies that taught me to make rapid decisions.
3 It was studying linguistics that helped me develop an interest in computing language.
4 It would be the dream of a lifetime to work at such a world-famous hospital.

E Your turn! Choose a job you brainstormed in 11A and write a job-application letter in about 280 words.

Before

List the character traits, qualifications, and experience that make you an excellent candidate.

While

Write four to five paragraphs, following the model in A. Use formulaic expressions and begin sentences with noun phrases (including *-ing* forms).

After

Post your letter online and read your classmates' work. Whose letter is most convincing?

8 What makes a restaurant special?

1 Listening

A 8.1 Listen to the start of a lecture on business practices. Which picture (1–2) does the speaker imply the dinner will be like?

B 8.2 In pairs, guess what happened next. Listen to check. Then answer 1–3.

1 Who came to the dinner?
2 What were they given at the end?
3 What was the true reason for the dinner?

C 8.2 Listen again. What do 1–4 mean in context? Choose a or b.

1 bland a ☐ smooth, not irritating b ☐ tasteless
2 shrug off a ☐ not care b ☐ brush off, remove
3 baffled a ☐ puzzled b ☐ frustrated
4 oblivious to a ☐ unaffected by b ☐ unaware of

D 8.3 Listen to the last part. Why didn't the companies sue the site? Tick (✔) the correct answer.

1 ☐ They probably wouldn't succeed.
2 ☐ It probably wasn't in their interest.
3 ☐ both 1 and 2

E **Make it personal** Does advertising work? In groups, discuss 1–3.

1 How effective do you think campaigns like the one described in A really are?

> Very effective! These days any video offering the unexpected goes viral almost immediately.

2 Which quotes (a–f) do you like most / least? Why? Take a class vote.

a 'The only people who care about advertising are the people who work in advertising.' (George Parker)
b 'Don't find customers for your product. Find products for your customers.' (Seth Godin)
c 'Advertisers constantly invent cures to which there is no disease.' (Author unknown)
d 'Ads sell a great deal more than products. They sell values, images, and concepts of success and worth.' (Brené Brown)
e 'Advertising teaches people not to trust their judgment. Advertising teaches people to be stupid.' (Carl Sagan)
f 'Let's gear our advertising to sell our goods, but let's recognise also that advertising has a broad social responsibility.' (Leo Burnett)

3 Guess why the quotes were all written by men. Similar opinions?

2 Vocabulary: Expressions with *take* for discussing events

A 8.4 Listen to excerpts 1–6. When you hear the 'beep', say one of the expressions below. Use the correct form of *take*. Continue listening to check.

take → (legal) action / a stand / matters into (its) own hands / offence / the blame / (the Internet) by storm

B In groups, use your instincts to guess the correct preposition (1–4). Search on the expression to check. Then change the sentences so they're true for you.

1 I wish more people would take a stand [**about** / **against**] GM foods.
2 In my country, it's easy to take legal action [**over** / **against**] cyber stalkers.
3 I take offence [**at** / **with**] jokes aimed at minority groups.
4 I sometimes get into trouble at work because I take the blame [**for** / **of**] my colleagues' mistakes.

C 8.5 Listen to two friends, Gary and Ruth, talking about a nightmare purchase. Take notes on 1–5. Then answer using expressions from A.

1 How popular does Ruth think a campaign like that would be in the US?
2 How did Gary react when Ruth mentioned the old washing machine?
3 Whose fault was the wrong delivery?
4 How apologetic was the manager?
5 What does Gary say he might do in the end?

D Make it personal Talk about bad service!

1 8.6 **How to say it** Complete the table. Listen to check.

Describing negative experiences	
What they said	**What they meant**
1 On ________ of that, (it took them three days to get back to me).	To make a bad situation worse or more painful …
2 To make ________ worse, (she said it was the delivery company's fault).	
3 As if that were not ________, (they charged my credit card again).	
4 To ________ insult to injury, (they didn't even apologise).	

2 What was the worst experience you've ever had at a restaurant? Think through a–b and make notes.

a the most relevant details (What / Where / When / Who / Why / How long)
b the outcome and what you learned from the experience

3 In groups, share your stories. Use *How to say it* expressions and ones with *take*. Who had the worst experience?

Common mistakes

The food was ~~tasteful~~ tasty / tasteless.

The decoration was ~~tasty~~ tasteful / tasteless.

I once had to wait an hour before my order was taken, so I took matters into my own hands.

What did you do? Grab food from the kitchen?

I stood up and yelled 'Fire'. So to add insult to injury, they accused me of creating a disturbance!

3 Language in use

A Read the cartoon. Do you agree? What advice would you give the waitress?

B 8.7 Listen to Raúl and his private English tutor, Julia. Tick (✔) the problems with his text.

- [ ] There are a few grammar mistakes.
- [ ] It's too wordy.
- [ ] It's too formal.
- [ ] The vocabulary is too simple.

C 8.8 Listen to the next part of their conversation. Underline the sentences in sections 1–4 of Raúl's draft handout that Julia suggests changing. Which reason in **B** does she give?

Guidelines for dealing with complaints – draft

Once you realise that a customer is dissatisfied, try to imagine yourself in his or her position, even if you're not to blame. Then follow these four easy guidelines:

1. It is critically important that your customers communicate how they feel. They need time and space to express their dissatisfaction. Then, apologise – even if you feel their criticism is unfair.
2. Listen actively. It is essential that you not draw any conclusions until you know all the facts. Then repeat your customer's concerns to make sure you have correctly identified the key issues.
3. If you can respond to the issue at hand immediately, do it. It is crucial that problems be resolved quickly.
4. A customer may insist that he or she speak to the manager. If that happens, try to find someone in a position of authority to support you.

D 8.8 Try to remember Julia's suggested changes. Cross out the words and write the new ones in Raúl's handout. Then listen again to check. Did you get them all?

E **Make it personal** In pairs, discuss 1–3. Similar opinions?

1. Which of Raúl's guidelines in **C** should companies follow more often? Would you add any others?
2. Should businesses refund or exchange damaged products with 'no questions asked'?
3. Do you notice the writing style of letters businesses send? How informal should it be?

> I'd add that a shop assistant shouldn't answer the phone when the customer is talking!

4 Grammar: The subjunctive

A Read the grammar box and tick (✔) the correct rules (a–c). Then, without looking back at 3B, rephrase the underlined parts of 1–4 using the subjunctive. Use the word in brackets.

The subjunctive: verbs and expressions with *it's*

I **wish**	(that)	**the shirt were**	on sale.
I **demanded**		**he give**	me a refund.
I **insist**		**the manager see**	me this instant.
I **suggest**		**we look into**	this matter.
It was important		**you not be**	rude.
It's essential		**she research**	her purchase.

a After *wish*, the subjunctive form for *he* and *she* is ☐ **was** ☐ **were**.
b After other verbs, and expressions with *it's*, the subjunctive is the ☐ **base** ☐ **past tense** form.
c When the first verb is in the past, the subjunctive form ☐ **changes** ☐ **doesn't change**.

» Grammar expansion p.152

1 <u>It's important for your customers to say</u> how they feel. (important)
2 <u>Don't jump to any conclusions</u> until you know all the facts. (essential)
3 <u>Problems must be resolved</u> quickly. (crucial)
4 A customer <u>may want to speak</u> to the manager. (insist)

B Read *Using the subjunctive*. Then complete 1–6 below. Imagine a context for each.

Using the subjunctive

The subjunctive is relatively uncommon in English, and is used in formal speech and writing. In conversation, other structures are frequently used:
It's important **for you not to be** rude. / **Please don't be** rude.
They suggested **speaking** to you. / They **said to speak** to you.

Plain English: All it's cracked up to be?

Writers often recommend a communication style that's short, clear, and to the point. But are we going too far in that direction? In this course, you'll learn how to make your language more emphatic – useful skills for writing and formal speeches.

Instead of:	It might be better to say:
1 Do your best to meet the deadline.	It's important … the deadline.
2 Don't be late.	It's essential … late.
3 He should seek help immediately.	I suggest … help immediately.
4 I'm sorry Dad isn't here to witness this day.	I wish … here to witness this day.
5 All the requirements must be met.	It's crucial …
6 She said the contract had to be revised.	She demanded …

I think in number 6, some lawyers might be talking about a client.

Common mistake

She suggested ~~him to take~~ *(that) he take* legal action.

C Make it personal Be convincing!

1 Choose at least one sentence from the right column of B, decide a context, and plan a short speech. Note down at most five key points.

2 In groups, deliver your speeches. Whose points were clearest? Who sounded the most formal?

Thank you very much for joining me here today. As I think most of you know, I'm the new school director. I'd like to begin by …

5 Reading

A Read the title. Does Barbara Apple Sullivan expect to be treated well? What clue is there? Read the first four paragraphs to check.

B In pairs, guess why Barbara had a 'reinvigorated customer experience'. Then read the rest to check. Make certain you understand the highlighted words, and search online for images, if necessary.

> I think she might have been given a free flight ...

The True Story Of Amazing Customer Service From – Gasp! – An Airline

1 **When Barbara Apple Sullivan accidentally dropped her passport in a Charles de Gaulle airport mailbox just before boarding a flight, she was certain she'd be stuck for days. But thanks to a Delta employee, she made it on board and had her future travel plans transformed forever.**

2 **'Keep Climbing.'**

That is the slogan for Delta Airlines' latest advertising campaign, which highlights its promise for a 'reinvigorated customer experience'. So often I have seen this television commercial and others like it, paying little attention to the message and the value proposition. My only takeaway was reassurance that the planes were pointed upward and not downward.

3 In such a saturated industry, it is difficult for any airline to differentiate the customer experience. The planes themselves are virtually identical. The food, if it exists, is universally awful. Airport security is conducted by an entity over which the airlines have virtually no control. And virtually everyone who flies has a personal horror story. Is it really possible to redefine the customer experience?

4 It was my personal experience with a single employee that emblazoned Delta's value proposition in my mind forever. Their promise came to life in a real, tangible way. More than any advertising, more than an impactful website, more than those tasty biscotti cookies served on the plane, this really was a reinvigorated customer experience.

5 Allow me to set the scene. To my horror, I inadvertently dropped my passport in a mailbox at Charles de Gaulle airport last Sunday morning (it was bundled with all my VAT refund envelopes). The instant the mail left my hand and dropped to the bottom of the mailbox, I realised my error. Two airport employees told me it was impossible to open the mailbox on a Sunday since postal workers, who do not work on Sundays, have sole authority to open the box. I was told I must wait until Monday, go to the US Embassy in Paris, and request an emergency passport before I would be able to fly. In desperation, I approached the Delta ticket counter and told them I had a BIG problem.

One gentleman behind the counter, Mr Karim Sayoud, took my problem as though it were his own. He calmed me in my increasing panic, explained what he could do and immediately called the US Homeland Security Customs and Border Control representative station at the airport.

Mr James Wilkinson from US Homeland Security came to interrogate me. All I had was my passport number. I had nothing else. No copy of my passport, no social security card, and the address on my driver's licence did not match my passport. After providing enough correct answers to convince him that I was in fact who I said I was, he agreed to let me travel, subject to the French authorities that retain final approval.

Karim Sayoud left his position at the Delta ticket counter, escorted me to Delta check-in, and he convinced his colleagues to accept my baggage (without the certainty that I would be on the flight) and issue a boarding pass. He then escorted me through French passport control and security, encouraging the authorities to let me through, and ultimately to the Delta gate agents. It was there that I was finally able to breathe a sigh of relief.

Sayoud didn't stop there. After I was successfully on the flight, he took it upon himself to make certain that my passport was retrieved from the mailbox the following day and returned to me in New York. He actually taped a handwritten note on the mailbox so the postal worker would see it and return the passport to Delta once it was retrieved. He phoned and emailed me multiple times each day updating me on the status. Lo and behold, my passport arrived at my address by FedEx – a true customer-service miracle made entirely possible by one dedicated employee.

—Barbara Apple Sullivan is CEO and a managing partner of Sullivan, a multidisciplinary brand-engagement firm based in New York City. Follow them on Twitter at @sullivannyc

C 8.9 Listen to and re-read the article. T (true) or F (false)? Correct the false statements.

1 Barbara accidentally dropped her passport in a mailbox when she was mailing letters.
2 Airport employees in Paris are allowed to open mailboxes if they have the keys.
3 Karim Sayoud first tried to reassure Barbara and then had a security and border-control representative interview her.
4 Whether Barbara was allowed to fly was ultimately up to US Homeland Security.
5 Karim Sayoud took multiple steps to make sure Barbara got her passport back.

D **Make it personal** In pairs, how unusual do you think Barbara's story is? If you'd had the same experience at an airport, train, or bus station, would you have got the same level of help? Why (not)?

> If this had happened to me, it wouldn't have occurred to me to ask Delta for help.

6 Vocabulary: Expressions of help

A Read *Describing helpful behaviour*. Then cover the table and use the cues 1–6 to retell Karim's story.

Describing helpful behaviour

Common expressions of help, like the one underlined in the text, often have similar meanings.

Karim Sayoud	**took it upon himself** **went to great lengths** **went out of his way** **went the extra mile** **moved mountains**	to make	sure Barbara got her passport.
	took it from there	and made	
	saw to it that	she was fully satisfied.	

1 When Karim learned about the problem, he [take / upon / himself] to ...
2 He then [go / extra / mile], left the counter, and ...
3 He [move / mountains] to make sure the authorities ...
4 On Monday, he [take / from / there] and saw to it that Barbara's passport ...
5 He [go / out / way] and even ... for a postal worker.
6 He then [go / great / lengths] to keep Barbara updated and ...

B **Make it personal** Share stories about Good Samaritans.

1 The unlucky people in the pictures were all helped by thoughtful people. In pairs, share what you think happened, using expressions from A.

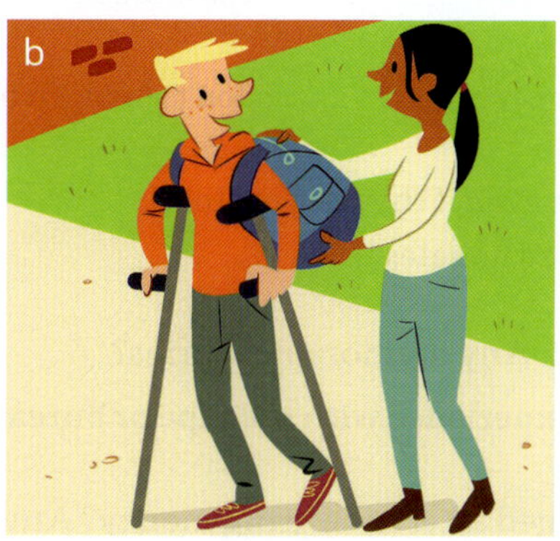

2 Has a stranger ever gone out of his / her way for you? Or vice versa? In groups, share your stories. Whose is the most remarkable?

> A man I'd never met before really went to great lengths for me once and ...

7 Language in use

A 8.10 Listen to two friends, Alba and Paul, discussing bureaucracy. In pairs, answer 1–2.

1 What was the problem?
2 Guess what Alba decided to do.

B 8.11 Listen to the complete conversation. Match the comments with the topics (a–f). There's one extra.

1 As much as you might try to plan your life, there are always unpleasant surprises.
2 However generous he may have been, for us it was a nightmare.
3 Whatever compromises you feel are reasonable, none will be convincing.
4 For all the good arguments you come up with, they just won't budge.
5 As exciting as it sounds, some things just aren't worth it.

a ☐ paying taxes
b ☐ getting an inheritance
c ☐ having a lot of money
d ☐ Spanish bureaucracy
e ☐ government bureaucrats
f ☐ Alba's uncle's restaurant

8 Vocabulary: Words for discussing money

A Read *Money terms*. Then complete 1–6 below with a form of the words in the box.

Money terms

Terms involving money can vary quite a bit across languages. For example, the Spanish verb *cobrar* can mean 'to charge (an amount)', 'to get paid (a salary)', 'to cash (a cheque)', or 'to collect (a debt)'. In English, these are all separate verbs. Always learn money terms in context. A noun and a verb may be identical or have different forms.

'I'm afraid they're going to *tax* (v) me a lot this year.' 'The *tax* (n) is very high, too.'
Tom might *inherit* (v) a lot of money. He's going to have a big *inheritance* (n)

borrow	charge (n / v)	inherit	loan (n / v)	profit (n / v)	tax (n / v)

1 *Stand by Us* Electronics has terrible customer service, but they certainly make a nice ________ .
2 If I ________ a lot of money, I'd leave my job the next day.
3 Never go to that shop on Church Street. They ________ me double for a purchase last week. I think they did it on purpose.
4 Ever since the recession, it's really hard to get a ________ . I don't think I'll be able to buy a house, there's so much red tape!
5 I never let people ________ my computer, even if they beg me to!
6 A great country to shop in is the UK. There's no sales ________ .

B **Make it personal** In groups, discuss 1–2. Any memorable stories?

1 Have you ever had a very (un)pleasant experience with red tape or bureaucracy? What was the situation?
2 Do you know of anyone whose life changed after inheriting money? Any interesting stories?

Yes, I had an uncle who became a well-known painter. When he no longer had to work, he started to spend his whole day taking art courses.

I really wish I could do that!

9 Grammar: Adverb clauses to emphasise conditions or contrasts

A Read the grammar box and complete the rules (a–c).

Adverb clauses to emphasise conditions or contrasts

1 **However** reasonable the price	**may** seem,	the watch still doesn't work.
2 **Whatever** discount you	**might** give me,	it won't be sufficient.
3 **As useful as** the manual	**may** be,	it isn't helping.
4 **(As) much as** you	**try** to please customers,	you're not succeeding.
5 **For all the** help you	**give** me,	I won't shop here again.

a Sentences 1–3 use the modal verbs ________ or ________ to express a condition.

b A condition can also be expressed using the ________ tense.

c Conditions or contrasts with *whatever* are followed by ________ , whereas ones with *however* are often followed by ________ or adverbs.

» Grammar expansion p.152

B Write the numbers from the grammar box (1–5) next to the sentences in 7B. Then rephrase each one so it begins with *No matter* ...

No matter how much you might try to plan your life ...

Common mistake

However ~~the price seems low~~ *low the price seems*, it's too high!

C Choose the correct answer (1–5) to emphasise a condition or contrast.

[1][**As important as / as much as**] it may be to be polite to customers, sometimes shop assistants are downright rude. However, anyone who has ever been to Japan knows that employees there have a few things to teach us. [2][**However / Whatever**] annoyed they may feel privately, you would never know it as the customer. [3][**Whatever / For all the**] questions you may have, they will always be answered with a smile. The reason is simple. [4][**For all the / As much as**] you may think it is unnatural or even super-human to be so polite, it is actually good for business. How do we know this? By asking customers, of course! [5][**However / Whatever**] surveys we've done on customer-service quality, Japan always comes out on top!

D Make it personal Discuss customer service where you live.

1 Tick (✔) the customer-service quality for your city for each kind of business. In groups, defend your choice. Use adverb clauses to emphasise conditions or contrasts, where possible.

Customer-service quality				
	Poor	Average	Good	Excellent
car dealers				
banks				
mobile phone carriers				
clothing shops				
electric companies				

2 Reach a consensus and share it with the class. How many groups agree?

Mobile phone carriers are the worst. Whatever problem you might have, they try to convince you it's your own fault.

Oh, but I've actually had a good experience with [name of company].

10 Listening

A 8.12 Listen to the start of Amber's call to a phone company. What's the problem? Guess what she says next.

B 8.13 Listen to part two. When you hear 'beep', choose Amber's response and write the number. Continue listening to check. There's one extra choice.

a ☐ You mean you save these conversations? I must have made a mistake. But could you please try to accommodate me?
b ☐ Could you please check if there's an earlier opening? It's essential that it be taken care of today.
c ☐ I have an important deadline. I'm not going to be home on 12th May.
d ☐ I'd like to wait if at all possible. I'm really quite worried about this.
e ☐ However limited the number may be, it's really important that you find a solution.

C 8.14 Guess the polite responses 1–5. Then listen to part three and circle the ones you actually hear. Which words make them rude in this context? Why did the speakers use this tone?

1 Mr Bell [**says** / **claims**] you recorded me.
2 I need my phone connected [**immediately** / **as soon as possible**].
3 [**I've already provided** / **I believe you have**] this information.
4 [**I'd really appreciate your accommodating** / **I insist that you accommodate**] me.
5 [**Could you possibly speak more softly?** / **I suggest you lower your voice**].

In the first one, Amber had made a mistake with the date, but she doesn't really believe it. So the word ...

D Make it personal In pairs, discuss 1–2.

1 Who do you sympathise with more, Amber or Ms McGuire?
2 Were you surprised by the outcome? Why (not)? Would it be different where you live?

I sympathise with Amber. It's natural to be upset after so many calls!

11 Keep talking

A Choose a type of business where you would like to have a real problem resolved. Note down the details. Be sure to include ...

1 the problem.
2 the steps you've already taken.
3 what exactly you'd like the company to do.
4 what action you'll take if they don't.

shop bank company car dealer

B Plan your phone call. Individually, review expressions from 10B and C, and try to imagine the conversation.

C In groups of three, role-play the conversation. Which of you should work for a phone company?

1 **A:** Place the call.
B: Respond as an employee.
C: Evaluate whether **A** and **B** are convincing and give suggestions for improvement.
2 Change roles until all the phone calls have been made. Choose one to share with the class.

[name of business] May I help you?

Yes, I'm phoning concerning a problem I've had with (a purchase) ...

12 Writing: A complaint letter

A Read Jacob Banks's complaint letter and match paragraphs 1–5 to their main function.

- ☐ give an opinion on the company's practices
- ☐ introduce the topic and create sympathy
- ☐ document evidence of previous steps
- ☐ make a strong request
- ☐ fully describe a problem

B Match the formal expressions 1–10 in the letter with these more informal ones with a similar meaning.

- ☐ you can help me
- ☐ even though
- ☐ I could easily have given
- ☐ I don't have to do that
- ☐ fix(ed) things (two expressions)
- ☐ If I'm not happy
- ☐ please write back
- ☐ take you to court
- ☐ without success

C Read *Write it right!* Then find two more passive expressions in paragraph 3 that both have the same meaning.

Write it right!

Complaint letters use formal expressions in the passive that mean 'I was told', but which avoid mentioning the person who gave the information:

I **was convinced (that)** the problem would be resolved promptly.

D In paragraphs 4 and 5, find ...

1 an example of a formal way to express a condition.

2 two examples of the subjunctive.

E Your turn! Choose a consumer problem you brainstormed in 11A and write a formal complaint in about 280 words.

Before

Plan the main function of each paragraph. Note down very specific details on the problem and what steps you've already taken.

While

Write five to six paragraphs to support your complaint, following the model in A. Use passive expressions from *Write it right!*, some formal expressions from B, and formal structures from D.

After

Post your complaint online and read your classmates' work. Whose letter got the most sympathy?

Ms Eleanor Fernández
Director of Customer Service

Dear Ms Fernández:

1 I am writing concerning the cancellation of my credit card on 5th September 2016. I have tried repeatedly, but [1]<u>to no avail</u>, to [2]<u>resolve the matter</u> with your staff. I am a university student, and as this is my first and only credit card, I am hopeful [3]<u>you will be able to assist me</u>.

2 On 1st September, I attempted to pay my monthly bill of £355.66, but mistakenly authorised a payment of £3,355.66. Within a day, my current account was frozen because of an overdraft, and my credit card was suspended. While my bank immediately [4]<u>rectified the problem</u>, cancelling payment and authorising a new payment in the correct amount, your company has refused to reinstate my card. In fact, the suspended card has now been cancelled because of 'possible fraudulent activity'.

3 On 2nd September, I spoke to Mr Ethan Adams, and I was led to believe that the problem would be resolved promptly. On 4th September, when I still could not use the card, I spoke to Ms Kira Russo. I was given to understand that I would have access to the card that very evening. However, when the card was not active on 5th September, I called a third time and spoke to Mr Sean McGee. [5]<u>Notwithstanding the fact that</u> I had been offered previous reassurances on two occasions, Mr McGee informed me that the card had been cancelled. When I asked to speak to a manager, I was connected to Ms Hannah Cook, who insisted that company policy had been followed, and I would need to apply for a new card.

4 I understand that fraud is a legitimate concern, and I appreciate the need for online security. Nevertheless, however reasonable your policies may seem, I believe that good customer service takes into account the specific situation, in my case a simple human error. [6]<u>I would have been happy to provide</u> whatever form of identification was required.

5 I insist that my account be reactivated immediately. In fact, it is imperative that this issue be resolved by 15th September so that I can pay my university tuition. [7]<u>In the event that I do not receive satisfaction</u>, I will have no choice but to post the incident on Twitter and YouTube, as well as [8]<u>consider legal action</u>. I sincerely hope [9]<u>these steps will not be necessary</u>.

Thank you very much in advance for your assistance, and [10]<u>I look forward to a response</u>.

Yours sincerely,
Jacob Banks

Review 4

Units 7–8

1 Speaking

A Look at the photos on p 72.

1 Note down milestones for each phase of life using some of these expressions.

act your age | come of age | come to terms with | conform to expectations | first-hand experience | get off track | make it through | the stakes are higher | take charge | young at heart | wise beyond your years

2 In groups, share insights about what (you think) it's like to be each of the ages in the photos.

> By the time you're in your 30s, the stakes are a lot higher if you feel you've chosen the wrong profession. I've decided to find a new job.

> I'm not sure I agree. Even if you get off track, you're still young and can start over.

B Make it personal Do you believe in nature or nurture? Give examples of people you know about.

> I believe in nature. Haven't you read those studies of identical twins separated at birth who turn out to be exactly alike?

2 Grammar

A Rewrite the opinions (1–6) using cleft sentences.

1 Your age doesn't determine how creative you are. *It's not your age that determines how creative you are.*
2 The recession prevents many young people from getting jobs even if they've tried many times.
3 Having friends makes a difference when life gets tough even if your family is supportive.
4 Your parents made you the person you are now even if school is an influence.
5 Getting old doesn't cause depression; you can enjoy life at any age.
6 We have to face the challenge, though, even if we don't want to.

B Make it personal In pairs, share two true opinions from **A**.

Given | In view of | So as to | With a view to | In an effort to | Thanks to | With the aim of

> It's your age that determines how creative you are. Young people have more ideas.

> I don't agree at all. My grandmother writes beautiful poetry.

C Complete the conversation with the verbs in brackets in the future perfect (simple or continuous) form, or the subjunctive. (Some have more than one answer.)

TEACHER: I suggest your son [1]__________ (try) to study harder before exams.
PARENT: Yes, I wish he [2]__________ (be) a better student. The problem is, he's on the football team and by the end of the year, he [3]__________ (play) 50 games. He's never home.
TEACHER: It's essential that he [4]__________ (improve) his marks. If not, he won't get into university. He's already failed maths twice.
PARENT: I know. I'm really quite worried. Next year, he [5]__________ (take) the same course for three years in a row.
TEACHER: It was important that he [6]__________ (study) for the exam last week, but I don't think he did.
PARENT: I promise I'll talk to him when I get home.

D Rephrase the sentences in **A**. Use the adverb clauses of condition (1–6) at the beginning or end of the sentence.

1 *However* + adjective / adverb ...
2 *For all the* ...
3 *As much as* ...
4 *As useful as* ...
5 *Whatever* + noun ...
6 *As much as* ...

However old you may be, it's not your age that determines how creative you are.

3 Reading

A Read the article on e-shopping. Note down five consumer problems and three actions you can take.

THE TRUTH ABOUT ONLINE SHOPPING

Nearly half of all online consumers have problems with online purchases, with issues ranging from unexpected fees to damaged merchandise. While there are more online customers than ever before, most never think about deliveries arriving late, not at all, or being left outside their homes without permission. Quality is hard to judge online, and some items may be better in a real shop. Returning a purchase may require that you pay shipping charges. And finally, some consumers are victims of outright fraud. Many of them have no idea of their rights.

In the US, you have various options. Your state may have a Consumer Protection Office that can mediate complaints and conduct investigations. The Federal Trade Commission investigates fraud and offers useful tips for getting your money back. There's even an e-consumer government website to help you file complaints against international businesses. But most important, the Better Business Bureau helps you locate reputable businesses so you will not need these other services.

B **Make it personal** Using your notes in **A**, share a story about an e-purchase. Include the problem, what you've done until now, and what you plan to do to resolve it.

For all the promises [name of business] may make, they never tell you about [type of problem]. When I bought ...

4 Self-test

Correct the two mistakes in each sentence. Check your answers in Units 7 and 8. What's your score, 1–20?

1 When I had children, my career came off track, something that was very hard to come to terms.
2 They say couples who have the same age get on best, but it's hard to meet people are my age.
3 When I'm old, I won't have been saving enough for retirement, but I will be working since my 20s.
4 My sister isn't the one who have problems because she's not the one who will have been taken care of our parents.
5 Would it be OK if I will apply for the job? I'm sure it will be a fascinating work.
6 We need to all take a stand about climate change and take legal action over companies that don't protect the environment.
7 It was important that you were not rude, but, unfortunately, you insisted that our manager not spoke at all.
8 I'm going to suggest her to go out of the way for our customers.
9 Notstanding the fact that I've written to the manager three times, it's been no avail.
10 By the time you open your new shop, I will be coming here for ten years and would really appreciate however discount you may be able to offer me.

5 Point of view

Choose a topic. Then support your opinion in 100–150 words, and record your answer. Ask a partner for feedback. How can you be more convincing?

a The 20s are the most important decade. OR
Childhood is far more critical than your 20s.

b In 50 years, many social changes will have occurred. OR
Change takes place slowly, and life won't have changed as much as people imagine.

9 Would you like to be a teacher?

1 Listening

A 9.1 Read the photo caption and guess the answer. Listen to the start of a radio show to check.

Homeschooling is becoming [more / less] popular in the United Kingdom.

B 9.2 In groups, complete the table. Then listen to the second part. How many of your ideas were mentioned?

Homeschooling	
What I (think I) know	What I'd like to know
It's popular in some European countries.	*Do parents prepare all the lessons?*

C 9.2 Listen again. Tick (✔) the advantages mentioned. How many of your questions from B were answered?

Homeschooling ...

1 ☐ enables students to do well academically later in life.
2 ☐ brings families closer together.
3 ☐ enables parents to cater to individual needs.
4 ☐ helps to avoid unnecessary interpersonal conflicts.
5 ☐ gives students more free time to pursue their own interests.

D 9.3 Listen to the third part. Circle the correct inferences.

Fadil feels that ...

1 parents [**worry** / **don't worry enough**] about protecting their kids from outside influences.
2 [**not all** / **most**] parents have the natural aptitude to be good teachers.
3 both parents [**generally** / **don't always**] agree on whether to homeschool.
4 kids need to interact with [**only a few** / **all kinds of**] people to develop emotional intelligence.
5 homeschooling might make kids [**self-centred** / **lonely**].

E **Make it personal** Share your thoughts on homeschooling. Any big differences?

1 Search on 'homeschooling' to answer any remaining questions you have from B.
2 Which of the advantages / disadvantages in C and D are the most important? Can you add others?
3 Would you like to have been homeschooled? Would you ever homeschool your own children? Why (not)?

On balance, I'm opposed to homeschooling, and it's not an option I'd choose for my children.

Really? But how can you be so sure?

2 Vocabulary: Verbs beginning with *out*

A 9.4 Read *Out*- verbs. Then complete 1–4 with forms of the verbs in the mind map. Listen to check.

***Out*- verbs**

The prefix *out*- in verbs usually means 'better', 'greater', 'further', 'longer', etc.
He's a savvy politician who always manages to **outsmart** his rivals. (= be smarter than)
In my neighbourhood, houses **outnumber** flats. (= There are more houses.)
Adele **outsold** every female singer on the planet in the mid 2010s. (= sold more than)

1 Schools have stood the test of time and __________ countless societal changes and paradigm shifts.
2 Do the advantages of homeschooling __________ the potential drawbacks?
3 Apparently, homeschooled kids tend to __________ their state school peers on standardised tests to get into university.
4 We need to expose children to different people and environments to help them __________ their immaturity.

perform	last
OUT	
grow	weigh

B Rephrase 1–4 using *out*- verbs. There may be more than one possible answer. Then ask and answer in pairs. Any disagreements?

1 Why are there more female than male teachers?
2 Is it a myth or fact that students who read widely tend to do better than those who don't?
3 When it comes to single-sex schools, are the pros greater than the cons?
4 In university shops, why do PCs tend to sell more than tablets?

C Make it personal 'Into' or 'out of' the mainstream?

1 9.5 **How to say it** Complete the table. Listen to check.

Drawing tentative conclusions

What they said	What they meant
1 It looks as __________ (it's crossing over into the mainstream).	It seems that ...
2 It would __________ that (the homeschool population is continuing to grow).	
3 This might have to __________ with the fact that (homeschooling offers both parents and children a great deal of flexibility).	Maybe this is related to ...
4 There might be some __________ to this.	Maybe this is true.

2 Read the headlines showing different educational trends in the United Kingdom. Which ones seem to be gaining popularity in your country, too? Note down some possible reasons.

1 Career-focused learning is back: Secondary schools, colleges, universities and companies push for a renewed emphasis on technical skills.

2 Not just for fun: Increasing evidence that music classes enhance performance in other subjects.

3 TAKING THE BULL BY THE HORNS: SCHOOLS RAMP UP ANTI-BULLYING EFFORTS

4 Size matters: Schools are packing more and more students into classrooms – and this is not good

3 In pairs, compare your ideas. Use *out*- verbs and *How to say it* expressions. Similar opinions?

Career-focused learning might have to do with the fact that these days, everyone needs to be an entrepreneur.

Yes, new tech start-ups are beginning to outnumber traditional companies!

3 Language in use

A Read the excerpt from an article on acupuncture and answer 1–2.

1 The writer most likely thinks acupuncture …
☐ definitely works. ☐ might work. ☐ is ineffective.

2 In pairs, looking only at the cartoon …
a summarise what acupuncture is.
b list three conditions it might be used for.

ACUPUNCTURE

Acupuncture, the stimulation of points along the skin using thin needles, is thought to be effective for a variety of medical conditions. But is it really? Patients are reported to have been cured of pain, but some scientists say research is inconclusive, and it's unclear if this is a placebo effect. The technique is believed to relieve neck pain, migraines as well as less severe headaches, and lower back pain, and while many patients are thought to be helped, these scientists say more studies are needed. Of course, this is a Western point of view. In quite a few Asian countries, acupuncture is mainstream medicine, and in Mainland China, Japan, Hong Kong, and Taiwan, nearly everyone will tell you that acupuncture is known to have reduced patient suffering.

B Which view of acupuncture do you agree with? Is acupuncture popular where you live?

> I don't know if acupuncture is effective. I'd like to see more scientific evidence.

4 Pronunciation: Stress on three-word phrasal verbs

A 9.6 Complete the text with forms of the verbs in the box. Listen to a conversation between Emma and Jakob to check. How many verbs did you know?

come down with	give up on	go through with	grow out of	watch out for

When Emma was in sixth form, she [1] _________ (= began to suffer from) migraines at least once a week. Her mum thought she would [2] _________ (= stop having) them, but she often missed school. The doctors couldn't help and Emma almost [3] _________ (= stopped hoping for) a cure. Fortunately, though, her mum [4] _________ (= was looking for) new treatments, and she discovered aromatherapy. Even though it didn't help right away, Emma decided to [5] _________ the treatment (= finish it to the end).

B 9.7 Listen to the verbs in A and tick (✔) the correct rule. Then repeat each one.

Three-word phrasal verbs are always stressed on the ☐ **first** ☐ **second** ☐ **third** word.

C **Make it personal** In pairs, discuss 1–3. Include three-word phrasal verbs, where possible.

1 Have you ever tried acupuncture or aromatherapy? Would you like to?
2 Why might some people be opposed to alternative medicine?
3 Do you know anyone who's had a medical problem that wouldn't go away? Would either treatment have helped?

> My grandmother came down with the flu and developed asthma, but I don't think acupuncture would have helped …

5 Grammar: Passive expressions with infinitives

A Read the grammar box and tick (✔) the correct rules (1–4).

Passive expressions in sentences with active and passive infinitives

The treatment	is	reported	to	work well.
		thought		have helped.
Patients	are	known		be easily influenced.
		believed		have been cured.

1 The blue phrases are ☐ **active** ☐ **passive**. They refer to the ☐ **present** ☐ **past**.
2 The red phrase is ☐ **active** ☐ **passive**. It refers to the ☐ **present** ☐ **past**.
3 The green phrase is ☐ **active** ☐ **passive**, and the purple phrase is ☐ **active** ☐ **passive**.
4 The green and purple phrases describe events that ☐ **happened in the past** ☐ **are happening now**.

Grammar expansion p.154

B Find four more examples in 3A of passive expressions in sentences with infinitives. In pairs, say why each infinitive is like the red, green, blue, or purple example.

The first one is 'Acupuncture is thought to be effective': I think it's red. The infinitive is 'to be' and it refers to the present. It's active because the subject is 'acupuncture'.

C Rewrite underlined sentences 1–6 from the forum to contain passive expressions and infinitives. Begin with the words in italics. How many infinitives are passive, too?

Eileen Finley, US
There are so many kinds of alternative medicine. [1]People think *homeotherapy* is helpful. It uses natural substances to treat infections, fatigue, allergies, and chronic illnesses like arthritis.

Héctor González, Mexico
[2]Doctors believe biofeedback assists *patients*. By using techniques such as visualising, relaxing, and imaging, it can treat asthma, migraines, insomnia, and high blood pressure.

Lester Silver, Canada
How about Bach flower remedies, the system of herbal remedies developed by Edward Bach? [3]Supporters report that they provide relief for personality problems and emotional issues. [4]We know that they've cured *many* people.

Patricia Moreno, Colombia
[5]We know that *Feng Shui* has helped some people, and I believe in it myself. It's an ancient Chinese practice where the furniture in a room is arranged and colours chosen to promote vital energy.

Betty Shih, Taiwan
Don't forget hypnotherapy! Hypnosis bypasses the conscious mind and draws on suppressed memories to help with phobias, weight loss, and stress. [6]People report that *it's* a miracle treatment!

D Make it personal What are the best alternative treatments?

1 Choose two treatments from C or search on 'types of alternative medicine' to find information about one of those below.

dance therapy fasting massage therapy Reiki vitamin therapy yoga therapy

2 Note down at least two reasons why they would be effective. For which ailments?
3 In groups, state your case. Use passive expressions with infinitives where possible.

Dance therapy is reported to be helpful for physical disabilities and eating disorders.

That may be, but it's also just fun and a great way to lose weight.

6 Reading

A Read the first three paragraphs of the article. In pairs, list three possible advantages and three disadvantages of single parenting. Then read the rest. Were any of your ideas mentioned?

Four Reasons It's Better To Be A Single Parent

By Kerri Zane

Although the gold standard in child rearing has traditionally been a dual family unit, being a single parent has myriad benefits. Rather than navigating the treacherous territory of constant parental compromise, you can independently make choices for your children that you feel are best. Eleven years ago, when my former husband and I split, I saw my divorce as a glorious opportunity to parent solo. No more discussing the finer points of gymnastics vs volleyball. I didn't have to debate dessert after dinner vs never ever letting sugar touch lips. And there was no longer a lengthy discussion over the reason my daughters needed braces.

While the state of rock-steady marital bliss in the United States continues to falter, more and more adults are joining the ranks of contented uncoupled family units. In fact, based on the latest Census Bureau statistics, there are over 14 million single-parent households with children under the age of 18. That is a lot of people and a good reason to celebrate. Which is why March 21st has been designated as National Single Parents' Day. It is a time to honour all those tenacious individuals who do what they do, day in and day out, to support, nurture and care for their kids.

As the single mom expert and author of the Amazon best-selling book, *It Takes All 5: A Single Mom's Guide to Finding The REAL One*, I would like to honour the day and offer you four solid reasons why it's better to be a single mom or dad than half of a parenting pair.

1. No Negotiations Necessary

While your married counterparts continue to disagree on the state of their children's welfare, you get to make unilateral choices. In the long run this is better for your offspring's well-being. A child's behaviour can be negatively affected by adult arguing. It will either leave them crying their eyes out or running for cover. With no one else in the house to challenge your choices, you may continue to be the cosy constant security blanket your children need. Granted, there is a financial price to pay when you are the sole provider, but children need to learn that sometimes we can't give them everything they want. And often times what they thought was a 'must-have', really isn't. Ultimately, if it is that important, you will find a way. Payment plans are designed for the single parent!

2. Stellar Independent Role Model

One of the best gifts I was able to give my two daughters was the knowledge that they can make it on their own. Change a light bulb without a dad in the house — snap Mom. Swoop a stylish up-do for your teen with no mom in sight — yeah Dad. You embody the idea that it's better to 'want' to be in a relationship because there is a loving bond, rather than you 'need' to be in a relationship because there is stuff to be done or procured. When your child sees you as a completely whole and independent adult, they will learn to emulate your healthy behaviours.

3. Relationship Options May Vary

Our society is shifting away from the bonds of matrimony. A recent Pew study revealed that just over half of adult Americans are married, the lowest rate in decades. Children will be enlightened and possibly relieved that they are no longer tied to that traditional lifestyle. Marriage is optional and sometimes not applicable. Long-term relationships without wedding bands can be stronger. My idols in this arena are Kurt Russell and Goldie Hawn; they've been together for nearly 30 years. These lessons are particularly important for girls, who've been raised on the fictitious belief that Prince Charming would sweep them off their feet to live happily ever after. There is a real possibility that they can become enormously disappointed when their fairytale ending turns into a hardcore courtroom reality.

4. Building a Better Body

Marriages are like your freshman year in college. You have the tendency to pack on the pounds. One study found that women could gain five to eight pounds in the first few years of their wedded bliss and a whopping 54 pounds by the ten-year anniversary mark. Their single counterparts stay slim. Most of us have an overriding desire to want to be attractive to prospective mates of the opposite sex. The result of a divorce? A slimmer, trimmer you — aka the Divorce Diet. Take a look at Tom Cruise who reportedly lost 15 pounds after splitting with Katie. Jennie Garth lost 20 and Demi Moore has been stick thin since the departure of her sweetheart, Ashton Kutcher.

Many reports will tell you that being a single parent is stressful. It is. But no more stressful than being a married parent. Ultimately, we all want to step into our own with confidence and take every curveball life throws us with our independent spirit intact. The best way to handle the inevitable life shifts is to stay positive, reach out for support from your friends and family, relish the time you spend with your children and most importantly, create a daily space for some much deserved me-time.

Happy National Single Parents' Day to you!

B Statements 1–6 are true, according to the author. Underline the evidence in the article.

1 Children benefit when only one parent makes all decisions.
2 Single-parenting can be financially challenging.
3 Relationships should be based on love rather than mutual dependence.
4 Women grow up believing that they're destined to find the perfect partner.
5 People tend to put on weight in marriage, just like when they start college.
6 Optimism and meaningful relationships can help you cope with life's changes.

C 9.8 Read *Common collocations and compounds*. Then listen to and re-read the article focusing on the highlighted phrases. In pairs, use context to work out what they mean.

Common collocations and compounds

Adjective–noun collocations and compound nouns are common, but distinguishing common expressions from an author's personal style can be hard. Memorise expressions you see frequently.

	Common	Writer's style
collocations	fictitious belief, overriding desire, prospective mate, lengthy discussion, unilateral choices	parental compromise, tenacious individuals
compound nouns	child rearing, fairytale ending, security blanket	parenting pair, divorce diet, life shifts

A 'fictitious belief' is obviously a belief that is false. I don't believe in Prince Charming!

D **Make it personal** In pairs, react to the author's article. Discuss 1–3. Use common collocations and compounds. Do you both agree?

1 How balanced is her presentation of single parenting?
2 How many of your points in A were mentioned? Which are most important?
3 Which statements in B do you agree with? Why (not)?

I don't agree with number 1. A good partner helps in decision-making and provides you with a security blanket, too.

But what about Kerri Zane's arguments? Don't you agree that ...?

7 Language in use

A 9.9 Match a–e to the photos. Then listen to conversations 1–5 and match them to the photos.

a a treadmill b stretching c weightlifting d sit-ups e abs

A

B

C

D

E

B 9.10 In pairs, do the quiz. Listen to a personal trainer to check. Any surprises?

Test your fitness IQ!	A fact	Hmm ... Not so simple!
1 Running on a treadmill will protect your knees.		
2 Calorie counters in fitness machines are usually accurate.		
3 You don't need to sweat to burn calories.		
4 Stretching before weightlifting prevents injury.		
5 If you do lots of sit-ups, you'll get toned abs.		

C 9.11 Read *Verbs ending in -en*. Then complete 1–5 with verbs formed from words in the box. Listen to check.

Verbs ending in *-en*

The *-en* suffix can be used to make verbs from adjectives or nouns.

1 Light and colour: *I'm going to have my teeth* ***whitened*** (adj: white) tomorrow.

2 Size, density, and movement: *Don't* ***lengthen*** (n: length) *your workout beyond your level of endurance and* ***lessen*** (adj: less) *your expectations for quick progress.*

3 Others: *Things have* ***worsened*** (adj: worse) *and his neighbour has* ***threatened*** (n: threat) *him.*

bright fresh soft strength weak

1 Most treadmills include padding that can stop your knees from hurting because, just like a cushion, it ________ any impact you may feel, unlike a hard surface outdoors.

2 Some machines can overestimate calorie count by over 40%! These numbers might put a smile on your face and ________ your day, but don't let them fool you! You can't count on them being right!

3 Sweating keeps you from overheating – and having to stop to ________ up every five minutes! But rest assured that you can burn hundreds of calories without necessarily dripping in sweat.

4 Some studies show that stretching before weightlifting won't necessarily enable you to perform better and might actually ________ your muscles!

5 Toning exercises will help you ________ your abs, but may not give you a really flat tummy.

D **Make it personal** Search on 'fitness myths' and find at least one more to share in groups. Whose was the most surprising?

Here's one to brighten your day! Working out actually lessens your craving for food!

8 Grammar: Overview of verb patterns

A Read the grammar box and write a–d in the white boxes for patterns 1–4. Then choose an underlined verb from 7C for each example.

Verb patterns with adjectives, gerunds, base forms, and infinitives

a	My coach	**makes**	me	**stay** focused.
b	Exercise	**encourages**	people	**to socialise**.
		will **cause**	your blood pressure	**to drop**.
c	Parents	should **discourage**	young children	**from overexercising.**
d	I	really **appreciate**	your	**helping** me.

verb + object + ...

1 ☐ infinitive (e.g., ________)
2 ☐ base form (e.g., ________)
3 ☐ *-ing* form (e.g., ________)
4 ☐ preposition + *-ing* form (e.g., ________)

Grammar expansion p.154

B 9.12 Circle the correct answer. Listen, check, and write a–d next to each underlined verb.

1 Maybe you won't dissuade ☐ me [**from giving** / **to give**] it a shot then.
2 I urge ☐ [**that you see** / **you to see**] your doctor before you begin exercising.
3 Have ☐ your doctor [**help** / **helping**] you choose the best exercise programme for you.
4 Sweat is a sign that your body is reminding ☐ itself [**to cool** / **of cooling**] down.
5 My doctor warned ☐ me not [**to stretch** / **stretch**] before weightlifting.
6 I won't insist on ☐ your [**listen** / **listening**] to me instead.

Common mistake

Can you help me ~~choosing~~ *choose* a good gym?

C Rephrase 1–7. Use the correct form of the verbs in brackets and begin with the underlined words.

Fact or myth?

1 You can lose weight faster by having cold showers. (help)
2 Take large doses of vitamin C and you won't get the flu. (stop)
3 Teenagers no longer develop social skills because of mobile phones. (prevent)
4 People still use their cars even if there are bike lanes available. (not dissuade)
5 Students remember information better when taking notes by hand. (enable)
6 Violent video games make children behave aggressively. (encourage)
7 Compared to maps, a satnav makes it easier for you to find your location. (let)

D Make it personal Fact or myth? In groups, do 1–2.

1 Individually, choose three statements from C. Write M (myth) or F (fact) next to each one.
2 In groups, support your opinion. Use verb patterns from A. Who's most convincing?

Cold showers really help people lose weight! They make your metabolism work faster.

I've heard that, too. I went on a 'cold-shower diet' once, but I gave up after a month!

9 Listening

A 9.13 Use the photo to guess what a raw vegan diet includes. Listen to Terri and Hugo and cross out the foods that don't belong.

B 9.13 Listen again. Terri most likely ...

- [ ] thinks Hugo has made a good decision.
- [ ] considers the diet a bit weird.
- [ ] is firmly opposed to Hugo's choice.

C 9.14 Listen to the rest. T (true), F (false), or NI (no information)? Correct the false statements.

1. A raw vegan diet contains no carbohydrates.
2. Carbohydrates aren't found in fruit.
3. A salad is a better protein source than fruit.
4. Adults usually find the diet easy to get used to.
5. Lack of vitamin D can have dangerous consequences in children.

D **Make it personal** In pairs, would you like to try a raw vegan diet? Support your opinion with at least three reasons.

I think it would be very hard to find places to eat.

Not any longer. There are lots of 'raw' restaurants these days.

10 Keep talking

A 9.15 **How to say it** Complete the table. Listen to Terri's responses to check.

Reacting to new information

What they said	What they meant
1 I should ________ judgment.	I should be more open minded.
2 Did I hear you ________?	You must be joking.
3 Who in their ________ mind (would eat so many bananas)?	You'd have to be mad (to eat so many bananas).
4 ________, but no thanks!	No way!

B In groups, report on out-of-the-mainstream choices!

1. Search for an article online on a topic below. Is it basically pro or con? Note down the main arguments.

FOUR WAYS TO GET OUT OF THE MAINSTREAM!

1. Leave your high-stress, high-paying job now! Be a 'taxi' tour guide or dog walker, instead.
2. Repelled by an image-conscious society? Support a ban on plastic surgery adverts.
3. Let your children be 'free to roam'. Reject structured after-school activities.
4. Become 'technology free'. Throw out your mobile phone and delete your Facebook profile.

2. Would you personally consider this choice? Support your 'decision' with information you've found. Use *How to say it* expressions where possible.

An article called [name] says being a 'taxi' tour guide pays well.

I should reserve judgment, but is that safe?

11 Writing: A report on pros and cons

A Read the report on the pros and cons of homeschooling. It can be inferred that the writer ...

a ☐ is for homeschooling.
b ☐ is against homeschooling.
c ☐ wants parents to make their own decisions.

Extensive research has been done on homeschooling, a growing trend in England and many other countries. Nevertheless, it is unclear whether observed benefits are actually caused by homeschooling, as opposed to other factors. For that reason, the decision to homeschool continues to be a very personal one. My neighbours struggled with this decision.

---

1 Among the many reasons given for homeschooling are the ability to ...

- customise the curriculum and offer more individual attention.
- experiment with pedagogical methods different from those used in schools.
- enhance family relationships.
- provide a safe environment for learners.
- impart a particular set of values and beliefs.

2 It is claimed that students who are homeschooled ...

- outperform their peers on achievement tests, regardless of parents' income or level of formal education.
- do above average on measures of social and psychological development.
- succeed at university at a higher rate than the general population, are more tolerant, and are more involved in community service.

3 Nevertheless, potential arguments against homeschooling are just as numerous.

- Time: Organising lessons, teaching, giving tests, and planning field trips are labour-intensive activities.
- Cost: Buying the newest teaching tools, computer equipment, and books can eat into the family budget.
- Effort: Ensuring adequate opportunities for socialisation with other children, including those from other countries and backgrounds, calls for careful planning.
- Patience: Separating the roles of parent and teacher requires a calm attitude.

I was homeschooled and it wasn't for me. Every child is a unique individual, as is every parent who homeschools. A child's needs and how optimum learning can be achieved remain the overriding concerns.

B Read the *Guidelines for good reports*. Then cross out two personal sentences in the report in A that don't belong.

Guidelines for good reports

A good report on a topic ...

- has a clear thesis and conclusion.
- is short and succinct.
- keeps the reader interested by avoiding repetition: different verbs or nouns start each point.
- does not include irrelevant personal information or opinions.

C Read *Write it right!* Then find the section that ...

a ☐ has items beginning with nouns.
b ☐ has ones with verbs.
c ☐ contains nouns with *-ing* forms.

Write it right!

For lists in reports, begin each item in a section with a similar style. For example, in section 1, all points begin with infinitives.

Homeschooling offers the ability **to** ...

- customise the curriculum.
- experiment with different methods.

Sections don't all need to be identical, just consistent. They may also begin with nouns or verbs.

D Rewrite the list with a consistent style. There may be more than one solution.

If you are considering homeschooling ...

- it's important to take into account the time involved.
- set aside money for materials.
- finding possible friends for your children is important, too.
- you should always be patient in your 'home classroom'.

E **Your turn!** Choose a topic that you discussed in 10B and write a report in about 280 words that includes two to three lists.

Before
Plan the main function of each list. Note down specific information for three to five bullet points. Search online for more details if necessary.

While
Write three to four sections, following the model in A. Include a clear thesis and conclusion, and refer to *Write it right!* for style.

After
Post your report online and read your classmates' work. Give suggestions for clarity and consistency.

10 Why do friends drift apart?

1 Listening

A 10.1 Listen to Henry reminiscing about his university years. How close is he to his old friends? Why?

B 10.2 Listen to the second part. Label Mike (M) and Bruce (B) in the pictures. There's one extra.

C 10.2 Match 1–4 with the topics a–d. Listen to check. Do you understand the expressions in context?

1 'The writing was on the wall.'
2 'What a riot he was!'
3 'Whatever became of him?'
4 'Go figure.'

a ☐ Henry's sister wonders what Bruce is doing.
b ☐ Henry was surprised by Bruce.
c ☐ Bruce was different from Mike.
d ☐ Henry and Mike didn't have much in common.

D 10.3 Listen to the last part. In pairs explain 1–2. Will Henry follow the advice? Why (not)?

1 what Henry meant by 'abducted by aliens'
2 Henry's sister's advice, 'Don't judge a book by its cover'

He might mean / be suggesting ...

E **Make it personal** Do opposites attract?

1 10.4 **How to say it** Complete the table with a form of *say* or *tell*. Listen to check.

Clarifying: Expressions with *say* and *tell*

What they said	What they meant
1 I guess it goes without ________ (that) ...	It must be obvious that ...
2 Truth be ________ , ...	Honestly, ...
3 There's no ________ why, but ...	It's hard to explain why, but ...
4 ________ what you will ...	You might have your reservations ...
5 Easier ________ than done!	That's easy to suggest, but hard to put into practice!

2 Note down answers to a–c. In pairs, tell each other about someone you see often, but who's very different to you. Use *How to say it* expressions.

a Who's the person? Are you in close touch with him / her out of choice or obligation?
b Do your differences bother you, or have they strengthened your relationship? In what way?
c Have you ever fallen out temporarily? What happened?

My friend María is my polar opposite. There's no telling why we're friends!

So are you saying you don't enjoy her company?

2 Vocabulary: Friendship idioms

A 10.5 Match each question or comment (1–6) to its reply (a–f). Listen to check.

1 The three of you were inseparable!
2 Bruce was the exact opposite, always the life of the party.
3 Our conversations never went beneath the surface.
4 You guys go back a long way, right?
5 Do you still see her?
6 OK, so you don't see eye to eye on everything. So what?

a [ ] Yeah, all you could talk about was soccer and video games.
b [ ] No, she was a breath of fresh air, though.
c [ ] We do! We went to high school together.
d [ ] Yes, what a riot he was!
e [ ] But it's important to agree on things, isn't it?
f [ ] Yes, we were birds of a feather.

B Rephrase underlined sentences 1–6 using highlighted expressions from A. Use the correct tense. Then choose two expressions to describe someone you know.

Five types of friends you need to have in your life. Who are yours?

INTERESTING CATEGORIES. HERE'S MY LIST. Louise762

1 THE HONEST CONFIDANT: GUY
[1]He's a welcome change. He's still the one I turn to when I need to hear the truth, and nothing but the truth.

2 THE SOUL MATE: LORNA
[2]Lorna and I are very similar in character. She's a terrific listener, and when we're having a serious conversation, [3]she can see beyond the obvious and have insights that none of my other friends can.

3 THE POLAR OPPOSITE: JULIA
It's funny how Julia and I have become friends even though [4]we don't seem to agree on anything. But, honestly, why would I want to surround myself with people just like me?

4 A FRIENDLY NEIGHBOUR: RON
Ron moved to the neighbourhood in 2005, so [5]we've known each other for ages! He's really helpful and dependable, and above all, a good listener.

5 A WORK PAL: HUGO
In an office full of boring people, Hugo is a breath of fresh air. [6]He makes me laugh! [7]He's a lot of fun! He's always telling jokes, even when we're stressed out.

> My next-door neighbour is a breath of fresh air. He's always in a good mood!

C Make it personal What's the nature of friendship?

1 In groups, explain what the quotes below mean to you.

1 'The best mirror is an old friend.' (George Herbert)
2 'A friend to all is a friend to none.' (Aristotle)
3 'And like a favourite old film, sometimes the sameness in a friend is what you like the most about her.' (Emily Giffin)
4 'I would rather walk with a friend in the dark than alone in the light.' (Helen Keller)
5 'In prosperity our friends know us; in adversity we know our friends.' (John Churton Collins)
6 'You will evolve past certain people. Let yourself.' (Mandy Hale)

> The first one must mean, 'An old friend sees you as you really are and reflects that back.'

> But do you agree? Don't friends sometimes see someone like themselves?

2 Vote on your three favourites. Why do they resonate?

3 Language in use

A 10.6 Listen to the start of a lecture. Which factor may be most important for longevity, according to the speaker? Which two photos (1–3) are her Aunt Agatha?

1

2

3

B 10.7 Listen to the rest of the lecture and complete the slide. Any surprises?

THE KEY TO LONGEVITY

- Regular [1]__________ __________ is just as important as diet and [2]__________.
- [3]__________ __________ can be much more harmful than [4]__________.
- The size of our [5]__________ __________ is slightly more important than the [6]__________ of our [7]__________ – but only during [8]__________ and old age.
- In other words: The more [9]__________ your [10]__________ are, the [11]__________ and [12]__________ your life may be.

C 10.8 Read *To as a preposition*. Then correct the mistakes, if any, in 1–5. Listen to check.

***To* as a preposition**

If *to* is followed by the base form of a verb, it's part of an infinitive:
I wouldn't **want to live** to a hundred if that means having a boring, overly healthy lifestyle.

If it's followed by the *-ing* form, it's a preposition:
I can understand why people **look forward to retiring**. There's more to life than just working.

It's easy to know which is which. Try putting a noun after *to*. If you can, it's a preposition:
I know I should **limit myself to (having) two cups** of coffee a day, but I can't!

1 What's the secret to living a long and healthy life?
2 Let me try to answer this question by way of a personal anecdote.
3 She came close to win a marathon.
4 Aunt Agatha managed to track down some of her school friends.
5 Social connections might be the key to have good overall health.

D **Make it personal** In groups, discuss 1–2. Similar opinions?

1 Re-read the sentences in the box in C. Modify them so they're true for you.
2 Which potential risks would you give up?

delicious, but fatty food   fun, but potentially dangerous sport
travel by plane, car, or motorbike   weekend parties, but not enough sleep
a well-paid, but totally sedentary job

The key to living longer is having a good time, so I'm never giving up parties.

4 Grammar: Degrees of comparison

A Read the grammar box. Then put sentences 1–7 in the categories below.

Degrees of comparison with *the* ... *the*, *more* / ... *er*, and *as* ... *as*			
1 **The more friends**	you have,	**the happier**	you'll feel.
2 **The healthier**	your diet (is),	**the longer**	you'll live.
3 I'm	**much / far / a (whole) lot**	**closer** to my sister **than (to)**	my mum.
4 She's	**a little / a bit / slightly**	**more traditional than**	we are. us.
5 Friends are	**every bit / just**	**as important as**	family.
6 Family is	**nowhere near**		friends.
7 Friends are**n't**	**quite**	**as close as**	family.

Grammar expansion p.156

Parallel or equal meaning	Big difference of degree	Small difference of degree

B Tick (✔) the sentence(s) that mean(s) the same as the four points in 3B.

1 ☐ Regular social contact is every bit as important as diet and exercise.
2 ☐ Social isolation is nowhere near as harmful as obesity.
3 ☐ For a small part of our lives, the size of our social network isn't quite as important as the quality of our friendships.
4 ☐ Meaningful relationships have a big impact on your health and lifespan.

C Rephrase the underlined sentences using the words in the box. Keep the same meaning.

1 The older   2 nowhere near   3 not quite   4 a whole lot   5 slightly   6 every bit

Marriage in later life

- [1]When you're older, you're more dependent on other people, and for many, this means one's husband or wife. So to what extent does marriage improve life expectancy?
- Marriage has traditionally been a non-biological factor that correlates positively with life expectancy. For one thing, [2]married people take risks far less often than single people. Marriage also gives you more social and economic support.
- However, [3]the health differences between married and single people are slightly less significant than they used to be. This may be because people are committing to each other in different ways.
- [4]Research also shows that people who are single, especially men, are living much longer lives than ever before. It would appear that they are taking more responsibility for their own health and well-being.
- [5]Widows and widowers aren't quite as healthy as people who are married. No one really knows exactly why. Maybe married people can count on an extended family to help them out. Besides, the widowed are more likely to be isolated, and [6]social isolation can be very bad for your health.

D Make it personal In groups, discuss 1–3. Any interesting ideas?

1 Were you aware of the research in 3B? Is it convincing? Why (not)?
2 Does being married help with social integration where you live?
3 In what ways might being married actually shorten some people's lives?

Common mistake

The sooner you start, ~~you will finish sooner~~ *the sooner you'll finish*.

Well, the less fulfilling your relationship is, the shorter your life might be! Doesn't stress shorten life?

That could be, but you don't have to stay in an unhappy marriage.

5 Reading

A In pairs, guess the author's answer to the article question. To what extent can nationality predict human behaviour?

B 10.9 Read and listen to the article. Tick (✔) all that apply. Does the author seem to agree with your answers in A?

The author compares Germans and Americans in ______ terms.

1 ☐ social 2 ☐ economic 3 ☐ historical 4 ☐ gender-related

Are American Friendships Superficial?

Why do many immigrants consider American friendships superficial?

1 I was speaking to a German woman who has lived in the United States for a decade and has made it her permanent home. She was describing her likes and dislikes about the US in comparison to Germany. For example, on the positive side, she was enthusiastic about the opportunities for work and advancement she had found here based on her skills and accomplishments – as opposed to Germany, where an insistence on the right credentials is often insurmountable. On the negative side, however, she complained that American friendships are superficial.

2 I have heard this criticism before, with variations – 'no deep friendships', 'people form and dissolve relationships too easily', 'you don't know if you can really trust people', and so forth.

3 She also described a misunderstanding with a co-worker, who referred to her as a friend. 'You're not my friend,' she said. 'You're an acquaintance. We go out for coffee together and chat about things. That's not friendship'. The woman was offended – not surprisingly. Telling someone in the US 'You're not my friend', is tantamount to saying 'You're my enemy.' It took quite a while for her to overcome this misstep.

What is going on here?

4 To begin with, in a conversation Germans tend to be quite direct. (An American might joke that their words are so long that there is no time left to beat around the bush.) Where an American might say 'From my point of view, I see it this way', a German might simply say, 'I think X'. Direct speech can seem inconsiderate to Americans. In this regard, Brazilians are to Americans as Americans are to Germans. Americans who are new to Brazil complain that 'You never know what Brazilians think', or even 'People are always lying to me'. From the Brazilian point of view, they're being considerate, modulating what they say according to the non-verbal reactions of the other person, so as to have an agreeable conversation.

5 Germany is also part of the Old World. A family may live in the same town, or even the same house, for several centuries; everyone knows everyone, and personal relationships develop gradually over extended periods of time. The United States has only been around for two centuries. We are a nation of immigrants, and time begins for many families with their arrival here. Our history of wagon trains and the conquest of the West involved a similar internal migration experience – breaking the ties of family and friendship, and then forming new ones.

6 American individualism means that we give more emphasis to our own needs in forming and dissolving relationships than do cultures organised around traditional forms and relationships. This means that people who don't know one another can form groups to satisfy common needs. In criticising what she viewed as the superficiality of our friendships, the German woman also praised the existence of numerous informal groups – around hobbies, interests, work, self-improvement, religion, and so forth – that make it possible to meet new people.

7 For generations, America has been the world centre of capitalism; and capitalism prizes a mobile labour force. Thus, it is not surprising that many Americans have developed the ability to form and dissolve relationships, as they are periodically uprooted to earn a living or advance a career in another city, state, or region.

8 I should also mention that, during her childhood, the place where the woman grew up was in East Germany. Before reunification, the Stasi (secret police) were an omnipresent danger. People never knew, if they told someone their true thoughts and feelings, whether the information could be passed on to be used against them. Trusting someone as a friend could mean putting your life in their hands – a much greater commitment than friendship here. Even though that time has passed, the more intense commitment involved in friendship lingers on.

9 German-English dictionaries define friend as *Freund* and vice versa. But clearly, despite many features in common, the two words are not equivalent. Friendship in the United States and Germany is similar but not the same. As I told the woman about her co-worker, 'She was your friend, but not your Freundin'.

C Re-read the article. Circle words or phrases that show the woman's views on friendship in Germany. Underline those for the United States.

D Scan the article and find ...

1 an expression that means 'equivalent to': ________ (paragraph 3)
2 an idiom that means the *opposite* of 'get straight to the point': ________ (paragraph 4)
3 an adjective that means 'pleasant': ________ (paragraph 4)
4 a verb that means 'remains, but is gradually disappearing': ________ (paragraph 8)

E **Make it personal** Friendships across cultures. In groups, discuss 1–2.

1 When it comes to making friends, is your country more like Germany or the United States?
2 Do you have any friends from other cultures? To what extent have they challenged your views on ...?

the relative importance of family
socialising and dating
gender roles
money

Here in [name of country], we would never tell anyone 'You're not my friend'. I think we're more like the US.

6 Vocabulary: Words with both prefixes and suffixes

A Read *Double affixation*. Then write the root words (1–7) as they are spelled in isolation. Were any letters dropped or changed?

Double affixation

Many adjectives, nouns, and adverbs are made up of a prefix, a root word, and a suffix:
In Germany, an insistence on the right credentials is often **insurmountable**.
Here, *in-* means 'not', *surmount* means 'overcome', and *-able* means 'that can be'.
So, *insurmountable* means 'that can't be overcome'. Remember: spelling sometimes changes, too.
I was shocked by their **unfriendliness**. (un + friendly + ness)

1 discouraging
2 ineffective
3 interdependence
4 unreliable
5 counterproductive
6 misunderstanding
7 impolitely

B 10.10 Match the three columns to find six words. Then write the full words with the correct spelling. Listen to two conversations about stereotypes to check.

Prefix		Root word		Suffix	
dis	in	1 mature	4 resist	able	ible
il	ir	2 taste	5 logic	al	ive
im	un	3 accept	6 expense	ful	ity

C 10.10 Listen again. Summarise each stereotype in one sentence. Any truth to them?

D **Make it personal** Complete 1–5 with popular stereotypes where you live. In groups, compare your ideas. Which ones are most common?

1 ________ are bad drivers.
2 ________ can be a bit rude.
3 ________ tend to be lazy.
4 ________ is a dangerous place.
5 ________ (You choose!)

Here in [name of city], [neighbourhood] is really dangerous.

That's just a stereotype! I live there, and I've never had any problems.

7 Language in use

A 10.11 Listen to the start of a radio show. Choose the correct answer.

'Six Degrees of Separation' means we're [further away / closer] to people than we think.

B 10.12 Look at the pictures on the right and read the conversation excerpts. Listen to the next part. Tick (✔) the callers that believe the 'Six Degrees of Separation' theory.

C 10.12 Listen again and note down key details. In pairs, summarise each story.

So in the first one, this man was in a bad mood and went out to eat ...

D 10.13 Read *Expressions with odds*. Then listen and match excerpts 1–5 with the correct pattern (a–e). Continue listening to check.

Expressions with *odds*

The word *odds*, meaning 'chances' is very common in English and takes various patterns.

The odds **of** see**ing** him were **50 to 1**.

What are **the odds that** I could get that job?

a ☐ the odds of [object] [verb]-*ing* ...
b ☐ the odds of [verb]-ing ...
c ☐ The odds are against you ...
d ☐ the odds that ...
e ☐ the odds are [number] to [number] that ...

E Make it personal In groups, use only the pictures from **B** and your notes from **C**, to decide which story is most surprising. Do you know of any similar experiences? Use expressions with *odds*.

Number 5 is the most surprising. What are the odds of falling in love with a place that quickly?

I think it's possible if you were looking to make a change in your life.

1 Had Sarah not come by with Tom, I wouldn't be married to her now! ☐

2 Should you need anything at all while Beth is away, just come over. You know I don't mind. ☐

3 Were I to have dialled a different phone number, my whole life would have been different! ☐

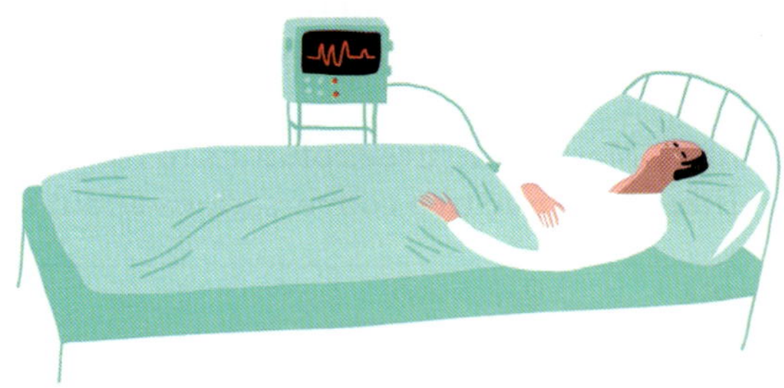

4 Had I called even a minute later, I might not have arrived in time. Eric saved my life! ☐

5 Were we to spend even one more day here, I'd never be able to leave. This is the most beautiful view I've ever seen. ☐

8 Grammar: Inverted conditional sentences

A Read the grammar box and choose the correct meaning below (a or b) for 1–5.

Inverted conditional sentences for present, past, or future time		
Were	**we to apologise**[1],	we could resume our friendship with Richard.
	I to have gone[2] home,	we never would have met.
Should	**you wish to come**[3] today,	just give us a call.
Had	**he contacted**[4] me on Facebook,	we could have seen each other.
	she not gone[5] to the party,	we wouldn't be married today.

Inverted conditional clauses can be used instead of *if*-clauses and sometimes add emphasis. They tend to be slightly more formal. *Had* is not contracted, and past sentences like *Were I to have gone* ... mean the same as *Had I gone* ...

Grammar expansion p.156

1 a ☐ If we apologised — b ☐ If we had apologised
2 a ☐ If I went home — b ☐ If I'd gone home
3 a ☐ If you want to come today — b ☐ If you came today
4 a ☐ If he'd contacted me on Facebook — b ☐ If he contacted me on Facebook
5 a ☐ If she'd gone to the party — b ☐ If she hadn't gone to the party

Common mistake

Had you not
~~Hadn't you~~ rung,
I would have worried.

B Underline the five inverted conditional sentences in 7B. Which sentence(s) with a form of *be* can be reworded with a form of *have*?

C Rephrase the underlined clauses 1–6 in the forum entries. Use inverted conditional sentences and a form of the verbs in brackets.

remember.me.id

Welcome to remember.me.id, our forum for people who almost meet, but don't quite succeed – the opposite of 'Six Degrees of Separation'! Register online and we will connect you.

David	1 If we'd talked just a moment longer (**have**), I could have asked for your number. You were wearing orange trainers.
Linda	2 If you want to get in touch at any time (**should**), I'd love to hear from you. We talked about astronomy on the number 15 bus.
Phil with the tattoo	3 If you hadn't got a phone call (**have**), I'm sure we'd be connected now. I loved talking to you.
Teresa	4 If I ever see you again (**be**), I'd be thrilled! I just love long beards.
Steve	5 If she'd tried, I said to myself (**have**), I'm sure she would have left a message. Please ring! You know who you are!
Wanda	6 If you take the same train again at 3.30pm (**be**), I'll be waiting for you with a smile!

D Make it personal Have you ever had an important 'missed connection'? In groups, share a true or invented story. Whose is most surprising?

1 When / Where / Why / What / Who? Note down a few details.
2 What would have happened had you been able to connect?
3 If you could go back in time, what would you have done differently?
4 Were you to meet this person again, what would you do?

When I was on the train last week, I saw an old girlfriend out of the corner of my eye. Had I reacted even one second sooner, I could have spoken to her!

9 Listening

A In pairs, imagine you want to persuade a slightly antisocial friend to come to a party you're giving. What strategies would you use?

I might say, 'I've only invited people you know'.

B 10.14 Listen to / watch the first part of a video on persuasion (0:00–3:05). What do the party invitation and restaurant tipping have in common?

C 10.14 Listen / Watch the first part again. Which statements do the speakers believe? Write Y (yes) or N (no). Correct the wrong ones.

1 Integrity is important when trying to persuade others.
2 Social plans don't involve obligation.
3 It's not only the size of a gift that counts, but also how the recipient feels.
4 Pleasant surprises make a strong impression.
5 It's usually not noticed when gifts are personalised.

D **Make it personal** In pairs, which statements in C do you agree with? Support your opinion with a personal story.

I definitely agree with number 1. I'll never forget the time that ...

E 10.15 Listen to / watch the 'persuasion of liking' from 7:40 to 9:05. How did liking crisps help the business students persuade others?

F 10.15 In pairs, can you recall why we like people? Complete the notes. Then listen to / watch the second part again to check.

We like people who ...
1 ______ . 2 ______ . 3 ______ .

10 Keep talking

A Choose two questions and note down at least three points for each.

1 How can we persuade our parents, teachers, or boss to give us more independence?
2 Why is it difficult, but important, to sometimes say 'no', even to those we like?
3 How have you been influenced by friends / family? Did they use strategies from 9E?

B Share opinions in groups, using these expressions. Any interesting stories or ideas?

They're far more likely to ... if ...	They persuaded me to ...
I'm nowhere near as ... by ... as ...	The more they ... , the more I ...

I got to know my friend Victoria when she cooperated with me on a project. The closer I got to her, the more she influenced me ...

11 Writing: A persuasive essay

A A persuasive opinion essay has a clear topic sentence, which may state subtopics to be developed in separate paragraphs. Read paragraph 1. What is the topic sentence?

B Read the rest. Then find three sentences in paragraphs 4, 5, and 6 that state each subtopic.

C Read *Write it right!* and write the strategy number (1, 2, or 3) next to the words in the box. Then complete 1–9 in the essay with an appropriate item.

Write it right!

A good persuasive essay appeals to the reader's feelings, and logically builds a persuasive argument. To do so, the writer uses several strategies.

1 Words and expressions that appeal to the reader's common sense, e.g. *undoubtedly*.
2 Conjunctions to link ideas, e.g. *as a result*.
3 Time markers to build the argument towards a conclusion, e.g. *next*.

☐ After all	☐ At this point	☐ Finally
☐ Therefore	☐ As we all know	☐ By now
☐ However	☐ Nevertheless	☐ Moreover

D Connect the pairs of sentences logically, using the words or expressions in brackets.

1 People love personal attention. Tips may be bigger if you give it. (as we all know, so)
2 I find it hard to say no. That's not such a good quality. (which, undoubtedly)
3 Friends understand us better than family. They tend to be more objective. (undoubtedly, and moreover)
4 My friends have persuaded me to be a bit calmer. You'd never know I was once a nervous wreck. (since, at this point)

E **Your turn!** Choose a topic that you discussed in 10B and write a persuasive essay in 280 words.

Before

Using your notes from 10A, plan four to five paragraphs.

While

Write your essay, following the model in A. Include a clear thesis statement, and start a new paragraph for each sub-theme. Use strategies from *Write it right!* to build your argument.

After

Post your essay online and read your classmates' work. Whose is most convincing?

The psychology of persuasion

1 Persuasion involves just a little bit of basic psychology, and this is true whether your target is a parent, a teacher, or even your boss. Research on the science of persuasion shows that we like people who are similar to us, pay us compliments, and cooperate with us. As a result, we are more likely to do what they request. How then can we apply this science in our everyday lives?

2 Let's look at an example, one we've all identified with at some point: How can we persuade our parents to give us more independence? Does this challenge have anything to do with being liked?

3 Undoubtedly, your first reaction will be 'no'. You may point out that your parents don't 'like' you, they 'love' you, and, not only that, their 'love' is permanent. 1 ____________, to agree to your request, they do need to 'like' you at the moment you make it. 2 ____________, it is possible to 'love' someone and not 'like' the person at every given moment. So let's look at the research step by step.

4 Nothing pleases parents more than to think that they and their children are alike. 3 ____________, not only have they invested a lot of time and energy in your upbringing, but you are likely to be here when they're gone – their legacy on earth, so to speak. In the case of children, if they are just like their parents, this also implies shared values, and shared values imply trust. 4 ____________, if you think like your parents, you are less likely to make decisions they would be against. Let's take a case in point: You'd like to borrow the family car for a long weekend. What similarities between you and your parents come to mind? Most people will think being cautious is a character trait to emphasise. 5 ____________, you might start by saying, 'You know how careful I am, Mum (or Dad). I'm just like you.'

5 Next come praise and admiration. You may be opposed in principle to excessive praise and feel pouring it on is 'false' or 'manipulative'. 6 ____________, is that necessarily so? What if the feeling is real? You might say, 'I've always admired you, Dad (or Mum) for thinking things over so carefully. It shows you're open to considering all sides of an argument.' Don't be surprised if your parent then announces that he or she admires this about you, too! Good feeling is being created all around, and you're well on your way to dissuading your Dad (or Mum) from saying 'no'.

6 7 ____________, people who lend a helping hand seem reasonable and thoughtful. Your parents are more likely to be persuaded if you appear to have these traits. Here you might start by saying, 'I know you get up really early on Mondays and don't want to spend Sunday evening worrying. So I promise I'll have the car back no later than 6.00pm.' 8 ____________, all three principles of persuasion are in place, and the odds are clearly in your favour. 9 ____________, you're nearly guaranteed a 'yes' answer!

Review 5

Units 9–10

1 Listening

A R5.1 Listen to a professor discussing traditional and innovative learning. Tick (✔) the statements that can be inferred. The professor probably feels ...

1 ☐ traditional techniques can be made to be innovative.
2 ☐ good lectures require very knowledgeable speakers.
3 ☐ it's easier to take notes than to participate in class.
4 ☐ a lecture is more innovative if it incorporates video.
5 ☐ the virtues of lectures need to be promoted more.

B Make it personal In pairs, discuss which statements in A you agree with.

There might be some truth to number 3.

Yes, note-taking discourages us from participating actively.

2 Reading

A Read the article. Underline at least one sentence in each section where the writer could have been talking about children.

HOW TO SET GOOD LIMITS WITH FRIENDS

Setting limits with friends may be difficult, but just as you would with your children, the sooner you establish them, the better. A number of years back, we befriended a new couple in the neighbourhood, who made it a habit to pay us a surprise visit every Saturday night. Had they not arrived with a delicious cake each time, we might have caught on sooner that they had an issue with boundaries. Here are a few pieces of advice based on this experience. They may not be innovative, but are known to work!

1 **Be direct.** If you're not clear, the other person may have trouble grasping what it is you're trying to communicate. Once you've planned what to say, go through with it, even if your message is that you find someone's behaviour unacceptable.

2 **Avoid guilt and self-doubt.** Don't let a fictitious belief that 'others come first' sabotage your legitimate need to act. Trust your instincts, which will outweigh any second thoughts you may have.

3 **Do not backpedal.** Despite the fact that you may have an overriding desire to please, don't allow yourself to be persuaded by your friends' point of view. In the end, they will appreciate your having held your ground. Consistency is every bit as important to friends as to children.

B Make it personal In pairs, discuss setting boundaries with friends. Is the advice in the article helpful? Use degrees of comparison where possible.

I've followed point 1. The more honest you are, the closer you and your friends will be.

3 Grammar

A Read the advice on how to lose weight. Complete 1–8 with the verbs in brackets and grammar patterns from Lessons 9.2 and 9.4. Some have more than one answer.

Top three ways to lose weight

1 You might not believe this, but adding foods to your diet [1]*is known* to *have helped* (know, help) people lose weight! Healthy fruits and vegetables make great snacks and [2]________ us ________ (help, appreciate) food even more.

2 Joining a gym may actually [3]________ us ________ (cause, avoid) exercise, contrary to popular opinion. That's because 'working out' sounds like work, so it [4]________ us ________ (encourage, dislike) it. You may [5]________ my ________ (give, appreciate) you the advice to just walk more. A fast-paced stroll [6]________ to ________ (believe, be) boring, but that's rarely true!

3 Many people [7]________ ________ (think, lose) weight just by drinking water. If that sounds odd, it's simply because it [8]________ us ________ (make, feel) less hungry.

B **Make it personal** Choose two sentences and, in pairs, explain why you agree or disagree.

> I disagree with number 1. Adding foods may be known to have helped people lose weight, but it's so easy to add the wrong foods.

4 Writing

Write your opinion on one of these topics. Follow the model in 2A, and include three pieces of advice.

a Setting limits in relationships b Giving honest feedback c Asking a parent to respect your privacy

5 Self-test

Correct the two mistakes in each sentence. Check your answers in Units 9 and 10. What's your score, 1–20?

1 Adele strengthed her fan base and sold out every other performer.
2 In the past, these types of treatments are thought to help people even if it seems unlogical.
3 My angry reaction to what you said might have to see with you refuse to listen!
4 Unmatureness often makes children to think only about themselves.
5 I love my work so there's really no telling to why I'm looking forward to retire.
6 More friends you have, more happy you'll be.
7 Jim is quite as close to us than he used to be.
8 My uncle was the laughter of the party – a true breath of cool air!
9 You should wish to come, accommodating you isn't unsurmountable.
10 I'm far qualified than my CV shows, and were you hire me, you wouldn't regret it.

6 Point of view

Choose a topic. Then support your opinion in 100–150 words, and record your answer. Ask a partner for feedback. How can you be more convincing?

a Society should discourage women from raising children alone. OR Society should make single parenting easier.
b Friends naturally drift apart after university. OR With a little bit of effort, university friendships can be lifelong.
c We're never more than six steps away from the perfect person. OR
Meeting the perfect person depends largely on effort.

11 What was the last risk you took?

1 Vocabulary: Risk-taking expressions

A 11.1 Read the quiz and, using your intuition, complete the highlighted expressions with *safe*, *safety* or *caution*. Listen to two colleagues, Phil and Lisa, to check.

Are you a risk taker or do you play it [1] ______?

1 What do you usually do with your savings?
- A Invest in a diversified portfolio.
- B Who needs savings?
- C Put them in a savings account. It's always a [2] ______ bet.

2 Which of these sounds like the most fun?
- A Sailing. But I'd never go by myself, just to be on the [3] ______ side.
- B Skydiving. You only live once!
- C Bowling.

3 On a game show, which of these would you be most inclined to do?
- A Take a 50% chance at winning £50,000.
- B Take a 10% chance at winning £100,000.
- C Take home £10,000 in cash. I might come to regret it, but I'd rather err on the side of [4] ______.

4 Your boss has made lots of decisions you disagree with. What do you do?
- A Meet one-on-one with him or her and voice my concerns.
- B Leave, even if I haven't found another job yet.
- C Nothing. I can't afford to leave without a [5] ______ net to fall back on.

B 11.2 Do the quiz in pairs. Have you got more A, B, or C answers? Listen to the results. How accurately do they describe you?

> I chose B three times. Well, while it's true I'm sometimes impulsive, I don't make risky decisions!

C 11.2 Listen again. Note down four more expressions with *safe*, *safety*, and *caution*. Which expression(s) in A can you replace with them in context?

D Rephrase 1–5 using expressions from A and C. There may be more than one answer. Then make each sentence true for you.

1 When I invite people round, I always end up cooking too much. Well, <u>it's better to do too much than too little</u>.
2 If you want to have good Italian food, try Massimo's. <u>You can't go wrong</u> if you eat there.
3 My friends say I should <u>stop being so careful</u>, leave my job, and start my own business.
4 I always put away 10% of my pay every month. That way I'll have <u>some savings for a rainy day</u>.
5 I love going to the gym. But I never work out more than an hour and always <u>take special care</u> to avoid injuring myself.

E Make it personal What makes people more / less prone to risk-taking?

1 Individually, tick the two most important factors. Note down a possible reason for each.
2 In groups, share your thoughts. Any major disagreements?

☐ gender ☐ age ☐ upbringing ☐ job ☐ marital status ☐ zodiac sign ☐ ______

> For me, upbringing is most important. If you're taught to err on the side of caution, you'll be that way for life.

> I don't agree. You can learn not to play it safe.

2 Listening

A 11.3 Listen to Phil tell Lisa about the promotion he's been offered. Order his concerns 1–4. There's one extra.

Phil fears he might ...
- [ ] not be able to overcome the language barrier.
- [ ] lack leadership skills.
- [ ] not be good at the job.
- [ ] miss his family and friends.
- [ ] have trouble getting settled in a foreign country.

B 11.4 and 11.5 Read and listen to *Intonation and intentions*. Then listen to four pairs of excerpts. When you hear the beep, choose Lisa's response (a or b). Continue listening to check.

Intonation and intentions

Changes in intonation may convey completely different intentions and / or emotions:

Phil: Blame it on my upbringing.
Lisa: What do you mean? (= 'Tell me more.')

Phil: I'm not sure I have what it takes ... you know, to be a sales manager.
Lisa: What do you mean? (= 'I disagree.')

1 'So ...' a ☐ Anyway ... b ☐ What's the problem?
2 'Oh, come on!' a ☐ Just say yes, please. b ☐ Don't be silly!
3 'Of course.' a ☐ Without a doubt! b ☐ Don't worry! You can trust me.
4 'What?' a ☐ You must be joking! b ☐ Please explain.

C **Make it personal** Get out of your comfort zone!

1 11.6 **How to say it** Complete the table. Listen to check.

Expressing hesitation and encouragement	
What they said	What they meant
Hesitation	
1 There's just too much at ________.	The risks are too high.
2 I'm not sure I have what it ________.	I might not have the necessary qualities.
3 I need to ________ on it.	I can't make a decision immediately.
Encouragement	
4 What do you have to ________?	What could go wrong?
5 What's the worst that could ________?	What's the worst case scenario?
6 Why not just ________ with the flow?	Why not just take things as they come?

2 In pairs, role-play one of the situations below.

A: Choose a situation and note down three things that might go wrong.

B: Offer reassurance and try to get A out of his / her comfort zone.

What might you have to lose if you ...?

spent all your savings on a great holiday created your own YouTube channel
told an old friend you had feelings for him/her started posting political views on Facebook
applied to sing in a reality show adopted two puppies from a rescue organisation

I'd love to spend a month travelling across Europe, but things are kind of up in the air at work. There's too much at stake.

Hmm ... If you did go, what's the worst that could happen?

3 Language in use

A 11.7 Listen to a programme on bike safety. It can be inferred that [**only the instructor has** / **both the instructor and participants have**] thought about safety before.

B 11.7 Use the pictures to guess the missing words in the safety tips. Then listen again to check.

BICYCLE SAFETY TIPS FROM OUR STAFF AND PARTICIPANTS

1

'You might want to take ☐ some basic precautions even when you're buying a new bike. Make sure the _________ of your _________ can support your _________.'

2

'I won't cycle ☐ on my first day in a new city. I explore the area on _________ to be sure I won't have any _________ when I'm cycling.'

3

☐ 'The driver could have looked before opening his _________. It was a close call! If drivers are looking at all, it's only for _________. So be careful!'

4

'They all should have mastered ☐ the basics in a few days, but one _________ had poor _________. So don't be too hard on yourself.'

5

'You might try cycling ☐ only during the day at first. Then make sure to buy a _________. Your _________ is reduced at _________.'

6

'It shouldn't be hard to remember ☐ one important rule, though. Always cycle _________, and not _________ traffic.'

C 11.8 Listen to an eyewitness account from two points of view. What safety rule did each person violate? Whose behaviour is more dangerous?

D 11.9 Listen to excerpts 1–6 from the conversation. Choose the missing phrase or sentence below for each 'beep'. Continue listening to check.

- ☐ froze in her tracks
- ☐ My hair stood on end.
- ☐ screeched to a halt
- ☐ I could feel the colour draining from my face.
- ☐ screamed at the top of my lungs
- ☐ swerved to avoid hitting me

E **Make it personal** Choose a situation. In pairs, role-play a real or imagined 'eyewitness account'. Use at least four expressions from D.

speeding bike or motorbike | distracted pedestrian | child in the road | reckless bus or car driver

You look shaken. What exactly happened?

I certainly am! You see, I was minding my own business and suddenly, I just froze in my tracks. This motorbike was coming right at me!

4 Grammar: Special uses of modals

A Read the grammar box and complete the rule. Then write a–d in the boxes next to the underlined examples in 3B.

Special uses of modals: expectation, suggestion, refusal, and annoyance	
a expectation	It **shouldn't be** dangerous. I think it's safe.
	She **should have landed** by now. I'll check the flight online.
b suggestion	We **might as well forget** it then. We wouldn't be happy with a car that doesn't have the latest safety features.
	You **might want to take** some precautions. I've heard travel there is dangerous.
c refusal	He **won't listen** to me. I've told him to wear a bike helmet!
d annoyance	She **could have phoned** at least. I was really worried something had happened to her!

Modal verbs have more than one meaning. *Should* also expresses [1]o__________, *might* and *could* also express [2]p__________, and *will* also describes a [3]f__________ event.

» Grammar expansion p.158

B Using your completed grammar box in A, say the function expressed by each word in bold (1–8). Then make four sentences true for you.

OUR CITY, THE TRANSPORT BLOG

- You [1]**should** watch out for pedestrians at all times. These days, people are on their mobile phones when they cross the street!
- It [2]**shouldn't** be hard to learn to ride a motorbike. It just involves good balance, like a bike.
- You [3]**might** as well put your energy into bike, not car, safety. Soon there's going to be nowhere to park around here.
- I'm afraid something [4]**might** have happened to the plans for more traffic lights. The city is doing nothing!
- If I hadn't looked up, I [5]**could** have been killed. It's the most dangerous junction in the city.
- The cops [6]**could** have been a bit more understanding. It's hard to move your car after a snowstorm.
- Starting next year, there [7]**won't** be any cars on Broom Street. They're turning it into a pedestrian walkway.
- I'm not letting my son drive until he's 21! He [8]**won't** wear his seat belt, even though he knows it's illegal.

C What are the people saying? Complete 1–3 with appropriate modal verbs. Which items in B are they talking about?

1 A ticket! You __________ want to be a bit more understanding. I __________ move my car until you plough this street!

2 Hey, watch out! You __________ have looked where you were going! It __________ be too hard to put that phone away for a second.

3 You __________ as well forget getting a licence! And I __________ let you in the car with me in the future either!

D Make it personal In new pairs, role-play your situations from 3E again. This time, comment with special uses of modals in A.

You won't believe what just happened. This motorbike was coming right at me, and I had to jump out of the way.

That's awful. He could have been a bit more careful. They're always speeding through here.

5 Reading

A Read the article on online dating up to the heading 'Big Mistake'. In pairs, brainstorm possible reasons for the author's mistake. Then read the next paragraph to check. Are you surprised?

> I think she might have stolen something from his house.

B Make sure you understand the section titles below. Then read the rest. Put the titles back into the article (1–7).

Ask the right questions	Be safe at home	Call for backup, Part 1	Call for backup, Part 2
Gentlemen first	Know when to bail	Pick a safe spot for your first date	

How to Stay Safe While Dating

by Ken Solin

Follow these tips to stay safe during your first few encounters with someone new

I was walking on California's Stinson Beach in August 2009 when I struck up a conversation with a woman who seemed utterly delightful. Captivated, I invited her to dinner at my house that evening.

Big mistake!

After dinner, she refused to leave. And, according to her, why should she? My acquaintance of 12 hours bizarrely insisted that we were living together. The situation felt menacing — would I find a rabbit stew boiling on the stove? — so I summoned my next-door neighbour, a woman, for help. The two of us spent 45 minutes coaxing my surprise head case to leave, but it took a threat to call the police to finally get her out the door.

Does it jar you to find a man writing about dating safety? Don't let it. Scary situations can pop up for anyone in the dating world — female or male, online or not. That's why everyone who is part of that world must take some basic steps to ensure his or her physical safety. At the very least, consider adopting the approaches below; all of them draw on my 12 years of recent online dating experience.

1 ______ When you've exchanged emails with a prospect and you feel it's time to furnish phone numbers, the man should offer his first. If he doesn't, the woman should ask him to do so. I can't think of any good reason why a legitimately eligible man would withhold his digits; if he does, that's ample cause to feel unsafe. Give the dude a pass.

2 ______ A busy daytime café is ideal. There isn't much privacy, but you'll be grateful for the presence of others if an unpleasant situation develops. If your date refuses to meet at a café or insists on a less public place, simply move on.

3 ______ I once had a coffee date with a woman who grew increasingly angry – and vocal – over her mistreatment by an ex-boyfriend. When she turned her attack on me, I got up and left – and was thankful for an audience to witness my exit.

4 ______ If a coffee date shows up with a bad attitude, a bad temper or a foul mouth, head for the door. Do likewise if he or she attempts to corral you into a relationship. If you feel truly threatened, explain the situation to the café manager and ask him or her to walk you to your car.

5 ______ I was enjoying a second date at a restaurant when my companion took a call during dinner. I was pretty sure I knew what was going on.

'I'm just fine,' she told the caller, then stowed the phone with an apologetic smile.

'What would your friend have done if you hadn't picked up?' I asked her.

'She had instructions to call the police,' she replied.

Good tip. Smart woman.

6 ______ Certain queries can reveal a lot of info in a short amount of time about a person you've just met. You might ask, for example, if your date has close friends: a 'yes' indicates he or she is capable of connecting with others; a 'no' suggests a lack of intimacy skills.

7 ______ As I learned the hard way with my would-be Glenn Close, it's unwise to welcome anyone into your abode unless you know them well. If you're unsure, consider asking another couple to join you.

My current girlfriend (whom I met online, by the way) invited me into her home after only our second date. I accepted, thanking her for her trust, but later mentioned that she could have been putting herself at risk.

We all want to believe the best about people, but a date you don't really know deserves only a modicum of trust. So rather than rolling the dice when it comes to your personal safety, try following the steps above. Who knows? They might even be a shortcut to finding the right person out there.

Note: Dating services' official rules for dating online are located under their websites' terms of use. They suggest appropriate behaviour, but screening is minimal – so I strongly urge you to use the tips above to create your own safety zone. Keep in mind that you can block any other member if you ever start to feel that safety is an issue.

C 11.10 Listen and re-read to check. Which tip do you think is most important?

D **Make it personal** What are the best safety rules? In groups, answer 1–3.

1 Should women and men follow the same safety advice? Why (not)?

2 Is any advice missing? Can you add at least one more piece?

3 What online dating safety stories have you heard or read about? Give advice. What new tips have you picked up?

OK, let's see. Men need to be careful with their phone numbers, too.

6 Vocabulary: Whether to look up words

A Read *Deciding when to look up words*. Then re-read the sentences in the article where the yellow highlighted words appear. In pairs, explain whether you will look them up and why (not).

Deciding when to look up words

Stopping to look up lots of words decreases reading pleasure. Before looking up words, ask yourself these questions:

1 Have you seen the word before?

Yes Go to question 2. **No** It may be infrequent. Keep reading.

2 Is it necessary to understand the word?

Yes Go to question 3.

No The sentence makes sense. Keep reading.

3 Do you want to learn this word immediately for active use?

Yes Look it up. Find the meaning that matches the text.

No Try to figure out the meaning from context and keep reading.

Coaxing must come from the verb *coax*. I've never seen or heard it before, have you?

No. But, following rule 3, let's not look it up. I wonder what it means, though.

I think it might mean 'to convince'. It's quite clear he's trying to get her to leave.

B 11.11 Listen to a conversation between two teachers and note down the words not chosen. Then find them among the blue highlighted words. Do you agree? If not, follow rule 3 in **A**.

C **Make it personal** Create your own safety tips! In groups, choose two topics and create five tips for each one. Use highlighted blue and yellow words where useful.

How to safely ...

be a celebrity | go on a crash diet | become a political activist | be a police officer | hire employees

First: If you want to be a celebrity, you might need to hire a bodyguard.

Yes, strange situations can pop up!

7 Listening

A In pairs, if you saw this sign at the beach, would you go in the water? Why (not)?

B 11.12 Listen to a couple talking at the beach. Note down one convincing argument each person gives. Are you more like Bob or Andrea?

C 11.13 Which of these are more likely to kill you than a shark attack? Listen to check. Were you surprised?

1

2

3

4

D 11.14 Listen to the end of the conversation. Which reason 1–3 does Andrea give for saying that the numbers 'can't be taken at face value'?

1 ☐ They don't take people's location into account.
2 ☐ Not all oceans have sharks.
3 ☐ The figures haven't been updated in a while.

8 Pronunciation: Stressing function words for emphasis

A 11.15 Read and listen to the rules. Then read exchanges 1–4 and guess the stressed words in the responses.

> As we saw on page 67, auxiliaries may be stressed for emphasis. Other normally unstressed function words like conjunctions, articles, and pronouns, are sometimes stressed, too.
> Bob: You worry too much. Come on! Have some fun!
> Andrea: I **am** having fun. But I want to have fun **and** be safe. And I want **you** to be safe, too.

1 Andrea: Do you want to get eaten by a shark? ☐
Bob: Do I want what?

2 Bob: There are an estimated 64 attacks each year, but few are fatal. ☐
Andrea: Few. Not none, so the odds might not be in our favour!

3 Bob: That doesn't make any sense! Sharks are colour blind! ☐
Andrea: Colour blind? They are?

4 Bob: It's written right here! The evidence is clear! ☐
Andrea: I think it's anything but clear.

B 11.16 Listen to check. In pairs, first repeat and then extend each exchange.

C **Make it personal** In pairs, choose a picture from 7C and role-play a conversation where you don't agree on risk. Pay close attention to word stress.

A: You're extremely risk-averse.
B: You don't mind taking risks.

Get away from that tree! You could be hit by lightning.

I could be, but I won't be! What are the chances of that?

9 Grammar: Definite and indefinite articles

A Read the grammar box. Then write a–f next to mini-dialogues 1–4 in 8A.

Definite and indefinite articles: general and specific uses

general	a count nouns	**Precautions** need to be taken.
	b non-count nouns	**Research** tells us that the risks are real.
specific	c first mention	Is this **a risk** you're willing to take?
	d adjective + number	**A record ten** attacks were recorded in 2016.
	e shared knowledge	**The study** was conducted in Japan.
	f adjective = group of people	**The rich** tend to live longer.

Grammar expansion p.158

B Correct the mistakes in article use in some of the underlined phrases (1–8).

Common mistakes

Mark gave me ~~an~~ *some / a piece of* advice. His ~~advices are~~ *advice is / suggestions are* always good.

Are you worrying about the right things?

These days, it's hard to choose what to worry about. [1]<u>Climate change</u>? Resistant bacteria? [2]<u>The flu outbreaks</u>? Whichever the answer, remember: Your brain is wired to conspire against you! Although [3]<u>human brain</u> can respond well to risk, it's not good at deciding which modern threats are actually worth worrying about. This is because our survival instincts are activated by the choices that kept our ancestors safe, in [4]<u>a world</u> where dangers took the form of [5]<u>predators</u>, not terrorists. As a result, we tend to overestimate the odds of rare events, such as [6]<u>the plane crashes</u>, while downplaying the real risks, such as lack of exercise. According to a recent study, for example, [7]<u>an astounding</u> 80–85 per cent of British schoolchildren are living [8]<u>sedentary lifestyle</u>.

C Read *Quantifiers and pronouns*. Then rephrase the underlined sentences in 1–5. Replace the bold words with those in brackets.

Quantifiers and pronouns

Notice the pronoun differences between count and non-count nouns.

Non-count	Count
The article offers lots of **advice**. Most of **it** is useful, some of **it** is not.	The article offers lots of **suggestions**. Most of **them** are useful, some of **them** are not. **One** of **them** in particular is terrible.

1 <u>There are a lot of **studies** on mobile phone use, but how reliable are they</u>? (research) I keep worrying about the risks posed by the radiation.

2 Exactly! And <u>let's not forget the WiFi **devices** we're surrounded by and the radiation they emit.</u> (equipment)

3 The recent unemployment statistics are quite scary, and I worry about losing my job. <u>Well-paid work isn't easy to come by these days</u>. (jobs)

4 <u>There seem to be competing **facts** about whether eggs are good for you</u>. (evidence) Why can't scientists decide?

5 <u>Digital songs are more affordable than they've ever been</u>. (music) How will artists make money?

D **Make it personal** In groups, which concerns do you share from C? What other concerns are important to you? Be careful with articles.

> Teenage obesity is a major problem. I read that an astonishing 17 per cent of teenagers are obese.

> Yes, schools need to pay more attention to teaching good nutrition.

11.5 Have you ever had an allergic reaction?

10 Listening

A 11.17 Listen to the beginning of a lecture on allergies. Complete the notes.

Per cent suffering in US [1] ________ *(Adults* [2] ________ *Children* [3] ________ *)*
Three main causes of fatalities: 1) [4] ________ *, 2)* [5] ________ *, 3)* [6] ________
Anaphylactic [7] ________ *: Name comes from* [8] ________

B 11.18 Listen to the second part and take notes. In pairs, share two important facts that you've learned. Were they similar?

Anaphylactic shock can come on quickly. It's important to seek help immediately!

C 11.19 These symptoms are mentioned in the second part. In pairs, brainstorm other possible causes for them. Then listen to check. Were your ideas mentioned?

cramps

hives

sense of impending doom

swelling

itching

wheezing

Wheezing, for example, might occur if you had asthma.

11 Keep talking

A In groups, choose a topic where you'd like to know more about safety. Choose from those below or think of your own.

home safety   sailing / operating a boat   horseback riding
side effects to everyday medications   hotel and holiday safety

B Brainstorm three specific questions about your topic you don't know the answer to. Search online by entering each question in a search engine.

C Share your information with the class. Be sure to explain any new words. Which topic did you learn the most about?

You shouldn't have any problems at a hotel if you make sure the entrance is in a well-lit area. Always err on the side of caution!

Also check that your door has a dead-bolt lock. That means one that has a heavy sliding bar that moves when you turn it.

12 Writing: A statistical report

A Read the report, underlining the numbers. Which is the most surprising fact?

B Read *Write it right!* Then complete 1–5 with a singular or plural form of the verb in brackets. Read the report again to check.

Write it right!

When you use numbers, subject–verb agreement can be tricky. Here are three rules to help you:

1 When you use fractions, percentages, or words like *half*, *some*, *most*, and *all*, the **object** of the preposition determines the verb:

Two thirds / 70% of the **voters are** undecided.

Half / Most of the **information** I got **is** useless.

2 After *one*, the verb is always singular:

One out of every three homes **has** Netflix.

3 *The number* takes a singular verb. *A number*, which means *many*, takes a plural verb:

The number of people with allergies **is** high.
And **a number** of them **have** severe reactions.

1 Seven per cent of children ________ allergies. (have)
2 A number of studies ________ that the number of children ________ rising. (indicate, be)
3 One in every 13 children under 18 ________ affected by allergies. (be)
4 In the US, many of the most common allergic reactions ________ from fish allergies. (come)
5 Three out of every 15 people with allergies ________ peanut and tree nut allergies. (report)

C Imagine you've been asked to write a statistical report on one of the topics in 11A to a specific audience responsible for safety, such as insurance companies, holiday resorts, or doctors. Your report will need to highlight possible dangers and give recommendations.

Before

Choose your audience and plan two charts to support your message. Search on questions designed to produce statistics, such as 'How many people ...?'

While

Write three to four paragraphs to summarise your charts, following the model in A. Address your audience in paragraph 1 and give recommendations in the conclusion. Use expressions with numbers from *Write it right!*, paying careful attention to subject-verb agreement.

After

Post your report online and read your classmates' work. Whose statistics best supported the report?

FOOD ALLERGIES:
please read carefully

Five out of every 100 Americans have food allergies – that's an astonishing 15 million people, or close to 4%. What's more, the rate is even higher in children. One in every 13 children under the age of 18 is affected. In other words, on average, over 7% of children have food allergies. In addition, a number of studies indicate that the number of children is steadily rising. Teachers: please review this information carefully.

Only eight foods account for 90 per cent of these allergic reactions: milk, eggs, peanuts, tree nuts (walnuts, almonds, hazelnuts, cashews, etc), soy, wheat, fish, and shellfish. Yet these foods can be very dangerous. Food allergies may cause anaphylactic shock, a sudden reaction that, if not treated quickly, may be fatal.

By age, allergies in children and teenagers break down as follows:

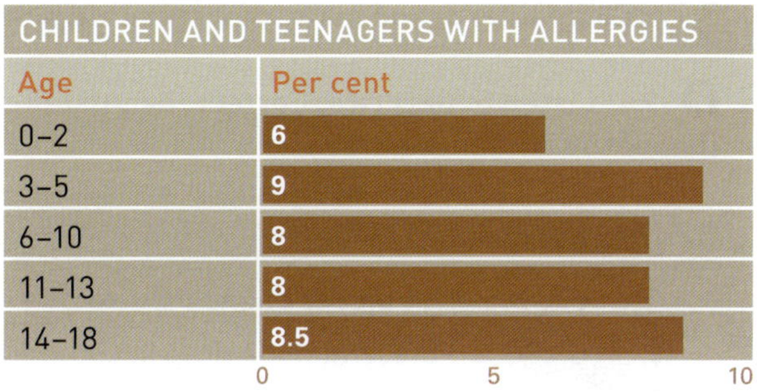

Among those diagnosed, the scope of the problem can be seen in this chart:

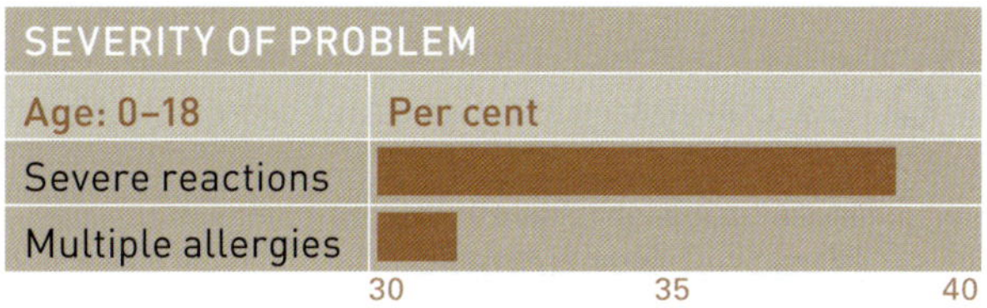

Some allergies can be outgrown, but fish and shellfish allergies are usually lifelong. In the US, many of the most common allergic reactions come from fish allergies – more than 6.5 million adults have them. Peanut and tree nut allergies tend to be lifelong also. More than three million adults report such allergies. Alarmingly, food allergies overall are so common that, in the US, someone ends up in the emergency room every three minutes, for a total of 200,000 visits a year.

Epinephrine auto-injectors can save lives! Should you be faced with an emergency, do not attempt to treat a student yourself. Take him or her immediately to the nurse's office and call 999. Every minute counts.

12

What brands are the wave of the future?

1 Listening

A 12.1 Look at the cartoon. What do you think the professor's lecture will be about? Listen to check.

> Maybe he / she will talk about how bad the economy is at the moment.

'What if we don't change at all ... and something magical just happens?'

B 12.1 Listen again. Tick (✔) the points the professor makes.

1 ☐ Innovation involves risk-taking.
2 ☐ It's hard to change well-established practices.
3 ☐ Companies spend many years planning changes.

C 12.2 Listen to part two. Correct the mistake in each line of the student's notes.

Microsoft

1 80s & 90s: high profits due to ~~PC~~ *software* sales
2 Mid 2000s – present: huge drop in computer sales, esp. laptops
3 *Surface* tablet: impressive sales at first
4 Future of PCs: 3D gaming won't increase sales

D 12.3 Listen to part three and complete the notes. Were you surprised?

National Geographic

1 Early days: American ___________
2 Challenge in the 90s: number of ___________ went down
3 John Fahey's role: change ___________ of company
4 Digital presence: top non-celebrity account on ___________

E **Make it personal** Brands that have come and gone! In groups, do 1–3.

1 Individually, search on 'brands that disappeared' to find an interesting story.
2 Read the case study and quickly note down the key points.
3 Share your stories. What should each company have done differently?

> Here's one ... the amazing story of Blockbuster, the video-hire company. They turned down a partnership with Netflix. Can you believe it?

2 Vocabulary: Verbs describing trends

A ▶ 12.4 Match the two halves. Listen to check. Then write the highlighted verbs under each graph.

1 Since the mid 2000s, sales of cell phones and tablets have increased worldwide,
2 The *Surface* line had a bumpy start,
3 If 3D gaming remains popular,
4 It seems the magazine had lost some of its edge,
5 *National Geographic* is the top non-celebrity account on Instagram,

a ☐ the decline in PC sales might **level off**.
b ☐ and the number of followers continues to **soar** month after month!
c ☐ but its sales eventually **skyrocketed**.
d ☐ while PC shipments have **plummeted**.
e ☐ and the number of subscribers began to **plunge**.

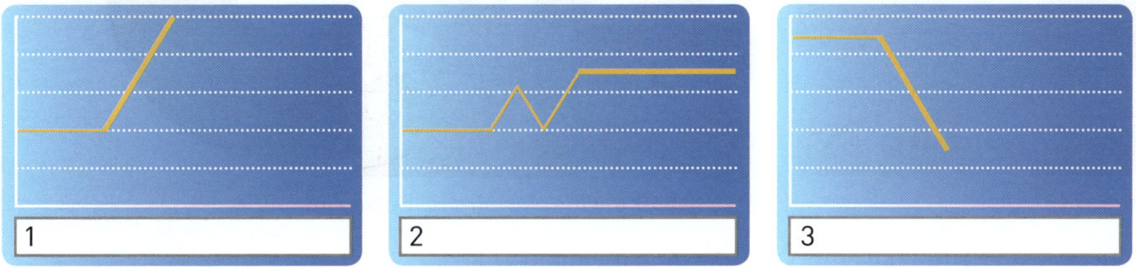

B Form sentences using cues 1–6. Notice the *Common mistake*.

Good news from around the globe:

1 Canada: number / traffic deaths / plunge / since 2006
2 Spain: unemployment / fall / from 2013 to 2016
3 India: generation of solar electricity / soar / over the past few years
4 UK life expectancy / rise / since 1990
5 US obesity rates / men / level off / in 2016
6 Globally: poverty / plummet / in the last two decades

Common mistake

Sales ^have plunged in / over the last three years.

C Make it personal Discuss trends in your region.

1 ▶ 12.5 **How to say it** Complete the table. Listen to check.

Expressing cause and reason		
	What they said	What they meant
1	(Many bankruptcies) _________ from (fear).	Negative outcome A is caused by B.
2	(Innovation) is _________ related to (risk and uncertainty).	A has a lot to do with B.
3	(Mobile computing) has _________ rise to (new challenges).	A has caused B.
4	(The TV channel) paved the _________ for (other innovations).	A made B possible.

2 In groups, change 1–6 in B to give true information for your region. Use expressions from C to explain the possible reasons. Can you think of any other trends?

> The number of traffic deaths around here has soared. It probably stems from raising the speed limit.

3 Language in use

A 12.6 Listen to a podcast about music and society. Note down one reason why each song below was influential.

Believe, Cher, 1998

Do They Know It's Christmas, Band Aid, 1984

B 12.6 Listen again. Tick (✔) the points the music critic makes.

1 ☐ Most singers use Auto-Tune these days, which is objectionable.
2 ☐ Auto-Tune has made singers less unique.
3 ☐ Fundraising songs should be as catchy as possible.
4 ☐ Music may have lost some of its impetus for social change.

C 12.7 Complete 1–5 with a form of the highlighted phrasal verbs. Listen to check.

bring about: make something happen
catch on: become popular
fall back on: use as a last resort
get across: make an idea clear or convincing
grow on: become more appealing over time
warm up to: begin to like something or someone

1 Cher didn't refuse to be 'auto-tuned', and the song instantly ________.
2 Today, most people – regardless of talent – can take a shot at singing if they can ________ Auto-Tune. It makes you wonder if singers are just one step away from being completely replaced by robots.
3 *Do they know …?* wasn't a tune I instantly ________, and I remember being underwhelmed when I first heard it.
4 But the song eventually ________ me, maybe because of the message it was trying to ________.
5 What's remarkable about *Do they know …?* is that it showed artists their influence could be used to ________ real change.

D Read *Transitive and intransitive phrasal verbs*. Then write 1–3 next to the phrasal verbs in **C**.

Transitive and intransitive phrasal verbs

Phrasal verbs can be transitive or intransitive:

1 Intransitive phrasal verbs don't take an object: Why did Abba **break up**?
2 Transitive ones need an object. Many are separable: They **called** the concert **off** / **called off** the concert.
3 Others are inseparable, including most three-word phrasal verbs: Can we **go over** the contract once more? (NOT ~~go the contract over~~); I'm **looking forward to** their next release.

E Make it personal In groups, agree on your two favourite quotes. Explain what they mean and why you like them.

1 'Music and the music business are two different things.' (Erykah Badu)
2 'There are two means of refuge from the miseries of life: music and cats.' (Albert Schweitzer)
3 'The trade of critic, in literature, music, and ... drama, is the most degraded of all trades.' (Mark Twain)
4 'Independent artists and labels have always been the trend setters in music and the music business.' (Shawn Fanning)

In the first one, I think she means that the music business is motivated by profit.

4 Grammar: Passive forms with gerunds and infinitives

A Read the grammar box. Underline the four passive sentences in 3C and write 1–6 next to each one.

Passive forms with gerunds and infinitives: after parts of speech and as subjects	
Use gerunds ...	Use infinitives and base forms ...
1 after certain verbs: Cher **enjoyed being played** on the radio again.	4 after certain verbs: Band Aid **hoped to be remembered** for the song.
2 after prepositions: She didn't object **to being 'auto-tuned'**.	5 after adjectives, nouns, and indefinite pronouns: The song is **unlikely to be forgotten**.
3 as subjects: **Being considered** cool again was her goal.	6 after modals: Its lyrics **should** not **be taken** at face value.
In negative sentences, the preferred form for *not* is before the infinitive: The singer was **disappointed not to be** invited to join the group.	

B Rewrite 1–6 in the passive, using *be*, *to be*, or *being*. Which books, if any, would you like to read?

Grammar expansion p.160

BOOKS THAT CHANGED THE WAY I ...

SET PRIORITIES: *THE ONE THING*, BY GARY KELLER.
Do yourself a favour and read *The One Thing*. In it, the author shows us [1]why people should set priorities in the first place, and [2]how we can accomplish this important task.

COPE WITH STRESS: *HOW TO STOP WORRYING AND START LIVING*, BY DALE CARNEGIE.
I read this book at a very stressful moment in my life. [3]I was so upset they didn't consider me for my dream job. Thanks to this book, I was able to pull myself together.

READ POETRY: *TRANSFORMATIONS*, BY ANNE SEXTON.
Up until recently, if someone asked me whether I enjoyed reading poetry, I'd usually reply: [4]'I'd prefer someone forced me to read the small print on a cereal box'. But *Transformations*, which turns well-known fairy tales into poems, taught me how to appreciate it!

FEEL ABOUT READING: *20,000 LEAGUES UNDER THE SEA*, BY JULES VERNE.
Over the years I've learned that [5]having people tell you what to read is a surefire way to make you hate books! *20,000 Leagues* ... was the very first book I chose to read, and this made all the difference! [6]I still recall that the author surprised me because I hadn't known that science fiction could be so engaging.

C Make it personal In pairs, has a book / film / play / article ever had an impact on the way you ...?

approach friendships / romance   cope with stress   deal with money   have fun   see the world

I don't remember ever being that influenced by a single book or film. How about you?

Actually, *Eat, Pray, Love* made me rethink my work schedule!

5 Reading

A Imaginative drawings of the future were once common. Look at two postcards of 'future' transport. In pairs, answer 1–2.

1 Where could the people be going?
2 What else might artists have imagined 100 years ago?

> Well, the first one looks like a flying train. Aren't they on top of a building?

B 12.8 Read and listen to the article. Underline details describing how the future will be. Which (if any) do you see in A? Are you surprised by anything in the article?

Here's how people 100 years ago thought we'd be living today

In 100 years, there will be flying taxis and people will travel to the moon routinely. Knowledge will be instilled into students through wires attached to their heads. These may sound like the predictions of modern-day futurists, but they're how people a century ago saw the future – otherwise known to you and me as the present.

These vintage European postcards illustrate a view of the 21st century that is remarkably prescient in some ways and hilariously wrong in others, says Ed Fries, who selected them from his private collection.

In the 10 years since he left Microsoft, where he was co-founder of the Xbox project, Fries has worked on what he calls 'a random collection of futuristic projects'. He's advised or served on the board of companies working on 3-D printing, depth-sensing cameras (like those used in Kinect), and headsets for reading brain waves. Earlier this month, he presented some of his favourite postcards at a neurogaming conference in San Francisco, using them to illustrate pitfalls in predicting the future that remain relevant today.

One thing you see in the cards is a tendency to assume some things won't change, even though they undoubtedly will. In one image, a couple flags down an aerotaxi. That's futuristic enough, but the man is wearing spats and carrying a cane, while she has a parasol and an enormous hat with a feather. Did they really think transportation would undergo a revolution while fashion stayed frozen in time? 'In every one of these you see a mix of a futuristic concept with stuff that looks to us to be very old fashioned', Fries said.

At the same time, there's virtually no hint in the postcards of the truly transformative technologies of the last century – namely personal computers and the Internet. Sure, there are video phones, but the image is projected on a screen or a wall. Moving pictures were just coming into existence, Fries says, so that wasn't a huge leap. But the idea of a screen illuminated from within seems to have been beyond their imagination.

All in all, people at the turn of the 20th century did a pretty good job of extrapolating the technology of their time, Fries says. But their imagination was limited by the world they lived in. The same is true today – at least for those of us who aren't the visionaries of tomorrow.

Fries thinks what sets those farsighted people apart has something to do with ignoring conventional wisdom. 'The future is changed by people who have a crazy idea and follow it wherever it may lead', he said. 'That's why I like hanging out with wacky people like at that neurogaming conference. One of them is probably going to change the world.'

C **Make it personal** In groups, search on 'vintage postcards of the future'. Share your favourite one.

> Here's one that's cool: a ship that turns into a train with wheels once it hits land. I wonder why those were never invented.

6 Vocabulary: Using a dictionary

A Read *Looking up words* and study the definition of *leap*. Answer 1–2.

1 Which questions from the box can be answered from the definition below?

2 Look up *leap* in a monolingual dictionary and find the noun. Is it countable or uncountable? How do you say, 'We took a chance'?

Looking up words

When looking up words, follow these helpful guidelines:

1 Study the examples, and consider these questions:
(a) Which prepositions are possible? (b) Does the word seem formal or informal?
(c) Does it have a figurative meaning, too?

2 Pay attention to collocations. What other words does the new word go with?

3 Decide the part of speech. Is the word a noun? If yes, is it countable or uncountable?

leap /li:p/ verb **Other forms: leaped** /li:pt/ **or leapt** /lept/; **also leaping**

1 to jump from a surface **2** to jump over something **3** to move quickly

Examples:

1 He leaped from the bridge.

2 He leaped over the wall.

3 The cat leaped into the air. / We leaped at the chance. (fig)

B Choose five highlighted words from 5B to look up. In pairs, explain what you learned.

> I chose *farsighted* and learned it has both a medical and figurative meaning ...

C **Make it personal** In groups, plan and draw your own futuristic postcard! Consider 1–3. Use highlighted words from 5B.

1 Study the postcards in 5A again. How might these areas be different?

2 Can you imagine fashion 100 years from now? Or would you prefer to draw current fashions like the postcard artists did?

3 Will there be anything truly transformative by 2050?

> I know it might sound a bit mad, but I think we should draw a ...

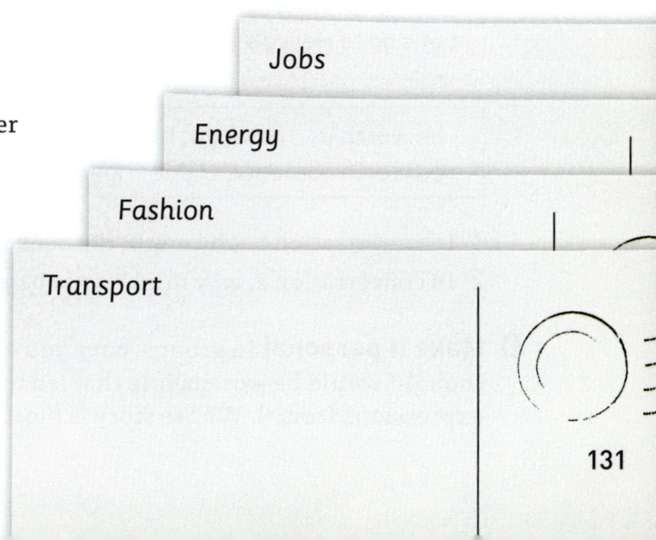

7 Language in use

A 12.9 What do you know about these people? Read the website and guess the missing words. Listen to check.

THESE 19TH CENTURY AUTHORS FOUND THE UNEXPECTED!

Dickens

1 Charles Dickens never would have imagined his [1]________. Since his father couldn't pay his debts, he **got arrested** in 1824 and **got thrown in** debtor's prison. His whole family, including Charles, **had** their home **taken away** and had to join the father in [2]________. Then, as a young man, the future [3]________ **was exposed** to terrible [4]________ conditions in a factory. As a result, he soon had a wealth of [5]________ for his 15 novels, among them *Great Expectations* and *A Tale of Two Cities*. It turned out the hardships of his youth were worth it.

Chopin

2 George Sand did not find what she was [6]________ when she travelled to the island of Mallorca, in the winter of 1838, with Polish [7]________ Frédéric Chopin. Sick with tuberculosis, Chopin **was being treated** in France, but **was getting pressured** by his doctor to find a milder [8]________. He thought a stay in Mallorca would be well worth the effort. They **had** their wishes **fulfilled** when they found a beautiful house in the town of Valldemossa. But, [9]________ for Chopin, he couldn't **get** his [10]________ **cured** because the humidity actually worsened it, and the couple had to return to France. Sand, though, now had material for a book: *A Winter in Mallorca*.

Sand

B Answer 1–6. Which story did you find more surprising?
Who ...

1 wasn't able to pay his or her debts?
2 lost their home and went to prison?
3 experienced bad working conditions?
4 encouraged Chopin to find a new climate?
5 was happy to find a beautiful house?
6 was still ill upon returning to France?

I found the Dickens story shocking. I had no idea that he'd spent time in prison.

C 12.10 Read *Expressions with worth*. Then listen to two conversations about *Great Expectations*. Answer 1–2, using the expressions in the box.

Expressions with *worth*

Worth expressions usually imply there's value in the effort involved. The expressions are often interchangeable. However, if you're not expressing effort, *worth* can sound unnatural. Compare:

Is it **worth it** to read this long book? It's 600 pages!

Let's go to Henry's for dinner. The food is really ~~worthwhile~~ **good**.

be worth it | be worth the effort / trouble | be worth + verb + *-ing* | be worth someone's time | be worthwhile

Common mistake

~~It~~ *It's* worth being frugal.

1 In conversation 1, why might the book be a good choice for Mike?
2 In conversation 2, why might it not be a good choice?

D **Make it personal** In groups, have you ever done something you never thought would be worthwhile that led to an unpredictable result? Use expressions from **C**. Whose story is most surprising?

I never thought it would be worth the effort to join a theatre group. But I ended up getting the lead in a play!

8 Grammar: The passive and causative with *get*

A Read the grammar box. Then rephrase the verbs with *get* in 7A with a form of *have* or *be*, and the ones with *have* or *be* with a form of *get*.

The passive with *get* and *be*; the causative with *get* and *have*

Passive: *get = be*	Tom	**was getting** **is being**	**hassled** **pressured**	a lot by his boss. to resign.
	I	**got** **was**	**fired** **left**	on Tuesday. without a job.
Causative passive: *get = have*	She	**got** **had**	her short story **accepted** her photo **taken**	by the magazine. as a result.
	We	**'ll be getting** **might have**	more work **assigned** our holidays **taken**	soon! away.

» Grammar expansion p.160

B Read *Spoken grammar: Using the get passive*. Then rephrase the underlined parts of 1–5 with a *get* passive or causative. In pairs, A: Read a sentence with emotion; B: Respond with feeling! Change roles.

Spoken grammar: Using the *get* passive

The *get* passive and causative, in spoken English, often convey nuances of meaning and register. For example:

a informality: Guess what! I **got accepted** into Oxford!
b emphasis: You **could get hurt** if you keep that up!
c negative intent: I **got** my wallet **stolen** as I was walking home.
d unintended consequence: Do you want to **get** me **arrested**?

1 Hey, you're going 90 miles an hour! Slow down. Do you want us to die?
2 Ouch! Some creep just stepped on my foot! I think he did it on purpose!
3 What! You're reading your boss's email? She could fire you and with good reason!
4 Fantastic news! They awarded me first prize for my painting!
5 Firecrackers are illegal! Do you want the neighbours to take me to court?

Hey, you're going 90 miles an hour! Slow down. Do you want us to get killed?

I'm sorry! I'm just worried we might miss our flight.

C ▶ 12.11 Guess what happened in pictures 1–4. Then listen to four conversations. After the 'beep', rephrase the sentence with *get*. Continue listening to check.

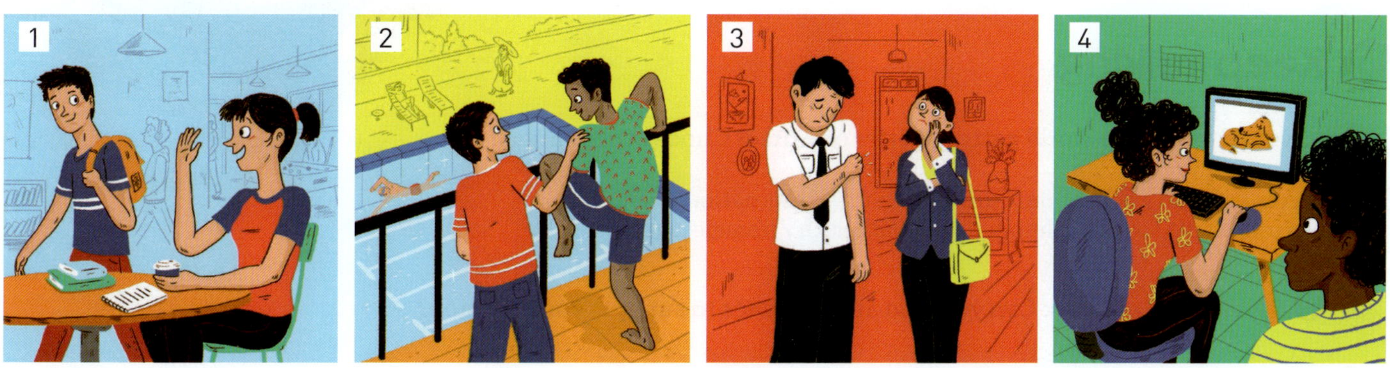

D Make it personal In pairs, using only the pictures, role-play new situations. Use the passive or causative with *get*.

Big news! I got my picture taken for the newspaper!

You did? That's awesome.

9 Listening

A 12.12 Listen to the start of a lecture on building a utopian society. In pairs, answer Professor Orwell's question.

B 12.13 Listen to part two. Complete Jennifer's reasons. In pairs, are any convincing?

There will be no ...

1 housing shortage because buildings will be ____________.
2 food shortage because people will have ____________.
3 pollution because everyone will have a ____________ for transport.

I think ... sounds ridiculous!

C 12.14 Listen to part three and take notes. Give one argument to show how ...

1 the housing crisis may diminish.
2 hunger will remain a problem.

D 12.15 Read *Whatsoever*. Then add *whatsoever* to 1–6, only if possible. Listen to check.

Whatsoever

Like *at all*, *whatsoever* can be used to emphasise negative ideas. Notice its position in these sentences:

I have **no** idea **whatsoever** what a utopian society is.

There's **nothing whatsoever** we can do to change the current situation.

It can also be used in questions with *any*:

Is there **any** doubt **whatsoever** that climate change is getting worse?

1 But rest assured, there's no connection to the famous novel, *1984*.
2 To me, a true utopia makes life just enjoyable and worth living.
3 I have no doubt that those things will come, too.
4 For one thing, the housing shortage will disappear.
5 There won't be any emissions where we live.
6 Is there any evidence that any of these changes might actually come about?

Big Brother is watching you

10 Keep talking

A In your view, is the world getting better or worse? Choose three areas.

access to quality education   animal rights   international relations
environmental issues   hunger   public health / homelessness

B Note down reasons. Can you find any evidence to support your opinion?

C In groups, share your ideas. Any disagreements?

I think the world is getting worse. For example, homelessness is on the rise.

Hmm ... What's your evidence?

11 Writing: An opinion essay

A Read Oscar's essay in response to Professor Orwell's question. In your opinion, is he ...

1 ☐ convincing?
2 ☐ somewhat convincing?
3 ☐ not convincing?

B Complete the essay with words from 10A.

C Read *Write it right!* Then rephrase 1–5 using verb or noun phrases. Scan the essay to check.

Write it right!

Good writers know how to use words and structures flexibly to avoid repetition. Verb phrases can be written as noun phrases without a change in meaning:

Verb phrase (verb + adverb)	Noun phrase (adjective + noun)
CO_2 levels have **risen steadily**.	There has been **a steady rise** in CO_2 levels.
Average earnings **dropped slightly**.	There was **a slight drop** in average earnings.

1 Life expectancy has increased steadily.
There's been a steady increase in life expectancy.
2 International relations have improved slowly but steadily.
3 There's been a significant decrease in the number of international conflicts.
4 The planet's temperature has risen steeply.
5 Homelessness has fallen sharply in some places.

D Your turn! Write an opinion essay in response to Professor Orwell's question in about 280 words.

Before
Decide how optimistic you feel about the future of the world. Then choose two to three issues from 10A and, using your notes, plan the content of each paragraph.

While
Write a four to five paragraph essay, following the model in A. Refer to *Write it right!* to vary your use of noun and verb phrases.

After
Post your essay online and read your classmates' work. What were the most pressing issues?

Is the world getting better or worse?

Let's face it. This year hasn't been the most positive of years. Last year was tough, too. But is the world really getting worse? When our social media feeds are filled with bad news after bad news, reasons for optimism can seem few and far between. However, if we look at the world as a whole, as opposed to individual countries, in my view things are actually getting better.

Take [1]________ for example. Although access to health care is still an issue in many countries, recent advances in stem-cell research, gene therapy, and nanotechnology mean we're inching closer to a cure for diseases such as Alzheimer's, Parkinson's, and multiple sclerosis, as well as some forms of cancer. There's also been a sharp fall in homelessness in some places. All of this might help to explain why there has been a steady increase in life expectancy.

Second, there has been a slow but steady improvement in [2]________. Since World War II, the world has seen no 'Great Wars', and the number of international conflicts has decreased significantly. Some historians refer to the period we are living in as the 'Long Peace'. While I don't quite agree since the world is still a dangerous place, in the long run, I feel globalisation will make it safer.

We're still faced with serious [3]________. In the past two decades, there's been a steep rise in the planet's temperature, which has caused glaciers to melt and seas to rise at unprecedented rates. The continued destruction of the Earth's biosphere and the extinction of an ever-increasing number of species are just some of the daunting challenges we're up against. Will we be able to meet them? Only time will tell, but at least awareness has increased.

Yet, despite all the problems in the world today, it doesn't seem as if we're on the edge of the apocalypse – at least not yet. In fact, looking back through the lens of history, it would seem to me that the opposite might be closer to the truth.

Review 6

Units 11–12

1 Listening

A R6.1 Listen to a conversation between two friends, Phil and Melinda. Her primary tone is ...

a angry and sarcastic. b angry, but resigned. b sarcastic, but hopeful.

B R6.1 Listen again and fill in the modal verbs. Then match them with their functions (a–e).

1 He ________ have just asked.
2 You ________ want to file a report.
3 This ________ be a bad corner.
4 They ________ come here.
5 It ________ be that hard to locate it.
6 He ________ have at least dropped the bag.

a ☐ possibility
b ☐ suggestion
c ☐ expectation
d ☐ annoyance
e ☐ refusal

C In pairs, role-play Phil and Melinda's conversation from memory.

> Stop, thief! Can you believe it? I just got my purse snatched!

2 Speaking

A Look at the cartoon on p. 126.

1 In two minutes, note down as many possible trends as you can imagine over the next ten years, using these words and expressions:

a steady increase a steep rise be closely related to bring about drop slightly give rise to level off plummet plunge rise significantly skyrocket soar stem from

2 In groups, share ideas. Similar opinions?

> Homelessness is going to skyrocket. There's not enough housing.

> Actually, I think it's likely to level off. Doesn't at least some of it stem from the recession?

B Make it personal Choose three question titles from Units 11 and 12 to ask a partner. Ask at least three follow-up questions for each. What did you learn about each other?

> What does the sea make you think of?

> Jellyfish! I'm always getting stung by them when I go swimming.

3 Writing

Write a persuasive paragraph summarising three trends you predict from 2A.

1 Note down evidence. Search online for one key fact about each trend, as necessary.

2 Express your arguments using verbs from the box. Change some to nouns to vary the wording.

decrease drop fall improve increase level off rise

'There will be a dramatic increase in salaries.'

4 Grammar

A Add or delete articles (1–9) where needed. Tick (✔) those that are correct.

Is there any doubt whatsoever that we have [1]homeless problem in the US? [2]A random study even showed that people walk by [3]the homeless without even looking. Participants who saw [4]the relatives on the street didn't even recognise them when they were disguised as [5]the homeless people! Nevertheless, every two years, [6]number of efforts is made in the US to count the number of homeless in major cities. [7]Last survey shows [8]a staggering 578,424 people were without [9]the shelter.

B In pairs, explain why the items are correct or incorrect.

Number 1 is incorrect. It has to be *a* homeless problem. It's the first time it's been mentioned.

5 Self-test

Correct the two mistakes in each sentence. Check your answers in Units 11 and 12. What's your score, 1–20?

1 When trying out a new recipe, I always play it safety since there's no safe net to fall back on.
2 We can't just do with the flow because there's much at stake.
3 Susan gave me some well-intended advice, but actually, most of them aren't too useful.
4 Apparently, one out of every three people have the itching when stung by a bee.
5 I really warmed up Auto-Tuning and didn't even realise they'd fallen it back on.
6 I enjoy to be recorded when I sing and don't hope to make any errors.
7 My brother was being hassle by his boss, and then he got fire on Thursday.
8 The new restaurant is expensive but worth, and the food is really worth the trouble.
9 There's nothing whatever we can do about the steady rising in pollution here.
10 We're having pressured by new boss more than ever.

6 Point of view

Choose a topic. Then support your opinion in 100–150 words, and record your answer. Ask a partner for feedback. How can you be more convincing?

a You think upbringing determines whether you're open to risk-taking. OR
You think age is the most important factor in risk-taking.
b You think online dating is generally safe and you should go with the flow. OR
You think online dating calls for detailed safety precautions.
c You think books are more influential than music in changing the world. OR
You think the power of music in promoting social change shouldn't be underestimated.
d You think limited access to quality education is a major social problem. OR
You think access to quality education has been steadily improving.

1 Subject-verb agreement with possessives
do after 1.2

In British English, it is ungrammatical to use a plural possessive adjective or pronoun to refer back to a singular subject. Indefinite pronouns are singular:		
Everyone should take	**his or her**	seat.
People should take	**their**	seat**s**.
In informal conversation, you will often hear sentences where a singular subject has the plural possessive *their* or *theirs*, but such sentences should be avoided in formal speech and writing.		

Common mistakes

Anyone who wants to open ~~their~~ *his or her* own business can.

Someone dropped ~~their~~ *a* wallet.

In other possessive constructions, the verb agrees with the subject of the sentence:		
One of my parents' friends	**has**	a great new idea.
Each of our team's members	**is**	sending in a proposal.

2 More on expressing continuity
do after 1.4

Use the past continuous to give background information, but use *used to* or *would* for repeated actions, and *used to* or the past simple to express a state:	
I **was going**	to school at the time.
I **belonged**	to a gym.
I **used to / would**	go there every week.
I **used to**	have a personal trainer.
Eventually I **decided**	to become a trainer, too.

Use modal verbs in continuous tenses to express ideas that are or will be in progress:		
Probability	You **must be moving**	soon. I can see you're packing.
Possibility	We **might be starting**	our own business, but things are a bit up in the air.
Advice	You **should be looking**	for a job. You're already 25!
Sometimes the continuous verb is close in meaning to a non-continuous form:		
Possibility	We **might start**	our own business if we find a good location.
But sometimes the meaning is very different:		
Obligation / Necessity	You **must move**	within three months. The landlord needs the flat.

How long ... ?*, *for*, and *since	
The present perfect and present perfect continuous have the same meaning when used with *How long ...?*, *for*, or *since*:	
How long **have you done** this kind of work?	I**'ve done** it **for two years**.
How long **have you been working** here?	I**'ve been working** here **since 2015**.
But use only the present perfect with stative verbs:	
How long **have you had** this car?	I**'ve had** it **for three years**.

1A Correct the two mistakes in each sentence. There may be more than one solution. (You may wish to review the rules on p. 9, too.)

1 One of my friends' classmate have an idea for a new start-up.
2 Everyone need to be cautious with their major decisions.
3 Many people worries about investing his or her money.
4 Two hundred pounds are a lot for someone to pay for their English course.
5 Having business strategies are important for anyone who wants their own start-up.
6 My teacher, as well as all my friends, think one of us have a great idea.
7 Keeping your fears in check are important if you're someone who are planning a lifestyle change.
8 Some of my parents' best advice were in his or her letter.
9 Everyone should take their umbrella because something tell me it's going to rain.
10 One of my sister's friends have told me that two years aren't long enough to learn English.

1B In pairs, explain the reasons each sentence is ungrammatical.

Number 1 is kind of hard. I wasn't sure about 'friends'.

You have several friends so that's correct, but 'classmate' needs an 's' because there are several pupils in the class. And then the verb ...

2A Circle the correct options to complete the texts about each first-time experience.

1 Speaking of 'firsts', I'll never forget the first time I [1][**acted / was acting**] in a play. I [2][**was living / would live**] in Spain, so the play [3][**used to be / was**] in Spanish. I [4][**'d been practising / 'd practised**] my part one last time before we [5][**went / were going**] on stage, but I [6][**was still / was still being**] nervous. I [7][**would worry /worried**] that [8][**I might be forgetting / I might forget**] my part. However, when we finally [9][**performed / were performing**] the play, it [10][**was / was being**] a fabulous success.

2 It may not seem like a big deal, but the first time I [1][**was / had been**] on an aeroplane was so exciting. I only [2][**used to fly / flew**] from Liverpool to Dublin, less than an hour away, but in those days, it [3][**wouldn't be / wasn't**] so common to fly, and it [4] [**used to be / would be**] much more expensive. When I [5][**got / was getting**] there, I then [6][**was having to / had to**] take a bus through the fields of Ireland up to Drogheda, where I [7][**was visiting / used to visit**] a friend. The fields [8][**went / were going**] on for miles. But what I remember most of all is that a girl [9][**had lost / was losing**] her rucksack, and the whole bus [10][**must spend / must have spent**] a half an hour looking for it.

2B **Make it personal** In pairs, share an experience about yourself beginning with 'Speaking of "firsts" ...' or 'It may not seem like a big deal, but ...'

Speaking of 'firsts', I'll never forget the time I spent the night in a sailing boat. The wind was picking up, and it had just started to rain when ...

Bonus! Language in song

♪ **Some people** want diamond rings. **Some** just want everything. But **everything** means nothing.

Rewrite the song lyric, half an hour changing the bold words in order to *only one of us*, *each of us*, and *most things*.
Add any other necessary changes.

1 Sentences with complements and conjunctions

do after 2.2

In conversation, repetition can be avoided both when you agree and don't agree.	
I actually like small flats.	I **do**, too. / So **do** I.
My mum doesn't throw anything out.	Mine **doesn't** either. / Neither **does** mine.
I don't like this neighbourhood.	But I **do**. Let's at least give it a chance.
I'm not happy in this flat.	But I **am**. And we just moved in last year.

You can also avoid repetition with possessives and with indefinite pronouns. When there is a compound noun, only the second noun is possessive.	
Possessives	My house is a lot smaller than my **sister's**. My garden is smaller than **hers** also.
	But my house is bigger than **Jim and Amy's**. And my kitchen is bigger than **theirs**, as well.
Indefinite pronouns	We don't have a garden, but my brother has **one**.
	Last year, we planted vegetables, but this year, we don't have **any**.

Finally, you can avoid repetition when referring to an entire idea or sentence.	
Do you feel like going out to dinner tonight?	I don't think **so**.
Would you consider renting one of these flats?	I guess / suppose **so**.
We have got a lot of junk here!	I told you **so**.
However, you cannot use *so* to refer to a specific noun.	
What was your reaction to *this neighbourhood*?	I like **it**.

Common mistakes

Our garden is nicer than my ~~sister garden~~ *sister's*.

I really like my new home, and my friends ~~like~~ *do*, too.

Do you like the flat? I think ~~that yes~~ *so*.

2 More on comparatives with *so* and *such*

do after 2.4

Use *so much* before comparative forms of adjectives, to compare non-count nouns, and to refer to a whole idea. Use *so many* when comparing count nouns.				
Adjectives	It's	**so much**	**harder**	living in a small flat.
			less expensive	here than in New York.
			more crowded	on the subway than the bus.
Non-count nouns	There's		**more information**	than there used to be.
			less time	than when we were children.
Ideas	We like it here		**more**	than we thought we would.
	We miss home		**less**	than we expected.
Count nouns	There are	**so many**	**more people**	that I can never get a seat.
	We have		**fewer services**	than we once had.

Common mistakes

It's so much ~~more noisy~~ *noisier* than what we were used to.

There are so many ~~less~~ *fewer* people than there once ~~was~~ *were*.

1A Rewrite the sentences, shortening them to avoid repetition.

1 My whole family has trouble throwing things out, and I have trouble throwing things out.
2 There aren't that many good English coursebooks, but I have a good English coursebook.
3 Several of my friends want to get married, but I don't want to get married.
4 A lot of people I know want to live on my own, and I want to live on my own.
5 I've looked at a lot of flats, and I hoped to find a flat, but I haven't found a flat. (two changes)
6 My friends say their ideas about the future have changed recently, and my ideas about the future have changed. (two changes)

1B Make it personal Change two sentences in **A** so they're true for you. In pairs, compare opinions.

My whole family has trouble throwing things out, and so do I!

I don't! My flat is so small I hardly fit in it myself.

1C Correct the mistakes in these shortened sentences.

1 Maybe you don't like small flats, but I like.
2 They haven't saved money for unforeseen events, but I've saved.
3 My view is nicer than Ted and Mary's, and my kitchen is bigger than them.
4 My neighbourhood is a lot more interesting than Sally and Bill.
5 We don't have a pool in our back garden, but my sister has.
6 My parents asked me if I wanted to move, and I said I thought yes.
7 We can't find a good moving company, but maybe you can recommend one good.
8 Our old flat had big wardrobes, but this one doesn't have some.
9 My boyfriend asked me if I wanted my independence, but I said I didn't think it.
10 I don't know for sure if we're buying this place. My husband wants, so I guess that yes. (two mistakes)

2A Complete the paragraph with comparatives containing *so many* or *so much* and the words in brackets.

Most major cities have changed substantially in the last 50 years, and Washington, DC is no exception. There are [1]*so many more people* (people) than there used to be, and it's [2]_________ (busy) all the time. It's true that the Metro, which opened in 1976, was a welcome addition to the nation's capital, one that makes it [3]_________ (easy) to get to work. But the trains are [4]_________ (crowded) than the old buses used to be. Since I still have to drive to a *Park and Ride* station to get the train, I'm aware that there's [5] _________ (traffic) everywhere, too. And forget about driving to work! There are [6]_________ (parking spaces) than there once were. In fact, there are hardly any! Everywhere, especially in neighbouring Maryland and Virginia, there are [7]_________ (buildings) and just [8]_________ (congestion) everywhere. I have to say I like the 'new' Washington, DC [9]_________ than the city I remember from my childhood.

2B Make it personal Rewrite the paragraph about a city you know, changing the details as necessary. In pairs, share your stories.

Most major cities have changed substantially in the last ten years, and ...

Bonus! Language in song

♫ So many tears I've cried. So much pain inside. But baby it ain't over 'til it's over.

Explain why the first sentence in the song lyric uses *so many*, but the second line *so much*.

1 More on subject and object questions do after 3.2

Clauses with question words can be embedded in both *yes-no* and information questions.		
Does	**whether I have good pronunciation**	matter?
How does	**where I study**	affect my test results?
Why is	**how my accent sounds**	important?
When does	**what we say**	offend people?

Common mistakes

Does ~~how do I pronounce~~ *how I pronounce* my 'r' really make any difference?

Why is what she ~~do~~ *does* your business?

2 More on participle clauses do after 3.4

Both active and passive participle clauses, including perfect participles, can also be negative.		
Active clause	**Not** living near a university,	Jack wasn't able to go to university.
	Not having driven in years,	I didn't feel comfortable starting again.
	After **not** being able to pay her bills,	Amy had to find a job.
Passive clause	**Not** respected by his boss,	Edward decided to leave.
	Not having been seen in a while,	Marie suddenly showed up.

'Dangling' participles, common in informal conversation where the subject is understood, may sound very natural. However, they are ungrammatical.		
Conversational, but ungrammatical	Not being outgoing,	it's hard to meet new people.
Written		**I** find it hard to meet new people.
For clarity, the closer the participle clause is to the subject, the clearer the sentence. For this reason, participle clauses often go at the beginning, and not the end, of a sentence: **Having loved** the violin as a child, **I** decided to study music and go to a conservatory.		

1A Rephrase the questions without the word *it*.

1 Does it really matter what you study at university?
Does what you study at university really matter?
2 Why should it be important how much you practise in public speaking?
3 When is it relevant whether you cram for a test?
4 How does it make you lose weight what you have for breakfast?
5 Why is it my parents' business what I do at weekends?

1B Correct one mistake in each question.

1 Do whether I can become bilingual really important?
2 How does what school do I choose affect my career?
3 Why does whether women has children keep them from finding jobs?
4 Does whether do I feel confident as a public speaker improve my performance?
5 How does what our teacher tell us about grammar help us speak more accurately?
6 Does how much TV we watch in English improves our vocabulary?

1C Make it personal Choose three questions from A and B to ask a partner.

Does what you study at university really matter?

I don't think it matters too much. Often you end up working in another area anyway.

2A Rewrite the paragraph, making the underlined participle clauses negative when the meaning requires it. Leave participle clauses that make sense as is.

My husband and I are both bilingual in Spanish and English, so naturally we wanted our children to be, too. [1]Having been raised bilingual ourselves, we weren't sure where to begin. So [2]knowing how to go about it and [3]having been given useful advice by anyone, we looked for books in the library. We decided we would both speak both languages. [4]After giving that a try, though, we didn't think it was working. [5]Knowing which language to speak, my children were confused, so we decided I would always speak English, and my husband Spanish. [6]Having tried that now for several weeks, we're all a lot happier.

2B Correct the dangling participles, changing any necessary words so each sentence has a clear subject.

1 Not being confident about my accent, it could seem to people that I'm shy.
Not being confident about my accent, I could seem shy to people.
2 Not having been elected president, Tom's attitude wasn't very good.
3 After dropping out of university last year, it was hard for me to find a job.
4 Not enjoying practising at all, my violin just sat in a cupboard.
5 Not feeling loved by his girlfriend, Greg's weekends were kind of depressing.

2C Make it personal Share something you didn't do or that didn't happen, and the result, with a partner. Begin with a negative participle clause.

Not having started my assignment until a day before it was due, I missed the deadline.

So what happened?

Bonus! Language in song

♫ And promise you kid that I'll give so much more than I get. I just haven't met you yet.

Rewrite the song lyric beginning with the participle clause, *Having not even met you yet …* Make any other changes needed.

1 More on emphatic inversion do after 4.2

When there is a subject and a verb in both clauses, adverbs and adverbial expressions sometimes invert them in the first clause and sometimes in the second. There is no rule. The expressions must be memorised.

First clause	**No sooner had I walked** in the door	than the police rang the bell.
Second clause	**Not until** I saw the strange objects	**did I believe** the news.

Other **first clause** adverbials are: *hardly (ever), never, seldom, rarely, only then, not only, scarcely, only later, nowhere, little, only in this way, in no way, on no account*

Other **second clause** adverbials are: *not since, only after, only when, only by + -ing*

Emphatic inversion and register

Emphatic inversion is used in conversation for dramatic effect:
Never in my life **had I met** anyone like him!

However, it is especially common in writing:
On no account can we claim that these events are real. (written, formal)
There's no way we can claim (that) these events are real. (conversational, neutral / informal)

Common mistake

Not since I was at ~~university, have~~ *university have* I had so little money.
Do not put a comma between the clauses when you use emphatic inversion.

2 More on formal relative clauses do after 4.4

Formal relative clauses often begin with prepositions. When the sentences are rephrased informally, the preposition goes at the end.

Formal	Jane met someone **with whom** she had a lot in common.
	It's an interesting dilemma **to which** I imagine there are no answers.
	That's the researcher **in whose office** we had the meeting.
Informal	Jane met someone (**who**) she had a lot in common **with**.
	It's an interesting dilemma (**that**) I imagine there are no answers **to**.
	That's the researcher **whose office** we had the meeting **in**.

However, sometimes formal relative clauses begin with indefinite pronouns or nouns.

Indefinite pronoun	The researchers, **some of whom** had different ideas, had trouble reaching a consensus.
	I looked at a lot of tests, **a few of which** seemed quite valid.
Noun	The test identifies **the frequency with which** we experience these emotions.
	We had a meeting this morning **the outcome of which** is still unclear.

These relative clauses have no informal equivalent, and the only way to express the same ideas more informally is to rephrase them:
The researchers had trouble reaching a consensus **since** / **because** some of them had different ideas.
The test identifies **how frequently** we experience these emotions.

Common mistakes

We've finished analysing the study, ~~which results~~ *the results of which* were very surprising.

The students, most of ~~them~~ *whom* are under 30, are very open to new experiences.

1A Rephrase the sentences so they're more emphatic, beginning with the words in brackets.

1 I haven't had a dream like this since I was a child. (not since)
2 I didn't realise the incident was serious until I saw it on TV. (only when)
3 I only came to understand the events later. (only later)
4 I absolutely didn't imagine our proposal would be accepted. (in no way)
5 Everyone started laughing, so we realised that Ron had made an April Fools' joke. (only after)
6 We almost never consider the consequences of our actions. (seldom)

1B In pairs, check the inverted subjects and verbs. Write 1 when the adverbial requires inversion in the first clause, and 2 for the second clause.

1C Rewrite the paragraph so it's more formal, using the adverbials in brackets.

I just couldn't have imagined some of the truly mean April Fools' jokes I've seen [1](never), but the perpetrators hardly ever suffered any consequences [2](rarely). Take the case of the friendly and genial office colleague at my former job. As soon as his colleagues had arrived at work, he would invite them to come to his cubicle for a piece of gum [3](no sooner ... than). Of course, they never suspected they might be chewing, and maybe even swallowing, something else [4](in no way)! But right when they put it in their mouths, we would hear a piercing scream [5](only when)! They almost never knew why it tasted so bad [6](seldom). You see, the gum was actually Play-Doh, a sticky substance used by children for art projects. My colleagues never found out that it began as a wallpaper cleaner in the 1930s [7] (hardly ever)!

1D Make it personal Using at least three adverbials, share a story about a prank or joke you've experienced.

Nowhere had I heard about the joke that my friend Hilary played on me!

2A Correct the sentences so that each one has a formal relative clause with *whom*, *which*, or *whose*.

1 There are many amateur personality tests, some of them aren't very rigorous.
2 That's the convention centre in it we stayed for the conference.
3 I studied the five domains into them our personalities can be classified.
4 Reliability is a trait which importance many people underestimate.
5 The scientist I work with him has just published an article.
6 The flatmates, I lived with them as a first-year student, were easy to get to know.
7 The woman I lived in her flat just got elected to public office.
8 Which speed the train was travelling when it crashed was very high.

2B Make it personal Make three formal statements about your class or classmates. Your partner will say which he or she agrees with.

Most of the people with whom we're studying English seem very motivated.

I totally agree. If you get to this level, you have to be!

Bonus! Language in song

♫ Never in my wildest dreams, did I think someone could care about me.

Which word or phrase in the song can be replaced by the word *little* without changing the meaning?

1 More on formal conjunctions and prepositions do after 5.2

Most conjunctions and prepositions are neutral in register because often the content of the full sentence determines the level of formality. However, some distinctions can be made.

To express purpose:		
Formal	**With a view to** **With the aim of** **In the interest of**	reducing costs, the post office has eliminated Saturday delivery.
Neutral	**(In order) to**	reduce costs, the post office has stopped delivering post on Saturday.
Other formal ways to express purpose: *so as to, in an effort to*		

To express reason:		
Formal	**In light of** **On account of** **Owing to**	increasing life expectancy / the fact that life expectancy is increasing, people need to save more money.
Neutral	**Because of** **As a result of**	
Other formal ways to express reason: *given, in view of, thanks to*		

To refer to something:		
Formal	**With regard to** **Regarding**	our communication of last week, we are still expecting a response.
Neutral	**As far as**	prices go, they couldn't possibly be higher.
	When it comes to	prices, they couldn't possibly be higher.
In formal speech and writing, shorter noun phrases, as opposed to longer clauses, are often used: In view of exorbitant prices, we need to take emergency measures. (formal) Because prices are through the roof, we need to act now! (informal)		

Common mistake

In light of / On account of / Owing to ^ *the fact (that)* you didn't pay your rent on time, we're going to have to evict you.

You may also say, 'In light of / On account of / Owing **to not having paid** your rent on time, you're going to have to move.' Remember: If you use a participle clause, it must have a subject!

2 More on objects + *-ing* forms after prepositions and verbs do after 5.4

When changing a noun to a possessive form in a more formal sentence, make certain the apostrophe is in the correct position.

Neutral to formal	They accepted	**our team's**	submitting a project.
	I read about	**the protester's**	disrupting the event.
	We're supportive of	**the employees'**	taking a longer holidays.
Informal	They accepted	**our team**	submitting a project.
	I read about	**the protester**	disrupting the event.
	We're supportive of	**the employees**	taking longer holidays.

Sense verbs are not followed by possessive forms:
I saw **the man** climbing in the window.
The cat is in our bed! I felt **it** tickling me.

1A Rephrase the sentences so they're more formal, using the words in brackets. Make any other changes necessary.

1 Because we need better security, we will be installing alarms throughout the building. (in the interest of)
2 Since you failed the final exam twice, I'm afraid you're going to have to repeat this course. (in light of)
3 In order to attract more customers, we're going to start doing more promotion. (with the aim of)
4 As far as the complaint you made recently about cockroaches, we'll send the exterminator this weekend. (with regard to)
5 Because we've had so many problems, we may have to postpone our holiday. (on account of)
6 As a result of having had very low sales, we can't offer rises this year. (owing to)
7 When it comes to the interpretation of dreams, I have some good books to recommend. (regarding)

1B Make it personal Rephrase the sentences so they are *less* formal. Then choose one topic to discuss with a partner. Any major disagreements?

1 Owing to the many world problems that face us, I don't think I'm going to have children.
2 In the interest of getting a good job, I'm going to delete my Facebook page so a potential employer can't see it.
3 Regarding understanding politics, I'm really not the slightest bit interested.
4 In light of the fact that we live a long life, I think it's silly to watch your diet too much.
5 So as to start over from scratch, I'm going to change schools.

For the last one, you can say, 'To start over from scratch, I'm going to change schools'. That could be a very good idea.

I'm not sure I agree. Even if things aren't going well, it's good to give things a chance.

2A Complete the sentences with an object and *-ing* form of the verb, adding any words needed. Then rephrase the sentences informally.

1 Jim witnessed *his daughter's getting arrested*. (daughter / get arrested) And now he's very upset with her.
Jim witnessed his daughter getting arrested.
2 All parents have an investment in ______________. (child / succeed) That's why they spend so much money.
3 I'm not happy about ______________ so often. (husband / travel) He's never around!
4 We're worried about both new ______________ so nervous. (managers / become) Maybe we're about to be fired!
5 The other team has an interest in ______________ the award. (our school / win) If we win, they won't have as much competition next year.
6 George resented ______________ with his old girlfriend. (Phil / go out) He was hoping to get back together with her.
7 Marcy was aware of ______________ about her behind her back. (classmates / talk) They would start whispering as soon as they saw her.

2C Make it personal Complete the sentences with the *-ing* form of a verb so they are true for you. Then share two with a partner.

1 I don't mind my teacher ...
2 I really appreciate my mother ...
3 I'm definitely going to insist on my children ...
4 I'm interested in our school ...
5 I'm uncomfortable with my neighbourhood ...
6 I'm grateful for my country ...

I'm grateful for my country('s) taking pollution seriously.

Bonus! Language in song

♫ All is quiet on New Year's Day. A world in white gets underway.

Create a new song lyric beginning with *In view of*, *thanks to*, or *given*. Do you like the way it sounds? Why (not)?

1 More adverb clauses of condition do after 6.2

Adverb clauses of condition also can be expressed more formally.		
As long as ...	**Assuming** (that) the film has subtitles,	viewers who don't speak the language can still enjoy it.
	Provided (that) your novel is accepted,	you'll be on your way to beginning a career as a writer.
	On the condition (that) the concepts are explained,	all students can understand and enjoy art.
(Even) if ...	**Supposing** (that) 50 per cent have a talent for music,	it's still true that the other 50 per cent don't.
Even though ...	**Despite the fact that** many young people don't like to read,	schools should still promote a love of literature.
	Irrespective of the fact that we have few museums,	our mayor realises the importance of art.
	Notwithstanding the fact that books are expensive,	public libraries are free.

Common mistakes

Supposing ~~the fact~~ (that) your class hates to read, they may still like comics.

Despite ^*the fact* that many cinemas have disappeared, some still remain.

2 More on emphasis do after 6.4

To emphasise a noun, you may begin the sentence with a *what*-clause.	
What a great **book**	it was.
What bad **English**	that actor spoke.
What bad **reviews**	the play got.
And to emphasise an adjective, you may begin with a *how*-clause.	
How bad the information was	that they gave us.
How right we were	about Jamie's novel.

Unlike auxiliaries to express emotion or emphasis (see p. 67), *what* and *how* clauses may begin a conversation. Compare:
A: *What a boring film that was!* I'm sorry we came to see it.
B: Yes, it *did seem* kind of slow, didn't it?

Common mistakes

What ~~a great~~ *great* art this museum has.

How enjoyable ~~was the play we saw!~~ *the play we saw was!*

1A Complete the paragraph to create formal adverb clauses of condition that mean the same as the words in brackets. Do not use the same words twice.

[1]________ (even though) increasing numbers of people move from country to country as they seek employment, newspapers and publishers have not kept up with the need to truly internationalise their offerings. [2]________ (as long as) they speak the local language, English speakers living abroad may wish to read books in their original version, but at least one prominent e-reader based in the United States has been known to offer only an English translation for certain titles! [3]________ (as long as) there is a potential e-reader audience for the original text, publishers should be obliged to provide it. [4]________ (even if) some people wish to read translations, it is still true that others don't, just as not everyone wishes to see dubbed films. [5]________ (as long as) publishers can break even on production costs, they need to remember that we live in a globalised age. [6]________ (even though) they undoubtedly have a large audience for the translation, they would do well to increase their marketing efforts to reach readers who can enjoy their texts in the languages in which they were originally written.

1B **Make it personal** Complete the sentences with true opinions. Use formal adverb clauses of condition. Then try to convince a partner.

1 ________________, all pupils should be promoted to the next year.
2 ________________, cinemas should remain open.
3 ________________, at least 50% of people my age don't enjoy doing crossword puzzles.
4 ________________, many people still never go to museums.
5 ________________, I could imagine reading a book a week.

2A Rewrite the first sentences in 1–6 for emphasis, beginning with the words in brackets.

1 That was a really great play! (what) I hadn't heard of the actors before.
2 The writer was awful in the way he expressed himself! (how) I'm not reading anything else by him.
3 There were scary actors that came on stage in the second act! (how) I didn't expect that.
4 She did a really bad job! (what) I'm hiring a different photographer next time.
5 You have an active imagination! (what) A film like that could never happen in real life.
6 The paintings in this exhibition were intriguing! (how) I loved the artist.

2B Complete the conversations. Use auxiliaries to express emotion or emphasis.

1 A: What a boring film that was. It didn't even have a plot.
B: But *it did have a plot*! I agree it was a bit slow, though.
2 A: How incompetent that actor was in how he delivered his lines. He couldn't even remember them.
B: But ________________. I read the play and they were correct.
3 A: What bad news I got today from the museum director. I can't even tell you.
B: But ________________. I'm always here to listen.
4 A: How stimulating our class was today. I love Shakespeare.
B: Are you sure? I thought you hated him.
A: But ________________. I just didn't know enough English to understand him.

2C **Make it personal** Using the models in B and C, make three true sentences with *what* or *how* clauses. Then share them with a partner.

What a boring class we had last week on English literature! I didn't learn anything.

But you did learn something! You told me yourself you'd never heard of George Eliot previously.

Bonus! Language in song

♪ Near, far, wherever you are, I believe that the heart does go on.

Identify the auxiliary used for emphasis in this song lyric. What is being emphasised?

1 Summary of future tenses do after 7.2

The future perfect emphasises the completion of an action and is often used with *by the time*. The future perfect continuous always implies the action is ongoing.
By the time I retire, I **will have had** at least three careers.
Unlike my parents, when I'm 90, I **will have been using** Facebook my whole life.

Going to and *will* are both used to make predictions. Use *going to* when you're more certain about your prediction or have present evidence. Always use a perfect tense with *for* and *since*.
A few years from now, our government **is going to run out** of money.
By 2050, people **will** still **be working** when they're 80.
By the time I'm 80, I **will have lived** here *for* 50 years because I have no intention of ever moving.
In the future, people **will have been working from home** *since* their very first job.

Common mistake

By the end of the century, 90-year-olds ~~will use / will be using~~ *will have used / will have been using* social media for many years.

2 More formal uses do after 7.2

The future perfect or future perfect continuous is sometimes used to speculate about past events and is usually more formal than the present perfect or present perfect continuous.	
Neutral	No doubt you**'ve seen** that film already and **have been telling** everyone else to do the same.
More formal	No doubt you **will have been** impressed by the performance and **will have been listening** to the orchestra's recordings.

When predicting the future, you may omit the word *going* for a more formal sentence. A contracted sentence is not as formal.	
Neutral	If we**'re going to be** happy in our old age, we need to focus on our relationships. (active) If we think we**'re going to be rewarded** for living to 100, think again! (passive)
More formal	If I**'m** ever **to get my degree**, I'd better start studying. (active) If we **are to live** longer, we need to change our eating habits. (active) Benefits **are to be paid** beginning at 65. (passive)

3 Cleft vs pseudo-cleft sentences do after 7.4

English has many ways to move information to the front of a sentence for emphasis. Sentences beginning with words like *what*, *when*, and *where* are called 'pseudo-cleft' sentences.		
Cleft sentences	**It's** younger people	**who** / **that** have a few things to learn. (subject)
	It's the unimaginable	(**that**) no one can predict. (object)
Pseudo-cleft sentences	**When** I'm really tired	is at the weekends.
	What I thought I once wanted	has all changed now.

1A Circle the correct forms.

Since I come from a family with lots of longevity, I [1]['ll live / 'm going to live] to be 100.When I [2][will start / start] my second century, I hope I [3][will still be able / will have still been able] to ride a bike. By that point, I [4][will have earned / will have been earning] the distinction of having been an avid cyclist for over 90 years, and I [5][will have been participating / will have participated] in at least 2,000 bike races! I [6][won't be racing / won't have been racing] any longer in my second century, and I [7][won't have been giving / won't have been given] any medals, but I [8][will have been passing / will have passed] the longevity test. I hope my friends [9][will have been exercising / will be exercising] for as many years as I have because I definitely don't want to do this alone!

1B Make it personal Rewrite the paragraph in A beginning with sentence 2, changing 'century' to 'decade'. In pairs, share your hopes for the next ten years.

When I start my next decade, I hope I ...

2A Rewrite the sentences to make them more formal.

1 No doubt your daughter has discovered a solution to peer pressure by now.
2 If we're going to be comfortable economically, we need to save money.
3 I'm sure older people have considered all the options before choosing a nursing home.
4 The government has planned for the fact that pensions are going to be cut back even further by the 2030s.
5 No doubt our planet has been suffering for generations, and we're just paying attention now.

2B Make it personal Choose three sentences from A and make them true. In groups, share opinions.

No doubt my friend [name] ...

3 Change the underlined parts of the responses to cleft or pseudo-cleft sentences. Begin with the word in brackets.

1 A: I just can't believe Bob didn't throw out the rubbish.
B: The small things always get to you. (it)
2 A: We're not ready to work until we're 75.
B: That's not a problem. We're not ready for global warming. (it)
3 A: Are you planning to do a Master's degree?
B: I'd love to, but I have no idea where I'll get the money. (where)
4 A: Do you ever think about the future?
B: Sometimes, but I really can't tell you what I'll be doing in ten years. (what)

Bonus! Language in song

♫ Wherever you go, whatever you do, I will be right here waiting for you.

Rewrite the song lyric ending with the words *for 50 years*. What tense did you use?

Unit 8

Grammar expansion

1 More on using the subjunctive do after 8.2

In formal speech, the subjunctive can be used with these verbs and expressions.	
Verbs	advise, ask, command, demand, desire, insist, prefer, propose, would rather, recommend, request, suggest, urge
Expressions with *it* ... *(that)*	It is best, critical, crucial, desirable, essential, imperative, important, preferable, recommended, urgent, vital, a good idea, a bad idea

The subjunctive can also be used in negative, passive, and continuous sentences. Remember that the subjunctive verb is not conjugated and remains in the base form.		
Negative	I suggest	(that) he **not speak** to me in that tone!
Passive	It's critical	(that) he **be fired** immediately.
Continuous	I absolutely insist	(that) you **be waiting** for me when I arrive.

Nevertheless, the subjunctive is limited in English. Do not use it to express the following.		
The future	I'm not leaving	until the manager sees me.
want, would like	I want	you **to refund** my money!
	I'd like (for)	
Emotion	I'm really happy	I **can exchange** this product.
	Sally was angry	the manager **didn't speak** to her yesterday.

In neutral or informal speech, the subjunctive is often avoided.		
Expressions with *it*	It's important	**for** shops **to respect** their customers.
	It's essential	she **expresses** her frustration.
Some verbs	I'd prefer	**for** your staff **to be** a bit more polite.
	I recommended	he **should see** the manager.
would rather	I'd rather	you **gave** me the money today!

Common mistakes

I'd like ~~that your manager~~ *(for) your manager to* speak to me now!

I want ~~that she~~ *her to* pay attention.

2 More on adverb clauses with *-ever* words to emphasise conditions do after 8.4

Nouns, adjectives, and adverbs may follow *however*. Be careful with count and non-count nouns.			
Non-count noun	**However**	**much** (money) you spent,	I won't be responsible.
Count noun		**many** times you try to persuade me,	we can't give you a refund.
Adjective		**calm** he may seem,	he's furious inside.
Adverb		**long** you might wait,	we can't see you today.
All of the *-ever* words may express conditions in the past, as well as the present or future. The meaning is sometimes clearest with *may* or *might*.			
Past continuous	**Whichever**	one you**'ve chosen** / **may have chosen**,	the purchase is non-refundable.
	Whatever	excuse he**'s given** / **might have given**,	I'm not really interested.

1A Correct the mistakes.

1 On top of that, when I wanted that the waiter apologise, he refused.
2 I suggest your staff to treat me appropriately!
3 I insisted the clerk didn't do that again.
4 The customer took offence when I requested for him to show me the receipt.
5 I demanded my sister gets a refund.
6 I suggest you no use that tone of voice with me ever again!
7 My boss insisted the customer was removed from the shop.
8 We were pleased the waiter be understanding when he talked to us.
9 I'll hold on until the owner agree to talk to me.
10 I'd like that this product be replaced right away.

1B Create sentences using the prompts. Which opinions can be expressed using more than one structure?

1 [important / an airline / go / extra mile / customers]
It's important (that) an airline go the extra mile for customers.
It's important for an airline to go the extra mile for customers.
2 [I / want / electric company / improve / where I live]
3 [I / rather / shops / not charge / so much / for high-quality merchandise]
4 [add / insult / injury / our government / would like / us / pay / higher / taxes]
5 [everyone / need / take / stand / and demand / restaurant service / improve]
6 [We / demanded / mobile phone service / improve / never / did]

1C **Make it personal** Make three sentences in **B** true for you. In pairs, share your opinions.

> Queues at [name of airport] are longer than ever. It's imperative airlines take a stand against inefficiency!

2A Respond to these situations. Begin with an adverb clause, using the words in brackets.

1 A man calls a shop ten times demanding to speak to the manager.
Manager to receptionist: ____________ (however, times)
2 A woman only wants to buy products she can return, but the shop has a 'no-returns' policy.
Shop assistant to woman: ____________ (whichever, one)
3 A young man is worried about buying a bed for his overweight father. She reassures him.
Shop assistant to man: ____________ (however, weigh)
4 A polite car salesperson tries to sell a young woman an overpriced car. In the end, she decides against it.
Woman to salesperson: ____________ (however, helpful)

2B **Make it personal** In pairs, exchange opinions on shops or restaurants near you. Use adverb clauses containing *-ever* words.

> Do you ever go to [name of restaurant]? Service there is really good.

> Yeah, well, however polite the waiters may be, the food leaves a lot to be desired.

Bonus! Language in song

♫ It's a bittersweet symphony, this life. Try to make ends meet. You're a slave to the money, then you die.

Which two expressions can be used to combine the last two sentences: *(as) much as*, *however*, or *for all the*? Create two new possible song lyrics.

Unit 9

Grammar expansion

1 More on passive expressions in sentences with infinitives

do after 9.2

More on passive expressions in sentences with infinitives					
Acupuncture The treatment It	**is**	reported	to	be	effective. I think I'll try it.
	was			have been	helpful in the past and still is.
	has been	shown		help	patients, including me.
	still hasn't been			have helped	people as much as some people claim.
	might be	thought		be	helpful, but I'm not so sure.
	may have been			have been	out of the mainstream, but it no longer is.

1 If you are unsure what a sentence means, try changing it to an active one.
Acupuncture **has been reported** to help patients, including me. (passive)
People **have reported** that acupuncture helps patients. (active)

2 Choose the tense based on the part of the sentence you wish to emphasise. Without additional context, the meaning may be clearer with only one verb in the past. Compare:

a Acupuncture **was reported** to help patients. (The reporting is in the past. Nothing is said about whether patients are still being helped.)

b Acupuncture is reported to **have helped** patients. (Patients have been helped in the past up to and including the present. Nothing is said about exactly when the reporting took place.)

Common mistakes

Acupuncture was known to ~~had~~ *have* helped people many years ago.

It was reported to ^ *have* cured many diseases.

2 More on verb patterns

do after 9.4

All verb patterns form questions in familiar ways. Only the first verb changes in the formation of the question.		
Does your coach	**make** you	**practise** a lot?
What will	**encourage** people	**to lose** weight?
Should teachers	**force** students	**to do** homework?
Has your brother	**appreciated** you	**teaching** him karate?

Passive questions are also very common.		
Have you	**been discouraged**	**from going** on a diet?
Will we	**be encouraged**	**to exercise** more?
Should students	**be forced**	**to take** so many exams?
Were you	**made**	**to wear** those ugly shoes as a child, too?

Common mistakes

Have you been discouraged ~~to try~~ *from trying* hypnotherapy?

Did your teacher make you ~~stayed / to stay~~ *stay* late?

1A Choose the correct meaning below for sentences 1–8.

1 Feng Shui was reported long ago to have existed before the invention of the compass.
2 It has been known to be effective for thousands of years.
3 The 1901 Boxer Rebellion in China was believed to have been caused by Westerners violating principles of Feng Shui during the construction of railways.
4 Feng Shui may have been thought to be a factor, but today the rebellion is known to have had broader causes.
5 Feng Shui may be seen to be an Asian custom, but Westerners practise it, too.
6 It still hasn't been shown to help people definitively, but it continues to be very popular.
7 Many other kinds of alternative medicine have been thought to have developed a long time ago, too.
8 They've been reported to have been tried in many countries.

1 Historians [**now report / reported earlier**] that Feng Shui was invented before the compass.
2 People [**once knew / still know**] that it is effective.
3 People [**originally believed / believe now**] that Feng Shui caused the Boxer Rebellion.
4 Historians [**no longer think / still think**] Feng Shui caused the rebellion.
5 People [**used to think / still think**] Feng Shui is an Asian custom.
6 Proponents [**once showed / are still trying to show**] that Feng Shui definitely helps people.
7 Historians [**used to think / may still think**] other kinds of alternative medicine are old, too.
8 Doctors [**report / used to report**] they've been tried in many countries.

2A Complete questions 1–5 using the verb patterns on p. 154 and forms of the words in brackets.

1 A: ______________ them recently? (anyone / really / appreciate / you / help)
B: Yes, my sister has. I helped her move just last week.
2 A: ______________ alternative medicine? (people / encourage – passive / try)
B: I think they should. It's been known to help many!
3 A: ______________ anything you didn't want to as a child? (you / ever / make – passive / do)
B: Yes, I was! My mum made me tidy my room every Saturday.
4 A: ______________ something new? (you / ever / discourage – passive / try)
B: Yes, unfortunately. I really wanted to be homeschooled, but my parents were opposed to the idea.
5 A: ______________ their wallet to a thief? (anyone you know / ever / force – passive / hand over)
B: Yes, my mum was mugged just a few weeks ago.

2B Make it personal Choose two questions from **A** to ask a partner. Answer with true information.

... something new?

Yes, I wanted to try rock climbing, but everyone said it was dangerous.

Bonus! Language in song

♫ Something in the way you move makes me feel like I can't live without you. It takes me all the way. I want you to stay.

Change the first sentence to a question so you are asking someone about yourself. Be sure to change all the pronouns, too.

1 More comparative patterns do after 10.2

More comparative patterns					
My friends are	half twice three times	as	**important**	**as**	my family (is).
My parents aren't			**sympathetic**		my friends (are).
I have			many **friends**		Bob (does)
They pay me			much **attention**		Ann (does).
I have	four times	more	**money**	**than**	my sister (does).
We have	**slightly / far**	fewer	**friends**		we used to (have).
I'm under	**much / far / a lot**	less	**pressure**		my friends (are).

Common mistakes

She criticises me half / twice ~~more than~~ *as much as* my mother.

He has ~~less~~ *fewer* friends than anyone else.

You may say *three times more*, but not *twice more*. *Less* is ungrammatical before a countable noun, even if you may, at times, hear native speakers say it in informal speech.

2 Summary of conditional sentences do after 10.4

Inverted conditional sentences are often distinguished from other types of conditional sentences only by register. The sentences below show a sequence from least to most formal.

Present or future meaning	**If you change**	your mind,	everyone **will be** happy.
	If you changed **If you were to change** **Were you to change** **Should you change**		we **would/could give** you a discount.
Past meaning	**If I had left** **Had I left** **Were I to have left**	a message,	I'm sure he **would/could have** come.

Present inversions with *had* and past inversions with *should* are restricted to highly formal or poetic usage:
Had he more money (present), I would marry him.
Should you have had second thoughts (past), I wouldn't have proceeded with the plan.

'I decided that if I could paint that flower in a huge scale, you could not ignore its beauty.'
Georgia O'Keeffe (1887–1986)

1A Write sentences with comparative patterns in blue from p. 156 and the information given. There may be more than one answer.

1 My class: 30 pupils – the other classes: 10 pupils
My class has three times as many pupils as the other classes (do).
My class has three times more pupils than the other classes (do).
2 Secondary school grades: important – university grades: double the importance
3 My friends: very understanding – my parents: not very understanding
4 Our cities ten years ago: high unemployment – now: double the unemployment
5 Me: three good friends; my best friend – 15 good friends
6 Your English: very fluent; my English – not as fluent

1B Correct five mistakes in comparative patterns.

A: People have far less friends and less support than they used to because everyone moves around so much.
B: But the good thing about the US is you can make new friends just by joining informal clubs.
A: Yes, but that's hard to do. I had twice more friends before I moved from London to Newcastle. And on top of that, now I have to drive such long distances everywhere.
B: It's true. I drive less miles when I want to see friends. But I have half of many as you! I don't know how you do it. Even though you just moved a year ago, you still have twice as much friends as I do!

1C **Make it personal** Choose two sentences from A. In pairs, share true information.

Our class has slightly fewer pupils than the other classes.

Do you really think so? It seems big to me!

2A Express present or future suggestions or requests informally or formally, according to the cues. Then underline the language in each sentence that shows the register.

1 Mother to child: [tidy room / take out for ice-cream]
2 Shop assistant to elderly customer: [need help / ask]
3 Employee to boss: [try new approach / double sales]
4 Teenager to younger sister: [not stop that this instant / get really cross]
5 Passenger to flight attendant: [have peanuts left over / give me some?]
6 Police officer to driver: [continue to argue / arrest you]

2B **Make it personal** In pairs, review your sentences in A. Do you agree the register is appropriate?

OK, number 6: Should you continue to argue, I'll arrest you.

Police officers are never that formal and polite! I have, 'If you continue to argue, I'll arrest you ...'

Maybe you're right. But it's good for them to be polite in my opinion!

2C Change your sentences in A to the past. Which now express a criticism instead of a suggestion or request?

Bonus! Language in song

♫ Where did I go wrong? I lost a friend, Somewhere along in the bitterness. And I would have stayed up with you all night, had I known how to save a life.

Rewrite the inverted conditional sentence using an *if*-conditional clause. Does it refer to present, past, or future time?

1 More on using modals do after 11.2

Modal verbs are very common and fulfill many functions. Below is a summary of common uses. Those with a star haven't been presented earlier in *Identities*.

Possibility	Jim **may** / **might** / **could have gone** home early.
Probability	Laura isn't here yet, so she **must be working** late tonight.
Certainty	Laura **can't / couldn't have taken** that train. I saw her on the earlier one.
Obligation	You really **must phone** your mother! It's been more than a month!
Advice / Criticism	You **shouldn't have let** so much time go by without talking to her.
Expectation	Fix your flat tyre? That **shouldn't be** too hard to do.
Ability	I **could speak** French when I was young, but I **can't speak** it any longer.
Implied *if*-clause	You just found out the airport is closed? I **could have told** you that! (if you'd asked me)
Request	**Could** / **Can** you **open** the window? It's boiling in here.
*Request / command with annoyance or anger	**Can't** you **sit** still for even a second! **Won't** you just **be** quiet and listen! You can ask questions later. **Would** you **watch** where you're going! You almost ran me over!
Future decision	I'**ll pick** you **up** after school. Phone me when your class ends.
Refusal	I **won't give** you any more money, no matter how many times you ask.
*Rhetorical question	**Must** I **listen** to that music blaring? I'm trying to concentrate! **Couldn't** you **have** at least **tried** not to spill your coffee? What a mess!
Habitual past action	I used to love to swim, and I **would go swimming** every afternoon.
Permission	Rows 15–30 **may** / **can** (less formal) now **begin** boarding.
Suggestion	You **might try** doing yoga to help you relax.
Invitation	**Would** you **like** to come to dinner on Saturday? We'd love to have you. We're thinking of going to the beach on Sunday. **Will** you **join** us?

2 Articles and subject-verb agreement do after 11.4

Use of the definite article and whether the verb that follows is singular or plural may differ in some cases from your language. Here are some tips to help you.

Countries: Memorise which countries have articles. All take a singular verb, even if they end in *s*.	The United States has 50 states. The Philippines is a country with numerous islands. Indonesia consists of many islands, too. Peru is famous for Machu Picchu.
Collective nouns such as organisations, companies, and shops take a plural verb in British English, and may or may not have an article. In American English, only collective nouns which refer to a category are plural; others take a singular verb.	The government's staff are based in London. Richmond have published *Identities*. Debenhams sometimes offer discounts. The young take too many risks. The couple are going to Ibiza on holiday.
Shared knowledge: Use *the* when you refer to something a second time or the listener knows what you're referring to.	Where are the children? I don't see them anywhere. I didn't eat the dessert. It didn't look very appetising.
Fractions may take a singular or plural verb. Expressions involving **time**, **money**, or **distance** generally require a singular verb.	According to a recent survey, two thirds of adults haven't got satisfying jobs, but one third of adults does. Thirty miles is a very long way to travel to school! Five pounds is a lot to pay for a fizzy drink!

'Before you marry a person, you should first make them use a computer with slow Internet to see who they really are.'
Will Ferrell (1967–present)

1A Rephrase the underlined sentences with modal verbs. There may be more than one answer.

1 A: Did you hear there was a motorbike accident this afternoon? I hope it wasn't Ethan.
B: I'm positive it wasn't. He's always so careful.
It can't have been.

2 A: Stop pointing that umbrella at me! Do you want me to lose an eye?
B: You needn't be so nasty about it.

3 A: I expect that Tom is here by now. His plane was due in at 4.00.
B: Yes, I was just thinking the same thing.

4 A: Aren't you able to talk more quietly? I'm trying to sleep.
B: Oh, sorry. I didn't realise we were talking loudly.

5 A: Excuse me, is it OK if I turn on my tablet?
B: Yes. Passengers are now allowed to use portable devices.

6 A: I still haven't run five kilometres in under 30 minutes.
B: Maybe a good idea is to run more at weekends.

7 A: I'm having Chloe and Alex over for dinner on Sunday. I'd like you to come, too.
B: Oh, I'd love to. Just let me know what to bring.

1B Make it personal Role-play the conversations with a partner. Use modal verbs in the cue sentences.

1 A: (Make a request)
B: Sure! That shouldn't be too hard to do.

2 A: (Express a possibility)
B: I could have told you that! I knew all along.

3 A: (Ask a rhetorical question)
B: You needn't be so sarcastic. How would I know it was bothering you?

4 A: (Ask permission)
B: Certainly! Go ahead.

5 A: (Make an angry command)
B: But we're not! I swear we aren't!
A: I saw you doing it. Stop it immediately!

6 A: (Make a suggestion)
B: That's a good idea. I think I'll try it.

2A Correct the mistakes.

1 Steak are a good source of iron.
2 The old is travelling much more now than in the past.
3 They say 25 per cent of the young people is unemployed, but everyone I know have a job.
4 The bicycles are usually safe, and bike I have has extra safety features.
5 Japan is the country that have to worry about earthquakes.
6 Ten pounds an hour aren't very much to earn in my opinion!
7 Half of all teenagers has nothing to do after the school.
8 The fruit are important for a balanced diet, but the fruit sold here are never fresh.

2B Make it personal Choose three sentences and start a conversation with a partner. Change them as needed so they are true.

Fish is a good source of protein, but the frozen fish sold here is tasteless.

That's a shame. You might want to try cooking fresh fish. It's easy!

Bonus! Language in song

♪ Oh, I would do anything for love. I would do anything for love, but I won't do that. No, I won't do that.

Which function is expressed in this song lyric: expectation, a suggestion, refusal, or annoyance? Underline the verb.

1 More on passive forms with gerunds and infinitives do after 12.2

Passive forms with gerunds and infinitives are also common in questions:

Gerunds …	**Infinitives and base forms …**
1 After certain verbs: **Did** you **like being videoed** by a total stranger?	4 After certain verbs: How **do** you **hope to be remembered**?
2 After prepositions: **Were** you **counting on being** promoted?	5 After adjectives, nouns, and indefinite pronouns: **Is** she the politician most **likely to be elected**?
3 As subjects: Why is **being chosen** important to you?	6 After modals: Why **might** he **be fired**?

After verbs and adjectives, be certain to use the correct prepositions:

Are you **terrified of being caught?**	Was she **worried about being fired?**
How did you **succeed in being considered?**	Why do your children **object to being left on their own?**
Is she very **discouraged at (by) not being chosen?**	Were you **congratulated on being elected**?

When the question is negative, the meaning may change based on the position of the negative:

	Meaning
Weren't you **relieved about being fired**? Our boss was a nightmare anyway.	The person *was* fired.
Were you **relieved about not being fired?** It's so hard to find a job these days.	The person *wasn't* fired.
Weren't you **hoping to be promoted?** I know you've been here a long time.	The person *wasn't* promoted.
Were you **hoping not to be promoted?** You didn't sound happy when they announced it!	The person *was* promoted.

2 More on the *be* and *get* passive do after 12.4

The *be* and *get* passives can both be used when talking about actions or something that has changed. But the two passives are not identical and are not always interchangeable.

The *get* passive shows greater informality, emphasis, and negative intent as explained on p. 133:
Get down from there! You could **get hurt**!

Only the *be* passive can be used with stative verbs, such as *say, tell, like, etc*:
He **was liked** by everyone in the class.
Those criminals **are known**, but the police do nothing about them!

Only the *be* passive is usually used for longer, planned events:
The new museum **was opened** in the summer of 2017.
The bridge **was built** to ease the flow of traffic.

The *get* passive is common with verbs like *killed, injured, wounded, paid, hired, fired, sacked*, and *accepted*, which have a clear beneficial or adverse effect on the subject. Neutral verbs, however, generally use the *be* passive:
Andy **got / was paid** £1,000 for just two hours of work. BUT
Her shoes **were purchased** at the expensive shop along the street.

1A Complete the passive questions using the verbs in brackets.

1 What university would you like ____________ to? (admit)
2 Do you mind ____________ to work late? (ask)
3 Do you object more to ____________ by your teachers or by your parents? (criticise)
4 How do you want ____________ of by people? (think)
5 Are you excited about ____________ for the football team? (choose)
6 Have you succeeded in ____________ for a job you really wanted? (hire)

1B Make it personal Choose two questions to ask a partner. Answer with true information.

What university would you like to be admitted to?

Well, I'd really like to go to ... , but it's very hard to get into, so I might have to fall back on ...

1C Choose the most logical response in italics (a or b) for conversations 1–4.

1 A: I'm waiting for an acceptance letter to the University of Nottingham.
B: a *Are you scared of not getting in?*
b *Aren't you scared of getting in?*
A: No, why would I be?
B: It's just that I've heard it's a hard university.

2 A: I've been working here for four years now.
B: a *Are you worried about not being promoted?*
b *Aren't you worried about being promoted?*
A: Not really. It would just mean more work if I were.

3 A: I ran into Andrea yesterday.
B: a *Oh, was she upset at not being invited to the wedding?*
b *Oh, wasn't she upset at being invited to the wedding?*
A: I think she was OK with it. This way she doesn't have to buy a gift.

4 A: I'm going to the conference tomorrow.
B: a *Didn't you mind being asked to give a presentation?*
b *Did you mind not being asked to give a presentation?*
A: I was relieved! I don't like speaking in front of lots of people.

2A Change the *get* passive to *be* when it is ungrammatical or unnatural. Tick (✔) if it is both correct and natural.

1 My house got broken into last week. They took all my jewellery.
2 I got told that flying cars will have been invented by 2050.
3 I think this shopping centre got opened around ten years ago.
4 The tickets got sold so quickly, we weren't able to buy any.
5 My dad got fired last month, but luckily he's already found a new job.
6 It's got said that global warming is the most serious threat to our planet.

2B In pairs, explain your choices in **A**.

The first one sounds fine with *get*. It shows emphasis, and it's used to talk about an adverse effect.

2C Make it personal Write three questions to ask a classmate about the future. How long can you continue the conversation?

Bonus! Language in song

♫ I want to thank you for giving me the best day of my life. Oh just to be with you is having the best day of my life.

Make the song lyrics negative. In which position does the negative make the most sense?

Selected audio scripts

2.2 *page 17 exercise 2A*

Notice th = /ð/ and th = /θ/ .

J = Julia, L = Luke

J: I've always believed that we attract whatever we think about, good or bad.
L: Mm-hmm.
J: So, when you can visualise your thoughts, you make them more concrete ...
L: In other words, you're saying that a vision board really can help you meet your goals?
J: Exactly.
L: The whole idea seems so far-fetched! You can stare at a picture of a new car till you're blue in the face, but it won't just fall into your lap. It's not enough just to put your mind to something. You've got to do your part and go the extra mile – you know, save money for a long time, if necessary.
J: Yes, of course, you've got to work toward your goals, even if they seem unattainable. But our minds help us do that. If you're clear about what you really want and stay focused, it really makes a difference. I've read lots of books about it.
L: Oh, come on! Surely you don't believe any of this stuff is based on actual research? If we got everything we thought about, we'd have no social problems, no poverty ... These people only want to sell books and get rich!
J: You're such a sceptic! Speaking of books, though. Remember that book I told you about? ...

3.2 *page 28 exercise 1C*

Notice the weak forms in Hugo's first speech.

H = Hugo, T = Teacher, M = María

H: Anyway, when I came back to Mexico, I was practically bilingual. Well, maybe not bilingual. My French – at least my spoken French – was much better than my English. But I've forgotten lots of words, and I'm not as fluent as I used as be.
T: So your French is a bit rusty ...
H: Yeah, that's the word. And I need to catch up on my reading. It's been a while!
M: You're right. Reading for pleasure is the only way to increase your vocabulary.
T: Well, definitely one good way. But do you agree with Hugo? Do you need to live in another country to master the language?
M: Well, I've never set foot in a foreign country. I've learned all the English I know in this school. And I ... I think my English is better than before.
T: Yes, it's improved by leaps and bounds! I mean, you need to be really advanced to use the expression 'set foot in'!
M: Well, if you say so ... I'm not a gifted learner, though. In the beginning I used to struggle a lot. I was always lost in class.
T: Well, it's natural to feel out of your depth sometimes.
M: I guess. Anyway, I've lost count of the number of grammar and vocabulary exercises I've done. Not to mention all the apps I've downloaded ...
T: Yes, I know you have! You've put a lot of effort into your work! And it's paid off! If you're willing to go the extra mile, you can make a lot of progress, whether or not you're naturally good at languages ...
M: Yes, and I don't think living abroad is automatically going to make you fluent. Take my dad, for example.
H: What about him?
M: He spent six months in the UK when he was in his twenties, but he keeps saying my spoken English is better than his.
T: Hmm ... interesting.
H: Did he use to hang out with a lot of Spanish speakers?
M: Yeah. I think most of his friends were from Mexico and Spain ...
H: So that might explain it.
M: But, honestly, why do you need to live abroad when you can access the Internet and immerse yourself in a foreign language without leaving your home? And YouTube is fantastic! When I watch videos, I feel as if I'm there.
H: Well, I'm not sure I agree. Even if you're exposed to a lot of English, it's not the same as actually living abroad. When you live in another country, you absorb the culture ... You, erm, you become 'one of them', and that's really important.

4.6 *page 40 exercises 3A and B*

Notice the *-ed* endings are pronounced /t/, /d/ or /ɪd/.

Welcome to 'Today in history,' where we review spectacular events you may not be aware of.

October 30, 1938, a day that will live in infamy! Orson Welles was only 23 when his theatre company decided to create a radio play based on a famous science-fiction novel. The show aired on a Sunday, at 8.00pm, and millions of Americans had their radios on as a voice announced: 'The Columbia Broadcasting System and its affiliated stations present Orson Welles and the Mercury Theatre on the air in *The War of the Worlds* by H.G. Wells.'

Orson Welles, no relation to the writer HG Wells, introduced the play, which was followed by a weather report and a music number. At one point, someone broke in to report that a certain observatory had detected a sequence of explosions on Mars, which, not surprisingly, took listeners by surprise. Then the music came back on, but it was followed by another interruption. Apparently, a huge meteor had crashed into a farm in New Jersey – except that it wasn't a meteor, but an army of Martians, which the radio announcer described as 'large as bears', with 'V-shaped salivating mouths' and 'eyes that gleamed like serpents'. Not only did the creatures look hideous, they were evil, too, annihilating whoever came their way and releasing poisonous gases into the air, which threw listeners nationwide into a frenzy.

As it turns out, the reports – which had chilling sound effects and incredibly convincing performances – were part of the radio play! The whole thing was so realistic that millions of listeners were under the impression that the US was, in fact, under attack. Panic broke out as thousands of people clogged the highways, desperately trying to flee the attack – where they were headed is anyone's guess, of course! Never before had a radio show inadvertently caused so much panic.

News that the show had wreaked havoc in the country eventually reached the studio, and only when Welles realised the seriousness of the situation did he interrupt the show to explain what was going on. The nation breathed a sigh of relief to learn that it was all fiction, of course, but the general public had a hard time believing that the show was never intended as a hoax. The radio station came in for a lot of criticism for unleashing terror across the country, and Orson Welles reportedly said that *The War of the Worlds* would be the end of his career. But the opposite happened. Welles eventually signed a movie deal which led to *Citizen Kane*, arguably the greatest American film of all time.

4.13 *page 46 exercises 9C*

Notice the links. Listen for more linked words in the text.

J = Julie, S = Seth

J: You know, it's not just criminal records. I think censorship has_its uses. In fact, I think_it's_essential_in_a civilised society.
S: You do? How? I think_it's just_a cover-up.
J: Well, for one thing, there's such a thing as too much information, most of which you have no need for whatsoever. We have no need to see sensitive government documents, for example.
S: I want to know what my government is up to! I'm not in favour of Big Brother!
J: That may be, but would you know what to do with the information you were given? You might get nervous. Overplay its importance. And you might exaggerate threats. Look at the famous radio play *The War of the Worlds* by Orson Welles. Not only were there no Martians, but there was no attack, either.
S: That's not the same as a real invader.
J: Well, maybe not, but let's take another example: parental censorship. I think it's a good thing.
S: What kind of parental censorship?
J: Like software that blocks access to certain sites. Kids don't have the maturity to know what they're looking at.
S: Don't you think it would be better, though, to talk to them? Why so much control? Seldom do kids not respond well when their parents trust them.
J: Hmm ... well, maybe. But how about reading? Shouldn't some novels be banned from school? And kids shouldn't be reading them at home, either, until they're 18. Books can be depressing. They might cause nightmares. And at the very least, they can have a negative influence on young people.
S: I just don't believe in any of this. Life isn't a bed of roses. Kids will be more resilient if they know what the real world is like! It's just not fair otherwise.
J: OK, one more example. What about history? Should textbooks be honest? This could be really scary. If teachers and textbooks were totally honest, kids might end up not trusting anybody. There's a lot of evil in the world, most of which we don't really need to know about.

S: I think it's the opposite. If we conceal information, kids will be suspicious as soon as they find out.

6.9 *page 67 exercise 8B*

Notice the /s/ and /z/ sounds and their different spellings. Find more examples in the text.

D = Donna, J = Jason

D: Hey, this is cool! An article on street art.
J: Street art?
D: Yeah, graffiti artists. Look. Bet you can't guess where they're from.
J: Well, their names are right there.
D: True, but what's in a name? Pick one. Let's see how you do.
J: OK. 'El Bocho'. He sounds Mexican. In the tradition of Diego Rivera. Didn't he do people like that, too?
D: You mean, short and squat? Well, I wouldn't say exactly like that! But anyway, El Bocho isn't Mexican. He lives in Berlin. And he's really well known in the Berlin graffiti scene.
J: You mean he's German?
D: Not exactly. He's from Spain originally. But his name does sound Mexican. Let me look it up. Wow, according to my dictionary, in Argentina and Uruguay, it means a person's head!
J: OK, let's keep going. Os Gêmeos. This artist must be Brazilian. I like him.
D: How do you know it's a him?
J: Well, aren't most graffiti artists men? Personally, I've never seen graffiti done by a woman. Anyway, I wonder what the name means.
D: I have seen some women graffiti artists. And, in fact, next I'll ask you to guess which of the remaining artists happen to be women. But to answer your question, the name means 'the twins' in Portuguese. Their names are Otávio and Gustavo Pandolfo, and they're from São Paulo. They've both been painting graffiti for almost 20 years.
J: Let's see. Maya Hayuk. She's obviously a woman.
D: You get a point! What did you think of her art?
J: Hmm ... I'm not sure.
D: Sounds as if you didn't really like it. Didn't the vibrant colours appeal to you?
J: I did like it. It's just that I really like graffiti with a message. And I'm having trouble figuring out what hers is.
D: Any idea where she's from?
J: Hayuk? Is the name native American?
D: I honestly have no idea. But she was born in the city of Baltimore and lives and works in Brooklyn, New York.
J: I think we've done enough guessing. Just tell me quickly about the others.
D: OK, There's Inti, from Valparaíso, Chile. His name comes from the Incan sun god and the Quechua word for 'sun'.
J: Interesting. The mural does seem very South American, doesn't it?
D: Yes, he also likes to draw political themes and represent South America around the world. And finally, we have two more women. Firstly, there's Olek, originally from Poland although she now lives in New York. I read she used to be essentially homeless until her art was discovered.
J: You're kidding! I love the bicycle.
D: It does look original, doesn't it? I wish I could buy one!
J: And the last artist?
D: Kashink from Paris. And get this? She's been drawing a thin moustache on her upper lip for a few years and 'wears' it every day.
J: Cool. I guess you could call that a kind of graffiti!
D: Yes. I bet you hadn't realised how creative graffiti could be.
J: Well, I had realised. But still, I always thought graffiti was mainly done on buildings.

7.1 *page 72 exercise 1A*

Notice the **sentence stress.**

H = Host, D = Dr Castro

H: And we're **very lucky tonight** to have Dr **Julia Castro** with us, **author** of *The* ***critical years*** *of our* ***lives***. **Thanks** for **joining** us, Dr **Castro**.
D: **Thanks** for **having** me.
H: So, **first**, can we **talk** about the **elephant** in the **room**?
D: Oh, the **article**! I had **no idea** it would be so **controversial**!
H: **Basically**, you went **against conventional wisdom** and **argued** that it's **not early childhood** that **sets** us up for **life** – or **adolescence** – but the **10 years** from **20** to **30** ...
D: Yeah, **most** people **still** seem to **believe** that the **first** few **years** are the **most important**, but the **critical decade** is **really** your **20s**. So I **guess** I **opened** a can of **worms**! You have **no idea** how many **angry tweets** I **got**!
H: But **what** about **milestones** like **graduating** from **high** school or **getting** a **driver's license**? These are **things** we **usually do before** our **20s**.
D: Yes, but I would **argue** that when we **come** of **age**, we **make** the **decisions** that have the **greatest impact** on our **future**.
H: **Why's that?**
D: Because **that's** when our **lives** either **take off** or **get** off **track**.

9.10 *page 100 exercise 7B*

Notice the 'disappearing' /t/s and /d/s.

H = Trainer, C = Colleague

T: Welcome back to *Fitness on the go*, the weekly fitness podcast for people on the run – just like you and me! Thanks for tweeting us your questions. We'll try to answer as many as we can today. So, let's get right down to it. Here's a tweet from @lazyrunner. Hi Lazyrunner. Hope you're with us today. Lazyrunner writes: 'Is it true that running on a treadmill – as opposed to, say, running on the street – is gentler on your knees?' Well, the thing about running is that it's a high-impact exercise, so it creates a lot of stress on your knees no matter where you run ...
C: You just talked thousands of listeners out of even trying!
T: But here's the good news: Most treadmills include padding that can stop your knees from hurting because, just like a cushion, it softens any impact you may feel, unlike a hard surface outdoors. That's why many people consider them to be safer than jogging outside.
C: Oh, well, maybe you won't dissuade me from giving it a shot then.
T: But that's only half the story. You see, a few studies have shown that people tend to take shorter steps, shorter strides, when they're on a treadmill, and this can actually increase the risk of injury. So, in a nutshell, the answer is, it depends. Either way, I urge you to see your doctor before you begin exercising.
C: Yes, that's critical! Have your doctor help you choose the best exercise program for you. Here's another tweet. 'Speaking of treadmills, can we trust those calorie counters?'
T: Treadmills and stationary bikes know nothing about your biorhythm, general health, and fitness level, all of which determine how many calories you're burning when you work out.
C: Yeah, that's what I thought.
T: Some machines can overestimate calorie count by over 40%! These numbers might put a smile on your face and **brighten** your day, but don't let them fool you! You can't count on them being right!
C: So, you're saying 100 calories might actually be 60?
T: That's right. But, you know, sometimes they guess right, so they're better than nothing.
C: Wow, I had no idea! Anyway, while we're on the subject of cardio, let's talk about sweating. Our next tweet: 'Is it true that you absolutely have to sweat to burn calories?'
T: You see, sweat is a sign that your body is reminding itself to cool down.
C: Like a biological response?
T: Yes. Sweating keeps you from overheating – and having to stop to **freshen** up every five minutes! But rest assured that you can burn hundreds of calories without necessarily dripping in sweat.
C: Oh, this is good news! Let me read another tweet. This one's from @robertbrown. 'My doctor warned me not to stretch before weightlifting. Has he lost his mind?'
T: Well, this is a tricky question, but your doctor might be on to something, Robert. You see, the jury's still out on how helpful stretching really is. Some studies show that stretching before weightlifting won't necessarily enable you to perform better and might actually **weaken** your muscles! This doesn't mean that there's no need to warm up, of course, but static stretching might–
C: What's that?
T: Stretching your muscles with your body at rest ... that might not be the best way to do it. But not all experts agree, your doctor for one, so, I won't insist on your listening to me instead!
C: OK, we have time for one more tweet before our commercial break. @Gwen_Chicago asks: 'I do 100 sit-ups every day. Will I get the abs of my dreams?'
T: Gwen, I hope you don't mind me saying this, but, no. Toning exercises will help you **strengthen** your abs, but may not give you a really flat tummy. If you want that, you'll have to incorporate cardio into your exercise routine ... and watch your diet, of course.
C: That's the hardest part. At least for me, it is!
T: Thank you everyone. We'll take a quick break and ...

Phrasal verb list

Phrasal verbs are verbs with two or three words: main verb + particle (either a preposition or an adverb). The definitions given below are those introduced in iDentities.

Transitive phrasal verbs have a direct object; some are separable, others inseparable

Phrasal verb	Meaning
A	
ask someone **over**	invite someone
B	
block something **out**	prevent from passing through (light, noise)
blow something **out**	extinguish (a candle)
blow something **up**	explode; fill with air (a balloon); make larger (a photo)
bring something **about**	cause to happen
bring someone or something **back**	return
bring someone **down**	depress
bring something **out**	introduce a new product
bring someone **up**	raise (a child)
bring something **up**	bring to someone's attention
build something **up**	increase
burn something **down**	burn completely
C	
call someone **back**	return a phone call
call someone **in**	ask for someone's presence
call something **off**	cancel
call someone **up**	contact by phone
carry something **out**	conduct an experiment / plan
cash in on something	profit
catch up on something	get recent information; do something there wasn't time for earlier
charge something **up**	charge with electricity
check someone / something **out**	examine closely
check up on someone	make sure a person is OK
cheer someone **up**	make happier
clean someone / something **up**	clean completely
clear something **up**	clarify
close something **down**	force (a business / store) to close
come away with something	learn something useful
come down to something	be the most important point
come down with something	get an illness
come up against someone / something	be faced with a difficult person / situation
come up with something	invent
count on someone / something	depend on
cover something **up**	cover completely; conceal to avoid responsibility
crack down on something	take severe measures
cross something **out**	draw a line through
cut something **down**	bring down (a tree); reduce
cut someone **off**	interrupt someone
cut something **off**	remove; stop the supply of
cut something **out**	remove; stop doing an action
cut something **up**	cut into small pieces
D	
do something **over**	do again
do someone / something **up**	make more beautiful
draw something **together**	unite
dream something **up**	invent
drink something **up**	drink completely
drop someone / something **off**	take someplace
drop out of something	leave
dwell on something	linger over, think hard about something
E	
empty something **out**	empty completely
end up with something	have an unexpected result
F	
face up to something	accept something unpleasant
fall back on something	use an old idea
fall for someone	feel romantic love
fall for something	be tricked into believing
figure someone / something **out**	understand with thought
fill someone **in**	explain
fill something **in**	complete with information
fill something **out**	complete (a form)
fill something **up**	fill completely
find something **out**	learn information
fix something **up**	redecorate (a home); solve
follow something **through** / **follow through on** something	complete
G	
get something **across**	help someone understand
get around to something	finally do something
get away with something	avoid the consequences
get back at someone	retaliate, harm someone (for an offense or wrong act)
get off something	leave (a bus, train, plane)
get on something	board (a bus, train, plane)
get on with someone	have a good relationship
get out of something	leave (a car); avoid doing something
get something **out of** something	benefit from
get through with something	finish
get to someone	upset someone
get to something	reach
get together with someone	meet / start a relationship
give something **away**	give something no longer needed or wanted
give something **back**	return
give something **out**	distribute
give something **up**	stop doing (immediately)
give up on someone / something	stop hoping for change / trying to make something happen

Phrasal verb	Meaning
go after someone / something	try to get / win
go along with something	agree
go over something	review
go through with something	finish / continue something difficult
grow out of something	stop doing (over time, as one becomes an adult)
H	
hand something **in**	submit
hand something **out**	distribute
hang something **up**	put on a hanger or hook
help someone **out**	assist
K	
keep someone or something **away**	cause to stay at a distance
keep something **on**	not remove (clothing / jewellery)
keep someone or something **out**	prevent from entering
keep up with someone	stay in touch
keep up with someone or something	go as fast as
L	
lay someone **off**	make redundant for economic reasons
lay something **out**	arrange
leave something **on**	not turn off (a light or appliance); not remove (clothing or jewellery)
leave something **out**	not include, omit
let someone **down**	disappoint
let someone / something **in**	allow to enter
let someone **off**	allow to leave (a bus, train); not punish
let someone / something **out**	allow to leave
light something **up**	illuminate
look after someone / something	take care of
look down on someone	think one is better, disparage
look into something	research
look out for someone	watch, protect
look someone / something **over**	examine
look someone / something **up**	try to find
look up to someone	admire, respect
M	
make something **up**	invent
make up for something	do something to apologise
miss out on something	lose the chance
move something **around**	change location
P	
pass something **out**	distribute
pass someone / something **up**	reject, not use
pay someone **back**	repay, return money
pay someone **off**	bribe
pay something **off**	pay a debt
phone / ring someone **back**	return a phone call
pick someone / something **out**	identify, choose
pick someone **up**	give someone a lift
pick someone / something **up**	lift
pick something **up**	get / buy; learn something; answer the phone; get a disease
point someone / something **out**	indicate, show
pull something **off**	make something happen

Phrasal verb	Meaning
put something **away**	return to its appropriate place
put something **back**	return to its original place
put someone **down**	treat with disrespect
put something **down**	stop holding
put something **off**	delay
put something **on**	get dressed / add jewellery (to the body)
put something **together**	assemble, build
put something **up**	build, erect
put up with someone / something	accept without complaining
R	
run into someone	meet
run out of something	not have enough
run something **by** someone	tell someone something so they can give you their opinion
S	
see something **through**	complete
send something **back**	return
send something **out**	post
set something **off**	cause to go off, explode
set something **up**	establish; prepare for use
settle on something	choose after consideration
show someone / something **off**	display the best qualities
shut something **off**	stop (a machine, light, supply)
sign someone **up**	register
stand up for someone / something	support
start something **over**	begin again
stick with / to someone / something	not give up / persevere
straighten something **up**	make neat
switch something **on**	start, turn on (a machine, light)
T	
take over from someone	take control from someone else
take something **away**	remove
take something **back**	return; accept an item; retract a statement
take something **down**	remove (a hanging item)
take something **in**	notice, remember; make a clothing item smaller
take something **off**	remove clothing, jewellery
take someone **on**	hire
take something **on**	agree to a task
take someone **out**	invite and pay for someone
take something **out**	borrow from the library
take something **up**	start a new activity (as a habit)
talk someone **into**	persuade
talk something **over**	discuss
team up with someone	start to work with, do a task together
tear something **down**	destroy, demolish
tear something **up**	tear into small pieces
think back on something	remember
think something **over**	consider
think something **up**	invent, think of a new idea

Phrasal verb list

Phrasal verb	Meaning
throw something **away / out**	discard, put in the bin / rubbish
tip someone **off**	give someone a hint or warning
touch something **up**	improve with small changes
try something **on**	put on to see if it fits, is desirable (clothing, shoes)
try something **out**	use an item / do an activity to see if it's desirable
turn something **around**	turn so the front faces the back; cause to get better
turn someone / something **down**	reject
turn something **down**	lower the volume / heat
turn someone **in**	identify to the police (after a crime)
turn something **in**	submit
turn someone / something **into**	change from one type or form to another
turn someone **off**	cause to lose interest, feel negatively
turn something **off**	stop (a machine / light)
turn something **on**	start (a machine / light)
turn something **out**	make, manufacture
turn something **over**	turn so the bottom is on the top
turn something **up**	raise (the volume / heat)

Phrasal verb	Meaning
U	
use something **up**	use completely, consume
W	
wake someone **up**	cause to stop sleeping
walk out on someone	leave a spouse / child / romantic relationship
warm (up) to something/ someone	begin to like something or someone
watch out for someone	protect
wear someone/something **out**	damage from too much use
wipe something **out**	remove, destroy
work something **out**	calculate mathematically; solve a problem
write something **down**	create a written record (on paper)
write something **up**	write in a finished form

Intransitive phrasal verbs have no direct object; they are all inseparable

Phrasal verb	Meaning
A	
act up	behave inappropriately
B	
blow over	pass, be forgotten
blow up	explode; suddenly become angry
break down	stop functioning
burn down	burn completely
break out	start suddenly (a war, fire, disease)
break up	end a relationship
C	
call back	return a phone call
carry on	continue doing something; behave in a silly / emotional way
catch on	become popular
check in	report arrival (at a hotel, airport)
check out	pay a bill and leave (a hotel)
cheer up	become happier
clear up	become better (a rash, infection; the weather)
close down	stop operating (a business)
come along	go with, accompany
come back	return
come down	become lower (a price)
come in	enter
come off	become unattached; appear a certain way
come out	appear; be removed (a stain)
come up	arise (an issue)
D	
doze off	fall asleep unintentionally
dress up	wear more formal clothes; a costume
drop in	visit unexpectedly
drop out	leave
E	
eat out	eat in a restaurant
empty out	empty completely
end up	do something unexpected; reach a final location / conclusion
F	
fall off	become unattached
fall through	fail to happen
fill out	become bigger
fill up	become completely full
find out	learn new information
follow through	finish, complete something
fool around	have fun (in a silly way)
G	
get ahead	make progress, succeed
get back	return
get by	survive
get off	leave (a bus, train)
get on	board (a bus, train); have a good relationship
get through	finish; survive
get together	meet; start a relationship
get up	get out of bed
give up	stop doing
go along	accompany; agree

Phrasal verb	Meaning
go away	leave a place
go back	return
go down	decrease (a price, number)
go off	explode, detonate
go on	continue
go out	leave (a building / home); socialise
go over	succeed (an idea / speech)
go up	increase (a price, number); be built
grow up	become an adult
H	
hang up	end a phone call
help out	do something helpful, useful
hold on	wait (often during a phone call)
K	
keep away	stay at a distance
keep on	continue
keep out	not enter
keep up	maintain speed / momentum
L	
lie down	recline (on a bed / floor / sofa)
light up	illuminate; look pleased, happy
look out	be careful
M	
make up	end an argument
miss out	lose the chance (for something good)
P	
pass out	become unconscious, faint
pay off	be worthwhile
phone / ring back	return a phone call
pick up	improve
play around	have fun, not be serious
pop up	occur unexpectedly
R	
run out	leave suddenly; not have enough (a supply)
rush off	leave in a hurry
S	
show up	appear; arrive at a place
sign up	register
sit down	sit
slip up	make a mistake
stand up	rise (to one's feet)
start over	begin again
stay up	not go to bed
straighten up	make neat
T	
take off	leave, depart (a plane); succeed, achieve success
turn in	go to sleep
turn out	have a certain result
turn up	appear
W	
wake up	stop sleeping
watch out	be careful
wear off	disappear, diminish slowly
wind up	become ultimately
work out	exercise; end successfully

Richmond

58 St Aldates
Oxford
OX1 1ST
United Kingdom

ISBN: 978-84-668-2758-4
DL: M-9664-2017
First Edition: March 2017

Publishing Director: Deborah Tricker

Editors: Laura Miranda, Shona Rodger, Jennifer Wise

Proofreaders: Fiona Hunt, Kate Mellersh, Tania Pattison, Sophie Sherlock

Project and Cover Design: Lorna Heaslip

Layout: Oliver Hutton (H D Design), Dave Kuzmicki

Picture Researcher: Magdalena Mayo, Arnos Design Ltd

Illustrators: Aviel Basil, Ricardo Bessa, John Holcroft, Oivind Hovland, Andres Lozano, lynton@kja-artists, sean@kja-artists

Digital Content: Luke Baxter, Anup Dave

Audio Recording: Motivation Sound Studios

Texts:

p. 32 https://www.mindtools.com/CommSkll/PublicSpeaking.htm © Mind Tools Ltd, 1996-2016. All rights reserved. "Mind Tools" is a registered trademark of Mind Tools Ltd. Reproduced with permission.

p. 43 http://www.scientificamerican.com/article/why-do-some-people-believe-in-conspiracy-theories/
Reproduced with permission. Copyright © 2016, Scientific American, a division of Nature America, Inc. All rights reserved.

p. 64 *The Way Up to Heaven* extract (first published in *The New Yorker*, 1954). Published in Penguin Books in the collection *Kiss Kiss*, a collection of short stories. Copyright © Roald Dahl Nominee Ltd, 1954. Reproduced with permission.
Illustration for *The Way Up To Heaven* copyright © Eleanor Percival

p. 76 http://listverse.com/2016/01/24/10-things-you-didnt-know-babies-could-do/
Reproduced with permission.

p. 86 http://www.fastcompany.com/3012939/the-true-story-of-amazing-customer-service-from-gasp-an-airline
Used with permission of Fast Company Copyright© 2016. All rights reserved.

p. 98 http://www.huffingtonpost.com/kerri-zane/5-reasons-its-better-to-b_b_2854313.html
Reproduced with permission.

p. 108 https://www.psychologytoday.com/blog/looking-in-the-cultural-mirror/201009/are-american-friendships-superficial
Reproduced with permission of Jefferson M. Fish Copyright© 2016. All rights reserved.

p. 120 http://www.aarp.org/home-family/dating/info-01-2013/online-dating-safety-tips-solin.html
Reprinted from January 9, 2013 AARP.org. Copyright © 2013. All rights reserved.

p. 130 http://www.wired.com/2014/05/victorian-postcards-predict-future/
Reproduced with permission Copyright © 2016 Condé Nast. All rights reserved.

Photos:
500PX MARKETPLACE/Brian Bonham; ALAMY/Kaleidoscope, Steve Stock, BSIP SA, Cultura RM, MBI, Home People, Rob Walls, Alex Segre, Image Source, David Cole, age fotostock, Peter Forsberg, Maurice Savage, RayArt Graphics, CBW, Stock Photo, blickwinkel, Blend Images, AF archive, Richard Levine, Vadym Drobot, Jack Sullivan, SilverScreen, Ian Allenden, Web Pix, Eden Breitz, David Levenson, Ferne Arfin, Ed Rooney, Xinhua, Mike Kiev, Roberto Herrett, Lynne Sutherland, ZUMA Press, Inc., Eric D ricochet69, Nicholas Stratford, Wavebreak Media ltd, World History Archive, Stacy Walsh Rosenstock, epa european pressphoto agency b.v., Clare Gainey; ARNOS DESIGN LTD./David Oakley; CARTOONSTOCK/Eldon Pletcher, Aaron Bacall, Fran; GETTY IMAGES SALES SPAIN/Howard Kingsnorth, HeroImagesCLOSED, Francisco Romero, Eyecandy Images, Hero Images, Thinkstock; GLASBERGEN CARTOON SERVICE/ Randy Glasbergen/www.glasbergen.com; ISTOCKPHOTO/Getty Images Sales Spain; OFF THE MARK CARTOONS/Mark Parisi; PBS/PBS Newshour; REX SHUTTERSTOCK/Ricardo Demurez / imageBROKER, Everett Collection, Blend Images, Broadimage, WestEnd61, SNAP; SHUTTERSTOCK NETHERLANDS,B.V.; WATCHMOJO/ www.watchmojo.com; ZUMA PRESS/Bryan Smith; Dr. Cialdini/ www.influenceatwork.com; Eleanor Percival; Chic by CHoice; Alinea Egmont; ARCHIVO SANTILLANA